From Odessa With Love:
Political and Literary Essays from Post-Soviet Ukraine

Vladislav Davidzon

From Odessa With Love:

Political and Literary Essays from Post-Soviet Ukraine

Vladislav Davidzon

Forward by Peter Pomerantsev

Preface by Simon Sebag Montefiore

Academica Press
Washington~London

Library of Congress Cataloging-in-Publication Data

Names: Davidzon, Vladislav (author)
Title: From odessa with love : political and literary essays from post-soviet ukraine | Davidzon, Vladislav
Description: Washington : Academica Press, 2021. | Includes references.
Identifiers: LCCN 2021942994 | ISBN 9781680539660 (hardcover) | 9781680539677 (paperback) | 9781680539936 (e-book)

With boundless devotion and fealty to Regina, my sovereign queen.

With gratitude to my family for all their support: to my mother Elena, my sister Natalia, aunt Marina and uncle Vadim.

To the blessed memory of Anthony Yakhnich, my grandmother Galina Seryabrikova -Rudderman, Nina Beilina and Tatyana Prudnikova.

And for David Samuels, for teaching me how to write.

Contents

VIII. Obituaries and Appreciations

IX. Conversations

Acknowledgments

Much gratitude to those whose support, love or violent opposition has sustained me though the writing of this book, from the hoodlums back in Brooklyn all the way up to Lords Oxford and Risby, who graciously hosted me in Westminster Parliament. This book owes its existence to the gallant encouragement of my dashing publisher and comrade-in-arms Professor Paul du Quenoy. I must thank him for proposing that I gather my disparate thoughts on Ukraine together that sunny afternoon in London over cucumber sandwiches and tea at the East India Club.

The moral, emotional and financial support of my family during strenuous times, especially that of my mother, my sister Natalia, my uncle Vadim and aunt Marina in Washington D.C. were crucial.

My father in law, George Semyonovich Prudnikov, took me into his home and taught me what it means to see life from the perspective of a real Odessan - a sailor!

My deepest thanks must go to Matthew Kupfer and Simon Albert for all of their generous efforts in reading earlier versions of the manuscript of this book. Any mistakes, errors or infelicities that remain in this volume after their graceful and generous editing efforts remain entirely my own fault. You are both gents and loyal friends.

Joseph Schwarzbach: even when you were very far away and ensconced in the pleasures of family life in Jerusalem, you have always been a pillar of support. The same goes for Victoria Kravets, who has followed a parallel life path to my own.

A mighty thanks to Martin Peretz for all his solidarity, honesty and gracious help. Marty: you are a real Mensch and I adore you.

My deepest gratitude goes out to Simon Sebag Montefiore and Peter Pomerantsev for their generosity in contributing a forward and preface to this book. It is a dream to have my first book appear in the world with endorsements from writers whose work I have have grown up reading - you are my kinsmen in terms of intellectual and aesthetic concerns.

Faina Kremerman and Alexander Geifman for inviting me out to attend a Wes Anderson film that spring day in 2010, and for much else besides.

Much gratitude to Dan Robins and Irina Dratva for their warm ironical company in New York City and for the boundless love that they have always shown in our histrionic correspondence.

The Bulgakov family have always shown amazing affection and generosity, wether on trips to Odessa and Kyiv or while vacationing in Greece. Anastasiya Bukovska and Danylo Kaptyukh for their friendship and hospitality in Kyiv and elsewhere.

Victoria Yakubova and Hervé Schneid in Paris, for all of their gracious assistance in times of trouble.

Dmytro Sikorsky, my fellow aesthete and collector in Odessa, you will always have my gratitude for filling me up with Bulgarian food at the Two Karls Cafe (which is helpfully located at the intersection of the streets once known as "Karl Marx" and "Karl Engels"). Marika Yamnizzki and Uliana Dovgan and our whole Odessa cohort - you are like another beautiful neurotic family.

My deepest respect to Peter and Martine Halban, perhaps the best people in London, you are a deeply civilizing influence on anyone lucky enough to find themselves in your orbit.

A deep bow to my friend and comrade in arms Adrian Karatnycky for all of his support over the years, I owe you a tremendous debt. This likewise goes for Alti and Berel Rodal, Rabbi Yaakov Dov Bleich, Mark Freiman and Wolf Moskovich and the rest of our comrades at the UJE.

I am tremendously grateful to Melinda Haring for all of her loyalty and solidarity in the face of existential danger. Likewise, my gratitude to John Herbst for his support at the Atlantic Council. My fellow innocent abroad Brian Mefford and I have shared many grand conversations and cold glasses of whisky during election monitoring missions.

A special thanks to all of the editors who have helped shape these pieces along the way: David Samuels, Peter Dickinson, Liel Liebovitz, Damir Marusic, Dominic Green, James Palmer, Ilya Lozovsky, Michael

Mosbacher, Claire Berlinski, Jacob Siegel, Adam O'Neil, Noam Blum, Park MacDougald and Mark Horowitz.

Matthew Torne and I have enjoyed many delightful and horrifying adventures together without ultimately having killed one another.

My gratitude to David Loyd Stern, whose moral support and American Midwestern decency were always crucial in getting me to calm down.

To my friends, colleagues, comrades, competitors and enemies among my fellow Eastern European journalists and experts: I raise a toast to all of you for your collegial support, love, and rancor. Mark Galeotti, Anna Nemtsova, David Satter, Devin Ackles, Anton Shekhovtsov, Andrew Wilson, Nataliya Gumenyuk, Polina Ivanova, Taras Kuzio, Ariel Cohen, Tom de Waal, Sam Sokol, Emmanuel Dreyfus, Alan Riley, Serhii Plokhii, Natalia Antelava, Roman Olearchyk, Vladimir Kozlovsky, and Richard Behar. I have learned a great deal from every one of you. So many of the individuals in our profession imbibe the worst and most misanthropic parts of Eastern Europe, yet all of you possess great and capacious souls!

To my pals in Paris who were comrades along the way and kept up my spirits in difficult times: Florian Hohenberg, Lex Paulson, Seb Emina, and Thomas Chatterton Williams. Greg Frolov and Anna Smailikova for taking care of me in Kyiv and for their excellent political advice.

Sophie Weisenfeld and Sam Oiknine must be thanked for taking me and Regina into their hearts and home in London and forging me into an angle in the Hexagon society.

To Emily Katz for her ingenious advice and support and Gilles Hertzog, a great dandy and friend.

Jason Stanley: I have argued with you about everything but I retain great affection for you.

Aleksander Roytburd in Odessa, director of the Roytburd Odessa museum of art - a true original who died tragically young as this book was going to print. And to our mutual friend Oleksandr Suslenskyi, who has always treated me like his 12th child, and demanded that Roytburd and I conclude our feud while waving his walking stick in our faces- with implicit threat of violence if we would not embrace.

Assorted friends, Odessans, fellow travelers and comrades on the path who have been indispensable in the creation of this book in one way or another include: Peter Culshaw, Alik Shpilyuk, Alexandra Koroleva, Helena Akhtiorskaya, Adrian Dannat, Christine Liubov Kaminsky, Alexa Chopivsky, Borislav Bereza, Bohdan Nahaylo, David Patrikarakos, Simon Waldron, Michael Gottlieb, Nada Gordon, Tamara Silverman, Tchavdar Georgiev, Yevgeniy Fiks, Will Murphy, Sheila O`Shea, Peter Webber, Thomas Eymond-Laritaz, Mr. Gray, Esther Adler, Michal Murawski, Val Vinokur, Vitaly Portnikov, Misha Gulko, Olga Gershenson, Olexo Gladushevskyy, Rabbi Stephen Berkowitz, Anne-Elisabeth Moutet, Martin Gimenez Larralde, Yaroslav Trofimov, Mark Gillespie, Anna Momigliano, Kate Tsurkan, Sophie Schultz, Joshua Dolgin, Eugene Ostashevsky, and Helga Landauer. A special thanks to Harvey and Irina Stein as well as the whole Oppenheim family back in New York City.

I am grateful to my teachers and professors. Some of whom - Morris Dickstein and Marshall Berman especially – I miss terribly and wish were still here to see this book come to fruition. A great clasp of the shoulder to Matvei Yankelevich for everything that he did for me when I was young and insufferable. I learned a great deal during my studies at CUNY at the CUNY BA program -thanks Director Kim Hartswick -with Professors Katie Siegel, Andre Aciman, Martin Elsky, Robert Cowan and Emil Draitser.

Finally: huzzah for the entire team at the *Odessa Review*, who made the life of our journal possible, especially Hennady Tanzzura, Lena Novitskaya, Vadim Goloperov, Larissa Babij, Katya Michaels, Masha Sotskaya, Christopher Pugmire, and Nika Minina. The final issue of the journal would not have existed without the generous assistance of Yegor Grebennikov.

Foreword: Odessa, Odessa!

Simon Sebag Montefiore

Odessa is a city of beauties and merchants, rebels and adventuresses, Ukrainians, Russians, Jews, Greeks, French, Caucasians, and Italians, of beaches and bourses, of gangsters and countesses, of fiction and poetry, of cosmopolitanism and brutality. It remains unique in the sphere of the ex-Russian and ex-Soviet empires. That is why this book is such a worthwhile and, indeed, essential enterprise.

I first visited Odessa when I was researching my first history book, on Prince Potemkin and Catherine the Great, the two leaders who were ultimately behind its creation. I stayed in the famed Londonskaya Hotel. I walked the Seaside "Primorskaya" Esplanade, the Potemkin Steps, the beaches and streets. In the city archives I was delighted to discover the only and last existing copy of an invitation from Field Marshal Prince Potemkin of Tauride to his wildly extravagant ball in the Tauride Palace in St Petersburg. This was an event attended by the Empress as well as the future Alexander I, shortly before Potemkin's final departure for the south, whence he never returned. The photo reproduction of that invitation is in my book.

Odessa history is particularly colorful. It started as an Ottoman fortress captured by Admiral José de Ribas, the Spanish adventurer turned Russian admiral under the command of Potemkin who, on hearing of its fall, ordered the creation of a new stronghold and city. De Ribas, himself a fascinating cutthroat (who later planned to stab or poison Emperor Paul I but died before the plot reached fruition), was the early driving force behind the Odessa project, but it was Catherine who named it Odessa after the Greek "Odessos." The city stalled under the feckless command of Prince Platon Zubov, who governed New Russia (*"Novorossia"*) after Potemkin's death. It was Alexander I's decision to appoint the competent

Duc de Richelieu as governor that really transformed Odessa into the multinational metropolis that dazzled the world, attracting Russian, Jewish, Italian, Polish, Greek, Georgian, and French settlers who quickly made it prosperous.

When Richelieu left Odessa to become prime minister of France, his compatriot Count Alexandre de Langeron, who had earlier fought in the tsar's armies, succeeded him. His tenure is immortalized in the city's Langeron Beach. By the time Nicholas I appointed the able and liberal Count (later Prince) Mikhail Vorontsov to manage Odessa, the city was becoming Russia's southern capital and its economic hub, the port for the export of over half its grain to Europe, which passed through the Straits. Vorontsov, known as Milord, presided over the city as well as his huge governorship that included Crimea, much of today's southern Ukraine and, later, the Caucasus. He ruled from his Vorontsov Palace that still just about stands, overlooking the port. He was accompanied by his pretty, clever, playful, and extremely grand wife, Countess Lisa Branitska. She was Potemkin's great-niece and had been born in the Winter Palace before growing up close to Catherine the Great herself. When Pushkin arrived in exile to report to Vorontsov, he embarked on an affair with Lisa. It was not the affair itself (the count had mistresses, too) but Pushkin's flaunting of it that outraged Vorontsov, who subsequently arranged for the poet to be dispatched to count locusts. Pushkin got his revenge by writing rude poems about Vorontsov and claiming paternity of his daughter.

By now, Odessa had a population that included all sorts of decadent aristocrats living far from Petersburg, alongside political rebels, exiled Poles, and others. Gradually a unique Russian-Polish-Jewish culture developed in the city, along with a highly educated intelligentsia and debauched aristocratic society, and, increasingly, a top strata of wealthy (sometimes Jewish) merchant princes, rich in grain and ships. At the other end of the scale was a bottom strata and underclass in the Moldavanka district, which included Odessa's famous caste of Jewish gangsters. The Ephrussi family, illuminated recently by the family memoir of Edmond de Waal, were amongst the wealthiest of these early oligarchs. Charles Ephrussi was later the model for Proust's Charles Swann in *À La Recherche du Temps Perdu*. Benya Krik, the fictional hero of Isaac

Babel's Moldavanka stories of Odessa, typified the Jewish gangsters of the city.

Politically, the city was now strategically important: indeed, in some ways, the Crimean War and the later war with the Ottomans in 1877-78 were concerned with the ability of Russia to exports its grain from Odessa through the Straits to the wider world.

The new dark times of revolution, repression, and intolerance began to transmogrify the city's enlightened atmosphere: in 1905/06, pogroms by vicious right-wing militias known as the Black Hundreds victimized the Jews. The crew of the battleship *Potemkin* famously mutinied there, which was why the name of Odessa's Steps changed from Richelieu to Potemkin. The 1917 Revolution ruined this colorful, outrageous, swaggering, and cosmopolitan city forever, but the stories of its best writer since Pushkin, Isaac Babel, immortalized the quaintly shady culture of its gangsters and beautiful molls in the Moldavanka in his brilliant *Odessa Tales*, which gave us the aforementioned Benya Krik and many other characters.

Odessa's worst tragedy came in 1941-43 when the city fell to the Romanian allies of Hitler's invading Nazi legions. The Romanians, both by diabolical design and in murderous frenzy, slaughtered the Jews of Odessa in scenes of turbulent bloodletting that horrified even the homicidal bureaucrats and killers of the SS. Some 80,000 died in the massacre.

After the fall of the USSR, many of the Jews who had returned to Odessa following World War II left for Israel or America. And yet Odessa is still Odessa; Odessans are still the graceful and elegant and playful products of their city's amazing history. The flamboyant men and the gorgeous women still walk with the swagger that distinguishes only the citizens of this great city.

Preface: The Tales of Vlad: Genius Loci

By Peter Pomerantsev

"Genius Loci." Genius of Place. It is the being, often but not necessarily immortal, that animates, protects and sums up a space, a city, square, suburb or glade.

"Zeitgeist." The spirit of the time.

Or maybe a spirit of the time.

Can we combine these two old ideas?

Into a being that appears, like Venus out of the waves, to define an age, a time, an era?

Our time, as many have noted, is out of joint. All of it; norms about how the truth is treated in public life; about whether it's ok to murder civilians with barrel bombs; on the question of where particular borders are located and where history is going; what is sane and insane; what is fact and fiction and what is the structure of the whole edifice of the "international rules based order" has been shaken. Reality itself has been rent.

Russian President Vladimir Putin's annexation of Crimea in 2014 signaled the inauguration of this miniature era. There was the very ambiguity of that invasion – with its Little Green Men in unmarked military uniforms who were neither Russian soldiers nor not Russian soldiers at the same moment and they were neither invading nor not invading. It served to demonstrate how the meanings through which we try to order the world and the dividing lines between peace and war, can easily be short-circuited. Putin's denial of his non-invasion, which was not so much a denial of facts but the denial that facts mattered, signaled the start of a time which went on to be called "post-truth." This topsy-turvy era also included Brexit and the victory of Leicester City in the Premier

League, the devastation of Aleppo, the expulsion of Rohingya, Q-Anon and Trump.

It was soon after the start of this strange era that I first noticed a curious apparition. It was, if I recall, at a conference of liberal intellectuals in Kyiv. It was full of *New York Times* columnists and Russian dissidents, important Ambassadors and French philosophers. And amongst the canapés there appeared a somewhat carnivalesque and fantastical figure. Dressed like an Edwardian dandy, in silk socks and bright trousers, maybe even wearing a boater of the type that Venetian gondoliers perch on their heads as they croon down the canals, he spoke in a transatlantic drawl I couldn't place. At first I thought the whole thing was an act, someone playing at a reincarnation of an early 20th century American in Paris. But it wasn't an act. It was Vladislav Davidzon.

With time, I got to know the apparition. He had (of course!) emanated from the two places most pivotal to the age. He was raised in Little Odessa, Brooklyn, the weird island of Soviet emigrés and post-Soviet corruption whose mafia-kitsch, money-laundering and strong-man respecting culture swirled around Donald J. Trump. Then he moved to the real Odessa, Ukraine, where the great drama of the Russian invasion had played out. The direction of travel, from Little Odessa USA to Big Odessa Ukraine, was itself emblematic: in "normal" times people move the other way. But in an age gone haywire wouldn't the Genius Zeitgeist do exactly that, move the wrong way along the lines of geopolitical logic? Reverse migration flows?

In your hands you hold the tales of Vlad. They are the stories of this time-out-of-joint as told from the places that defined it. But as for all "genius Loci," the mission of this book and of its author is not purely descriptive: the aim of this thorough and analytical reporting is to set the age to right, to undo the damage.

You might not agree with everything.

But that is not the point.

Read this book.

Read it and understand that it is important if one wants to understand where we are now.

You do not choose the times you live in,
You only get to breathe and die in them.
Времена не выбирают,
В них живут и умирают.

– Aleksandr Kushner

Introduction
By Vladislav Davidzon

The revolutionary Odessa of Isaac Babel — that city of adventure and political intrigue — may be history, but in many ways it continues to live on with us. Even today, it is still possible to experience the charm and romance of old Odessa in modern Ukraine, as well as the political machinations that a senior Ukrainian intelligence officer once admitted to one of the individuals profiled within in this book "constitutes a state within the state". Odessa remains a key city to understanding our fantastical present for many reasons. An important one being that it remains a magnetic place where central figures of the age find themselves. It is universally known as a city of characters- this is doubtless true - yet it is also a city where characters from other places congregate. French philosopher Michel Onfray, former Georgian President Mikheil Saakashvili, Russian performance artist Petr Pavlensky and Belarusian writer Svetlana Alexievich all appear as characters in this volume.

This book represents a love letter to the city of Odessa, which is undoubtedly the most storied metropolis in Eastern Europe, and also to Ukraine, which is likely by any measure the most dynamic country in the region. This volume is a missive, a postcard sent home from a town full of spies, mobsters, thieves, operators, artists, musicians, hustlers, and political schemers. The Odessa port is a central hub of Black Sea criminality and the book does contain some of my favorite pieces on the fabled mafioso of the city.

Two of my grandparents were born in towns that now find themselves within the borders of the modern Ukrainian nation-state. In 2010, while I was still a student in Paris, I began spending my summers in Odessa with my future wife, Regina Maryanovska-Davidzon. What first began as a brief sojourn to the land of my ancestors would soon lead to my dedicating a decade of my life to observing the tumultuous developments of Ukrainian politics and culture as the country attempted to transform itself after the 2013-14 EuroMaidan Revolution. The subsequent invasion of Ukrainian territory and annexation of the Crimean peninsula by Moscow would ironically continue the process of the creation of the Ukrainian political nation.

At the end of 2015, my wife and I decided to take a leap of faith and move back to Odessa. We had been dividing our time between Paris and Kyiv. I would make monthly reporting trips to Ukraine while running the English-language division of a Ukrainian television station in Paris. When the television channel was closed down due to mismanagement in Kyiv (as well as the fact that the oligarch who partly owned it was being banished to Switzerland for his political misdeeds), we thought it was the right moment to return to Ukraine.

It was a remarkable time. We founded a literary magazine which we hoped would chronicle the development of contemporary Ukrainian culture at a moment when the Ukrainian arts scene was experiencing a post-revolution Renaissance. The *Odessa Review* would be a sort of cultural guide to the city of its name. Yet the magazine quickly morphed into a regional and finally national cultural journal of ideas and aesthetics. It would cover Ukrainian innovations in every art form and craft, starting with music and interior design and concluding with the practice of human rights law in the country.

Many of the pieces collected in this volume first began life as essays or feuilletons in the *Odessa Review*. Others came out of my reportage for American publications. Ukrainian politics in a time of war and the construction of the modern, independent Ukrainian state were always wild, the political life of Odessa was infinitely more surreal and fun. In 2016, former Georgian President Mikheil Saakashvili was appointed governor of the region, turning the city into a strange — and, ultimately, unsuccessful — experiment in political and economic reform. Suddenly, the city was the center of political life. What occasionally seemed to be every journalist that I had ever met was arriving in the "southern Palmyra" to report on the raucous developments.

The moment was characterized by the most glorious parties, continuous frenetic happenings and anti-corruption conferences that were bizarrely filled up with oligarchs and mobsters. As well as the internecine scandals and political intrigues at which Saakashvili was an indisputable master. Odessa was now the center of gravity in Ukrainian politics as it grew increasingly obvious that Saakashvili was preparing to use the region to springboard himself into power in Kyiv. His plan ultimately failed for reasons which are discussed in the chapter devoted to his legacy in the city. Yet the Saakashvili sojourn did represent an idealistic moment when Western reformers were flocking to Odessa and Ukraine more broadly with hopes of pushing through a reform agenda. Some of the articles in this volume date from that moment. The fact that such a moment was somewhat squandered - at least on the regional level- represented a tremendous missed opportunity. Still, escapade was glorious while it lasted. Which is important.

This book represent a distillation of 10 years' worth of my coverage of Ukrainian politics and culture. It operates on the assumption that the reader already has a basic understanding of the events that transpired during that period. It was a time of hope. The fervor of the Revolution of Dignity was followed by the Russian invasion and the grievous emotional blow of the annexation of Crimea and the protracted conflict in the Donbas. I have chosen from amongst my favorite pieces, which I hope will remain timely and of interest to students of Ukraine and Eastern European political history irrespective of the book's framing. Many of the pieces included here are of comparative historical interest to students of Ukrainian politics, even if some of the details in regard to "Russiagate" and "Ukrainegate" would be superseded later as the stories took on a world historical importance.

From among my published articles, essays, dispatches, reports, reviews, retorts, and profiles, I have selected those that I thought were the most salient for understanding this remarkable moment. Mostly, I have avoided including any analysis and reportage dealing with Russia or Belarus that do not directly engage with Ukrainian developments. Shrewd readers will notice that this volume largely does not engage with what was arguably the most fantastical event of Ukrainian politics of recent years: the 2019 election of President Volodymyr Zelensky. A television actor had literally stepped out of the television set and into the halls of power. Those events — as well as the majority of my writings on Jewish-Ukrainian relations — will be included in a forthcoming volume. The story of those years concludes with a bizarre historical escapade in which I played a role: that is the "Ukrainegate" scandal and the impeachment of American President Donald Trump.

Odessa Story:
Reading Isaac Babel in Ukraine

This essay from the Autumn of 2011 was my first publication on Odessa, a review of Charles King's Odessa: Genius and Death in a City of Dreams, as I began spending my summers in the city. It was also the first article commissioned from me by the Jewish magazine Tablet, whose European Culture correspondent I would become and where I would publish many of my essays and articles over the next decade. Even as the adventure concludes on a somewhat somber note, the essay would foreshadow many of my interests and concerns over the next decade, especially my fascination with the intersection of literature and politics in the city, the texture of Jewish life in Ukraine and the specter of organized crime in southern Ukraine.

The article is noteworthy for its portrayal of the widespread frustration with the brazen and endemic corruption that was normalized under the presidency of Victor Yanukovich and which would erupt into political revolution less than two years later.

Odessa was the epicenter and staging ground not only of the Russian Jew's secularization but also of his masculinization. The great voice and chronicler of this dual evolution was Issac Babel, whose stories I re-read with great pleasure while sitting in cafés on tourist-thronged Deribasovskaya Street, in a post-Soviet Odessa that has lost most of its Jews but is in many ways unchanged from the city that Babel described with such pungent and precise language, and to such mythic effect. The title character of the "Rabbi" story in Babel's *Red Cavalry* cycle is the crooked and ancient Hasidic Rabbi of Zhitomir. This wizened last representative of a dying dynasty tartly interrogates the protagonist of the story—a traveling Jewish war correspondent who has dropped in to share a Shabbat meal and to drink the wine that "won't be offered"—about "where this Jew has come from?" The answer, "Odessa," propels him into knowing perorations of lyrical exasperation: "The Godly city, the star of our exile, that reluctant wellspring of all our troubles!"

The rabbi's sickly-idiot son is in the corner of the room desecrating the holy day by smoking. It is apparent even to our passing Jewish war correspondent that he will be of no use in continuing the family line or propagating the law. The rabbi and the other men in the room spit words of toxic condemnation on him but the traveling war correspondent pleases the rabbi with his erudition—"What did this Jew study?" he is asked; "Bible," he answers—and his comportment. The pathos of the scene is to be found in the mutual understanding between the rabbi and the soldier-intellectual, one lucidly perceiving the new path his people must take, the other regretting the passing of ancient traditions. At the end of the story the war correspondent returns to his unit of the Red Cavalry to write an article for its newspaper. Like me, he is behind deadline and he must spend the entire night at his typewriter.

Yet Odessa was never *just* the wellspring of all our troubles. Built by Italians and Greeks, its original ruling class was the cream of exiled European aristocracy. (The first several governors were French.) Populated to this day by hundreds of nationalities, it was the Black Sea gateway to Constantinople. It was the regional outpost of European trade and thought, and every idea, innovation, caprice, and whim of Europe was there taken up, second hand, from the holds and decks of the ships docked in the port on their way to being spread, along with the occasional bout of plague, throughout the Russian Empire. Demographically the most Jewish city besides Minsk at the edge of the empire, Odessa was the only place inside the pale of settlement where Jews weren't prohibited from living in town. In fact they had been actively incentivized to do so, and Odessan Jewry was among the most emancipated and disabused throughout the Russian Empire. Babel's ancient rabbi was not wrong to be suspicious of his guest.

The "star of our exile" is, along with Alexandria, Thessaloniki, New Orleans, and Naples, one of a constellation of glittering and flamboyantly raucous port towns that fascinate and inspire the continuous composition of enough history books and reminisces to fill whole libraries.

Odessans are curators of their own mythic past par excellence. One Soviet-era Odessa professor made his vocation in writing 30-odd books about "Criminal Odessa." (Naturally, I was warned off by other historians from using these as source material, as half the stories had been made up.)

The latest English addition to this literature and an excellent guide to the city is Charles King's 2011 chronicle, *Odessa: Genius and Death in a City of Dreams*. A readable distillation of Odessan folklore and yarns nimbly unspooled by an academic clearly having fun on his sabbatical abroad, it is a treasury of salty anecdotes, such as the unlikely tale of the Sioux circus performer traveling with a Russian troupe in the Crimean port town of Sevastopol. The native American had found himself sacked after a night-long vodka-fueled bender; the circus had departed, and his costume had been stolen so he walked naked through the city. The British Consul took pity on him and lent him the ferry money to Odessa, where, as a member of the Sioux nation, he was entitled to services from the American consul. The American diplomat then took him to see an Orthodox Jewish tailor who made him a new costume. We know all this from diplomatic archives: The consul had requested an official reimbursement of $75 from the State Department to cover the cost of the costume.

King's book also unearthed for me the amazing fact that Catherine the Great's campaign to wrest control of the Crimea and the surrounding territories from the Turks was waged by a ragtag assortment of regular army, irregulars, conscripts, and mercenaries that also included "a company of Jewish lancers" drawn from regional farmers who owned horses. Jews of what would become the Odessa region were in fact the first Jewish soldiers in the Russian Army.

Built on the dusty steppe amid borderland anarchy and casual banditry, Odessa retains the entrepreneurial scheming spirit that has always been its most beloved characteristic. Babel's most famous and adored literary creation is the swaggering wiseguy Jewish gangster Benya Krik of the *Odessa Tales*. As the scene of some of the worst pogroms of the Russian Empire, Odessa harbored Jews who had to get tough fast. Marvelously, and sometimes not, much of the character of the city remains unaffected: Picaresque kleptocracy and violent crime have remained steady features of Odessan life for two centuries. The talk of the town this summer was renewed efforts by the local authorities to expropriate businesses and redistribute them to members of the president's Party of the Regions. From the largest corporate enterprises to my fiancée's friend's graphic design shop with its four employees, no one was safe. The tax police come first asking for the receipts, and the goons arrive shortly thereafter.

The current president of the country, Victor Yanukovych (who is widely alleged to be the de jure political head of the Donetsk mafia clan) has been tried and convicted and jailed for multiple violent crimes, including assault. After the 2004 uprising known as the "Orange Revolution," 2007 marked the Ukrainian public's one concerted effort at democratic intervention into a political process it feels it has no control over. Viktor Yushchenko's ineffectual reign, after clawing back the presidency in the wake of mass demonstrations over a rigged election, and the collapse of the government from infighting between him and fellow revolutionary, braided former Prime Minister Yulia Tymoshenko, dampened any further enthusiasm for democratic politics amongst the Ukrainian people. Tymoshenko's politically motivated trial for corruption in signing off on Russian natural gas contracts as prime minister was this summer's televised grand spectacle. (Sample dialogue from the proceedings: Judge: "You will stand when addressed by this court and refer to me as 'your honor' as legislated by the Ukrainian Law codex!" Tymoshenko: "Honor cannot be legislated; it must be earned.") This month, she was sentenced to seven years in prison.

Over dinner, I asked a TV journalist friend who understands the Ukrainian and Odessan political situations intimately to explain the specifics of the corruption and graft to me. He spent the rest of the meal drawing an intricate Venn diagram with sub-graphs and charts on the white table cover to illustrate the mind-bogglingly complex interrelations of the various oligarchs, local political fiefdoms, competing mafias, rogue intelligence services, London-based gangsters, Russian political machinations, and operations of the state. Every time I spoke with a young person about what they thought of the political situation, what was reflected back was apathy and exhaustion. Everyone made the comparison to Russia. In almost every case the person making the comparison would tell me that Ukraine used to be better off politically and economically, but now the situation was approaching what they called "Russian levels of corruption and political instability."

The dreaded regional prosecutor's office was across the street from my Odessan apartment on graceful, cobblestoned Pushkinskaya Street. While eating my lunch at the café on the corner one day, I asked the owner of the café why no one protested the ongoing usurpation of their businesses. She just shrugged fatalistically as if I had asked her why she did not flail at the trade winds, and then said with typical Odessan brio, "What am I supposed to do? Not serve them soup?"

Odessa's last Jewish mayor, the infamous and flamboyant Eduard Gurvits, who served three terms in the 1990s, began accumulating his fortune during Perestroika when he was the manager of the city's paint factory. (In the late '80s, he would often be seen walking the streets of his wealthy cul-de-sac hocking paint.) A constant thorn in the side of both regional and national authorities, he was swept from power for a second time this past November. Already holding an Israeli passport, he absconded to the land of milk and honey immediately after the elections. Safely out of the reach of the authorities, he finances the city's only legitimate anti-government, dissident television station. This summer, my fiancée, a native of the city, would occasionally come home from an evening out with her Odessan friends to tell me that another acquaintance or a friend of a friend who had worked as an aide to Gurvitz had been jailed.

On another occasion, my fiancée's friend invited us to attend the local Chabad synagogue and the Shabbat dinner afterwards. His name was Yoel, a pleasant, black-frocked Chabadnik who teaches math at the university. His parents live in Denver, and he is waiting to immigrate to the United States with his young bride and their daughter. The crowd at the synagogue was split between the black-coated Hasidim and the rougher looking gentlemen with arm-length prison tattoos. When I marveled at the sheer quantity of prison tattoos exposed by short-sleeved shirts, Yoel explained that the Odessan community's unique nonchalance and acceptance of "problematic social pasts" was one way it distinguished itself. This respect is a prerequisite for reestablishing a functioning community when the majority of Odessan Jewry is to be found in New York, Haifa, Montreal, and Berlin. Mass immigration has brought the proportion of the city's Jews down from a high of 41 percent between the wars to the estimated 4 percent they make up today. There are not that many Odessan Jews left. It is a way also, he told me, to integrate the community's base of potential donors.

"Men in this community who have not done any time are the exception to the norm," Yoel told me as I gawked across the hall at a gentleman with a boxer's face and a tattooed neck "Since the professions were closed off to us, many here had to figure out alternative ways to make a living. The breakdown really runs along generational lines. The guys here in their twenties sat in jail for making money, that is, for the prosecution of economic crimes. Those in their thirties sat in jail for the anti-Semitic prosecution of economic crimes. The ones in their forties who did time were 'politicals.' Anyone older than that who spent time in jail— the dissidents—those guys immigrated."

Hearing of my exotic travels, occasional Russian passport problems, and jocular interest in crossing over to the Transdniesterian border to buy false Moldovan papers, Yoel very kindly offered to make introductions to the Chabadnik whose business it was to acquire "any papers in Eastern Europe you might need for less than 800 American."

As we walked slowly to his house after services, I was introduced to Yasha. Handsome and strapping in his late forties, he had come to pray wearing a sailor shirt, designer jeans, and sandals. A naturalized Dutchman, he had made his money importing luxury cars from Europe and often commuted between Amsterdam, New York, and Odessa. He extended a powerful hand, proffered a steely stare, and greeted me with a barrage of piercing questions: "Bro, you circumcised? If not, it's time. You aren't a boy anymore. I did it at 42. Why do you keep using *their* name? You should carry your real name with pride!"

I was later told that the wrong answer to his question could have had perilous ramifications: During the alcohol-drenched revelry of the previous year's Simchat Torah party, he and a group of the congregants, carousing with the zeal of the newly religious, had seized an uncircumcised teenager and had prepared to perform the operation with the kitchen knife they had been cutting meat with. Only the timely physical intervention of the Israeli rabbi had saved the kid from entry into the covenant.

After the kiddush at Yoel's apartment, I spoke with his brother-in-law, a journalist and spokesman for a political party. The contrast between him and the effete, evenly spoken, intellectual Yoel could not have been more striking. His head was shaved down to military-length stubble, and his enormous muscles strained his tank top. He had sat all through dinner with a Glock pistol tucked into the back of his jeans. He told me that journalism was a different vocation here, carrying a weapon was mandatory, and that the rules and values of the profession were not ones I might understand. I pressed him to explain, but he refused to elaborate. We spent the rest of the night talking about our mutual love of Muay Thai boxing and resolved to go to the gym together.

A few nights before I left, my friends and I were again standing in the middle of Deribasovskaya during the annual klezmer festival. We stood in a ring at the side of the stage speaking with the king of Russian klezmer, Psoy Korolenko, after his show when a group of passing young men turned and without breaking their strides screamed at us, "One grave for all the *Zhids*."

This is when I realized that things change very slowly in Odessa, and that it was time to get back to New York.

Table Magazine 2011

Putin Makes Peace, but Not Before His Minions Try To Kill Poet Boris Khersonsky

This article was published in February of 2015, right as the Minsk II accords were being signed by Russia, Ukraine and the so-called "Luhansk and Donetsk People's Republics." The agreements were about to temporarily halt the fighting taking place in Eastern Ukraine at a time when the Russian regular army was inflicting heavy casualties on the Ukrainians. Boris Khersonsky is the most renowned Russian-language poet living in Odessa and one of Ukraine's best known writers. I grew up and attended school in New York City with his niece Yelena Akhtiorskaya, who fictionalized the poet's life in her scabrously funny novel "Panic in a Suitcase."

As Vladmir Putin celebrates yet another diplomatic victory by force, one element of that victory has gone largely unreported in the Western media: the terrorist bombing campaign, widely ascribed to clandestine Russian intelligence services, that has been carried out weekly across southern Ukrainian cities such as Kherson, Zaporizhye, and Dnipropitrovsk. On Tuesday, on the eve of the Minsk II negotiations, the latest of these attacks targeted the home of the famous Russosphone poet and clinical psychologist Boris Khersonsky in Odessa, where about a dozen similar bombings took place in the last two months. The doors, floors, and windows of Khersonsky's apartment were blown out, and extensive damage was done to some of the rooms. (The same floor of the building also housed a hostel that is currently hosting refugees from Donetsk and Lughansk.

The bomb had been hidden under a pile of garbage bags that lay between the apartment and the hostel. Khersonsky no longer lives at the apartment, but the apartment constituted the poet's official registered address in city records. His ex-wife Tatiana Khersonska was present at the time of the explosion and has suffered acute hearing loss. The attack took place as heads of state Francois Hollande, Angela Merkel, and Petro Poroshenko arrived in the capital of Belarus on the eve of the second round of Minsk protocol negotiations that would reward Putin for sponsoring the violence of Russian-backed separatists and for a string of similar attacks.

Stylistically a quirky classicist, Khersonsky is likely Ukraine's best-known Russian language poet. A graphomaniacally productive writer, he is the author of over two-dozen volumes of poetry (including an excellent bestiary and the slyly heterodox *Hasidic Sayings*), as well as collections of essays and memoirs. Over the last year, he has been an exceedingly candid commentator in his defense of Ukrainian sovereignty. Now one of the numerous death threats that the outspokenly pro-Ukrainian poet had received over the last several months has been acted upon. The blast took place after Khersonsky posted a widely read post denouncing the bombings.

In addition to being a poet, Khersonsky is often quoted in places like *The New Yorker* on questions relating to Odessa's literary history and the city's tradition of multicultural tolerance. When Odessa erupted in deadly violence last spring, Khersonsky was cited in a piece in *The Wall Street Journal* reminding readers that the port retains its identity as a cosmopolitan and fiercely autonomous city:

Odessa is very different from heavily ethnic Russian Crimea as well as the industrial Donetsk region with its own significant Russian population and Soviet Nostalgia. Although it is mostly a Russian-speaking city, it is a true melting pot of cultures, where no single national idea predominates. "Separatism here is inspired from the outside," said Boris Khersonsky, a prominent Odessa poet and psychologist, who is Jewish. "Odessa would like to be independent from everyone."

Khersonsky is also the real-life model for the character of Pasha, a stubbornly recalcitrant poet who refuses to emigrate to America with the rest of his family, in his niece Yelena Akhtiorskaya's critically acclaimed novel *Panic in a Suitcase*.

The poet's son Michael Khersonsky is a filmmaker who has recently left war-torn Ukraine to work in documentary film production in New York City. His wife and baby son were out of the apartment at the time of the explosion. Michael informed me that the family was being helped by multitudes of people who answered a message that he had posted on Facebook. He added, "I am very grateful to them. We are being assisted by the city authorities and by cadres of volunteers. Unfortunately, no one can provide us with the main thing—a guarantee of our safety." He said, "I am very worried about my family and loved ones."

This vicious, squalid, and brutal attack was a targeted assassination attempt against a very great poet and his lovely family who belong to the core of Odessa's artistic intelligentsia and cultural life. While it is certainly a case of moral senselessness, the assault's logic was not arbitrary. Odessa, as has become widely known over the past six months, is a critical junction for the expansion of the so-called "Novorossiya," or "New Russia," the fledgling state entity that the Kremlin is attempting to fashion in southern Ukraine. Along with the besieged port of Mariupol, Odessa is Ukraine's last remaining port in the wake of the Crimean annexation. Without an exit onto the Black Sea, its export economy would quickly collapse. The linking of the Crimean peninsula to mainland Russia across the Kerch Strait is an engineering problem of famous proportions. The costs of both of Moscow's recently proposed bridge-and-tunnel projects are estimated to run into the tens of billions of dollars. It is widely believed that the Kremlin would instead prefer to annex a direct road linking the autonomous Moldovan breakaway region of Transnistria and the Crimean peninsula that the Russians have already taken—and that the world seems prepared to let them have.

Last spring, Russian intelligence services attempted to foment a separatist rebellion in proudly Russophone Odessa, utilizing the same techniques that they had used successfully in the armed takeover of the cities of Luhansk and Donetsk. Those attempts sputtered to a halt outside of Donbas, though not before 48 citizens of Odessa lost their lives in street clashes. After the rebellion fizzled out, the Ukrainian interior ministry culled the higher ranks of the Odessa police force of pro-Russian officers and influences.

Yet the terrorist bombing campaign carried out around the large population centers of southern Ukraine has succeeded in terrorizing both its ordinary and extraordinary citizens alike. It is a craven tactic, but it looks likely to pay dividends to its Kremlin sponsors in the social flight of people like Khersonsky, who have chosen thus far not to emigrate. In his social network profile, Khersonsky wrote candidly that when he is asked what he would do if a "Donetsk-style scenario" played out in Odessa, he replies that he will "tuck the cats under my armpits and leave." That he could "not and would not want to live under the Putinist regime. Which would be a most difficult decision—especially in relation to the cats."

After the bombing, Boris Khersonksy struck back by publishing a poem:

> explosions norm of life coming to terms with them you
> stop noticing man it be your end
> the sapper and demolition man arm-in-arm in the park
> whisper in each other's ear what are they saying
>
> get the gist of the action shovel means undermine
> conspiracy means undermine, underhanded means overkill
> granny grew plain dill* under the rain that fell mainly
> elderly lady means elderberry, God means year
>
> you get the gist of death out of the blue avalanche
> gist of vodka for mortals to handle loss
> mind means undermined means over and out
> black square of a mustache means till death do we part
>
> sapper and demolition pal arm-in-arm in the alley
> terminating angel beholds them holds them with love
> we are unfreebirds good night sweet prints turning read
> shines the black sun the no one's rose of a shell shard

(Translated from Russian by Vladislav Davidzon and Eugene Ostashevsky.)

Ukrop is a slang neologism that literally means "dill" in Russian. It is a derogatory term for Ukrainians with roots in the fighting of the Donbas, which was later appropriated by the Ukranians and became something Ukrainians refer to themselves as. It now adorns patriotic T-shirts with a picture of dill and the word *ukrop*.

Tablet Magazine 2015

One Night in Odessa

The war in Ukraine has divided numerous families along political and cultural lines. This includes my own. Intense national debates followed in the wake of the 2014 Maidan Revolution as well as the Russian military invasion that followed it. These were part of wider cultural changes and transitions that roiled the country and many of these discussions were very much long overdue. However, some of the over-earnest political debates that took place in the overheated atmosphere of 2015 - when the previously mostly integrated Ukrainian and Russian worlds began to separate inexorably - can seem fairly surreal in hindsight.

On our way to my mother-in-law's house on a trip by car to Odessa, we were warned that a distant relative from Donetsk had overstayed her welcome. We were instructed not to specify the length of time we would be staying, so that our visit might be used as a salubrious opportunity to cleanse the spare bedroom of Ludmilla.

My wife's very distant relative, whom she had not seen since she was a teenager, turned out to be a plump, cheerful, and not entirely unpleasant woman in her mid-50s. The late-Soviet-style black bob haircut should have warned me at the time. The war had depressed the Donetsk fur business, and the chance of being killed by an errant shell had been drastically increased as skirmishes raged around her apartments in Horlivka and Donetsk. As a result, she had spent several months camping out in the apartments of unhappy relatives in Moscow and Odessa while ostensibly trying to open up another fur outlet.

Ludmilla invited me to visit her in the Donbas, so that I could see how things were with my own eyes. My newly discovered relations would put in a good word for a border pass and protection papers for me with rebel leader Zakharchenko. He really is a nice guy, I was informed, his reputation to the contrary notwithstanding. Nothing bad would happen to me in Donetsk, she insisted, despite my American passport or my camelhair coat.

Forty minutes after my father-in-law left the house to drive her to the bus stop, we received a phone call informing us that Ludmilla had missed the last bus back to Donetsk. She had mixed up the bus schedule—Donetsk was now an hour ahead of Ukraine, having recently switched onto the Moscow time zone. The only other bus went through Mariupol, which would require going through a Ukrainian army checkpoint. My livid father-in-law attempted to catch up with the bus by speeding through traffic, but after half an hour of futile chasing he capitulated to the inevitable. Ludmilla returned to the kitchen to continue drinking the Odessa region's surprisingly palatable Shabo sparkling wine, and to persist in arguing about politics with my mother-in-law and wife. The awesome screams and sounds of titanic battle that emanated forth from the kitchen for the rest of the night would have terrified all but the bravest members of the human race.

"There is blood on Poroshenko's hands!," Ludmilla screeched.

Shouts of "We are a rich region! We don't want to feed Kyiv anymore! Your oligarchs have gotten fat off of our people long enough!" were countered with haughty retorts that "Parasitical Dombass takes more in infrastructure funds from Kyiv than it pays back in taxes!" "One day Yatsenyuk and his ilk will be shot by a Russian tribunal," mixed with cries of "Your precious criminal Yanukovich was a bandit" and "The Ribbon of Saint George"—the orange-and-black band commemorates the Soviet victory over the Nazis and has been appropriated by the pro-Russian Baltic and Ukrainian Dombas separatists as well as the Kremlin during the Victory Day festivities—"was worn by Andrey Vlasov's treasonous killers as they massacred innocents!"

Unperturbed, Ludmilla took another tack. "We don't go to their land, to Kyiv, to kill. To kill our brothers on their own territory!" she exclaimed, her eyes glittering with her delight in the battle.

"If by 'your territory' what you mean is the land of sovereign Ukraine," riposted my mother-in-law.

"I don't consider myself a Ukrainian, but I was born in Ukraine and I speak Ukrainian ..." Ludmilla whispered, switching into a few words of Ukrainian with a trembling voice.

"We wanted federalization. All we wanted was federalization! Federalization! Fe-de-ra-li-za-tion!"

"Then why did you march with Russian flags?," my otherwise placid wife interceded, repeating arguments that themselves are being repeated word for word across a hundred thousand Ukrainian households.

"You can't protest freely in your beloved Russia!," my mother-in-law accused.

Ludmilla did not give in. Was all this not a double standard? Was this all not cosmic injustice? Why could their side not go out to demonstrate if we pro-Ukrainians could stand around all day on the Maidan? Why could one side not have a referendum?

"Life was good under Yanik! Not at all like under your Yushchenko, let alone your baby-killing Poroshenko!"

"They don't even import Poroshenko's horrible Roshen chocolate into Europe!"

"No, it is the Russian chocolate that is the crappy chocolate!"

Chocolate aside, the assertion that life was indeed better for Yanik's clan and his constituents in the Donbas under his kleptocratic reign was doubtless true. "Do you have any idea how many furs I sold then?," Ludmilla demanded with rueful disbelief.

Ludmilla was incensed. "The ousting of Yanukovich was a great coup" was parried with "he fled his responsibilities as head of state and was impeached." Allegedly, Right Sector leader Dmytro Yarosh had walked into Yanukovich's office on Feb. 21 and told him that it was time for him to leave. "Yanik did not flee his office out of cowardice, he was coerced! Yarosh even admitted to this once in a television interview!"

There seems to have been an ominously voiced Russian made-for-TV interview about the incident. In the interests of fairness and to determine if this was true my mother-in-law agreed to watch the entirety of a rambling YouTube interview with Yarosh. Thirty minutes later Yarosh had yet to make the self-incriminating comments about forcing Yanukovich to flee for Russia. My wife gently insisted that there might be a cultural clash between East and West and a problem with the cities of the Dombass, with vestiges of the region's historical criminal mentality still prevalent in the eastern coal mining towns of Eastern Ukraine.

"This is all pure Russophobia!," exclaimed Ludmilla.

"I am not Russophobic, even though I am Russian!," my Jewish mother-in-law insisted passionately to her ardently pro-Russian relative (who was herself half-Polish, half-Greek, which debunks all arguments about ethnicity.) As the conversation grew even more heated, both sides began using slang neologisms and argot for the other.

"If we want to clean up the city, the region and the country, let's start with our kitchen and stop calling Western Ukrainians 'Banderovtsiy,'" my wife insisted.

"You all think that we in Donbas are backwards retards!"

"I don't divide people into the first and second sort," Ludmila sniffed. "I am Russian and I like it in Donetsk! One day there will be a trial in The Hague! For Poroshenko, for Yatsenyuk, for Arsen Avakov! One day there will be a tribunal! Poroshenko will beg for mercy from the firing squad and Yarosh will put a revolver to his temple!"

And what about the perfidious Joe Biden? I wondered.

"Yes, Biden!," Ludmilla eagerly assented. "What do you think Biden does here? Why does he keep coming here? Why all those meetings in Kyiv? The Kyiv Junta are going to sell the Donbas to the Americans on a 50-year lease!" she warned darkly, despite a certain lack of evidence.

The argument degenerated over the presence of marauding Russian soldiers on the separatist side and the alleged existence of crack American divisions and mercenaries on the Ukrainian side. The question of NATO special operations "ghosts" fighting on the Ukrainian side drove the argument in the direction of pure epistemology: How do we know what we really know? Do Western Ukrainians really want to make speaking Russian illegal? How do we know if Biden really did not send NATO ghost legions into the Donbas?

The debate raged inconclusively for several hours, concluding only when my mother-in-law began yelling about the "zombifying" powers of Russian television. She then began grasping theatrically at her chest while reaching for her heart medicine and valerian root pills. "Don't get agitated," Ludmila tried to soothe her. "It's bad for the heart. Take your pills! After all, I am being shelled by Ukrainian troops all day, and I am not getting hysterical in the middle of the kitchen."

My wife and I left as soon as possible.

Ludmilla stayed.

I have since been informed that the argument has continued unabated at every meal for the past three months.

Tablet Magazine 2015

A Close (and Surprisingly Positive) Encounter with Odessa`s New Police

The reform of Ukraine`s deeply corrupt police force was a major social objective in the wake of the Maidan Revolution of Dignity. The reformist government which came to power set its sights on nation wide police reform. Before the Maidan, the police basically functioned as a parasitical pyramid-bribe-extortion racket on the general population. The reform was a project to which Ukraine`s Western partners devoted tremendous resources. The Georgians had successfully gone through the same process several years earlier, and former Georgian cabinet ministers arrived in Ukraine en masse to help facilitate the modernization process. Some serious accomplishments aside, for various reasons the reform process would run into difficulties and would mostly fail over the next six years. Large numbers of the corrupt police officers were very difficult to get rid of, especially in cities outside of Kyiv. The national police reform also focused on intentionally recruiting "sexy" officers and played up the newly attractive police force in public relations campaigns. In Kyiv and Odessa, the police brigades were swiftly repopulated with attractive young people, some of whom had very interesting pasts as I learned when the beautiful police spokeswoman whom I was interviewing turned out to be a former pole dancer. The large proportion of former strippers in the new Kyiv force soon became apparent to the general mirth of the population, which may or may not constitute a policy failure. This very pleasant midnight meeting with the new police took place in the Autumn of 2015 in a moment of excited expectation, which alas, ended in disappointment.

The reorganization and reform of Ukraine's catastrophically corrupt police force was the top priority when President Petro Poroshenko appointed Eka Zguladze first deputy Interior Minister of Ukraine.

Poroshenko wants to emulate the relative success that Georgia's Rose Revolution reformers garnered in modernizing their small post-Soviet country. Zguladze is just one of the many Georgians who have been drafted by the new Ukrainian government to kick reforms into high gear.

In January 2015, Ukraine's Ministry of the Interior began recruiting the first of approximately 2,200 new patrol officers in Kyiv. The first battalions were inaugurated on July 4. The rigorous selection process included a ten-week training program accompanied by a battery of exams. In an effort to ensure moral rectitude in the new force, the officers are paid almost $400 a month, roughly three times more than new recruits previously made.

The glistening new patrol police can also be seen cruising the streets of Cherkasy, Kharkiv, Lviv, and Odessa. By the end of the year, there should be at least 10,000 new officers.

American and Canadian trainers provided state-of-the-art training and equipment. The newly reformed police were carefully instructed to be polite and, in marked contrast to the previous force, only use force with cause. The photogenic new cadres proved to be wildly popular, especially in Kyiv, and spawned a cottage industry of laudatory news articles about the populace lining up to take photos with them.

However, some influential Ukraine experts have argued that police reform is of relative insignificance in comparison to the scope of the nation's wider corruption issues. In addition, more than 100,000 of the old police remain on the job, and Ukraine has more than four times as many security officers per capita than comparable West European countries. Police forces operate on a mafia-like system of tributary patronage. Much like feudal vassals, law enforcement agents are expected to deliver a set amount of tribute to their commanding officer each week. Each rank kicks up tribute to the rank above it, forcing officers to extract the required amounts from citizens in the form of coerced bribes. The result is universal complicity, with the rot rising to the highest levels of the force. Without a wholesale purge of the old corps, the argument goes, any change is akin to applying a band aid to a gangrening limb.

Those arguments certainly have merit, but they fail to understand the visceral symbolic importance of the actual experience one has when encountering the new police instead of the old guard (with whom one tried to minimize interactions at all costs).

My wife and I had our first experience with Odessa's new police last week. It was admittedly anecdotal and perhaps random, yet it left us exceedingly impressed.

At 2:30 am on November 3, I was pleasantly immersed in my writing and oblivious to the raucous scène de ménage taking place between the neighbors. Abruptly, my wife strode out the front door in her slippers and bathrobe. Neglecting to relate her intentions to me, she marched purposefully down the stairs. I barely caught up with her before she began knocking on the neighbor's door. When the door creaked open, she warned them in no uncertain terms that they had five minutes to stop shrieking before she would call the police. "Wait for me the next time you do that!" I reproached her worriedly. Unflappable as only a French-educated daughter of an Odessa sailor and now filmmaker could be, she riposted that she could handle her own conflicts.

Our clamorous neighbors did not put an end to their fracas and my wife followed through with her promise. Ten minutes later, a pair of good-looking and clean-cut young men in their late twenties arrived. Surprisingly, they had distinctly unpolice-like manners. After having a stern talk with the neighbors, the exceedingly polite officers in their snazzy blue American uniforms and peaked caps arrived at our door to complete the complaint form.

The officers were nothing like the arrogant, paunchy, agitated, ill-mannered officers with greasy uniforms that one was used to. Slim and athletic, they also spoke grammatically correct Russian and Ukrainian.

They read out our rights to information under the Ukrainian constitution and asked us to sign the complaint. Afterwards, they made small talk and politely inquired where they could see my wife's films.

Every previous encounter with Ukraine's Security Service or police I've had has concluded with a radically unpleasant denouement. That is with them being flippantly nasty, demanding a bribe, or deploying domineering power maneuvers for the simple sadistic thrill. Once as I was passing through Kyiv's Boryspil airport several years back, a border guard informed me that he could strip me naked and confiscate me if he felt like it. In most civilized countries, that approach would be considered a case of egregiously bad manners as well as being manifestly bad for business.

Instead, the new recruits smiled at my jocular inquiries about their California police trainers and laughed at my jab about having paid for their uniforms as an American taxpayer. The old *militsiya* would have clubbed me on principle. They gamely discussed their training at 3 am—the black beating heart of the journalist never ceases beating—and addressed my queries as to whether they had successfully gotten rid of the pro-Russian influences and sympathizers in the force. By the time we had filled out the complaint, I was about ready to invite them in for a nightcap.

The Atlantic Council 2015

An American Innocent Abroad
Meets a New York Dandy In Odessa

Along with its hard-nosed skepticism, Odessa is renowned for an acerbic sense of humor, expressed most characteristically in its love of iconic set-piece anecdotes. Odessa has a way of drawing innocent and often colorful travelers into humorous adventures. For instance, Mark Twain's visit to Odessa in 1867 may have entailed far more anecdotal episodes than his book "The Innocents Abroad; or, The New Pilgrim's Progress" reveals. This encounter with a Cowboy in Odessa seems to emanate straight from his imagination — but it surely happened!

Today, as I was returning home from my office, dressed in a sober black business suit and black tie after attending an earlier meeting at City Hall, I ran into a personage wearing an entirely different sort of suit.

Arriving at the entrance to my apartment building, I saw a man with a droopy mustache. He turned out to be an American dressed in a cowboy hat, denim jacket over well-worn jeans, a plaid shirt and cowboy boots, the outfit topped off with a Wyoming State belt buckle. Intrigued, I struck up a conversation with the stranger, and eventually inquired about his profession.

"Well, I am what I look like," he replied. "I am a cowboy from Wyoming, on the South Dakota border, where I have 3000 head of cattle!" We had a conversation about this being his first trip to Europe, and I took the opportunity to tell him that Mark Twain had visited Odessa in the nineteenth century. "Really?" the Cowboy exclaimed with amazement. "I like Huckleberry Finn, and all that good stuff... He reminds me of my younger self!"

I asked the Cowboy to stay on the corner as I ran upstairs to my apartment to get him a hard copy of this magazine as a souvenir of his visit.

He assured me that he would wait, but when I returned a few minutes later, he was gone.

Disappointed, I looked all around the street to find him. Somewhat dejected, I made an inquiry with a pair of old men smoking on the corner.

"Did you see that gentleman in the cowboy hat? Where did he go?"

"Well, I have never seen a gentleman before. There are no gentlemen here other than yourself," one of the Odessan jokesters replied.

"There was a cowboy here!" I tried to convince him. "The one from Wyoming? He had a droopy mustache and a pair of cowboy boots."

"Listen, there are no cowboys in Odessa. Cowboys live in the desert, with horses," he tried to assure me.

"But he was really here, the Cowboy..." I began to protest. "He had come to Odessa to find a mail order bride! He told me he was going to take her back to Wyoming."

But the shrewd old Odessite would have none of it: "It must have been a mirage. You are imagining him, there never was a cowboy. It is because of your glasses, you cannot see straight..."

I am comforted by the conviction that somewhere, the Cowboy is telling his friends of his encounter with a New York dandy in Ukraine and trying to convince them that it really happened.

The Odessa Review 2017

Russian Conceptual Artist Petr Pavlensky Gives Sensational Lecture On Violent Political Art, Evening Ends With Lethal Brawl

The lecture of Russian conceptual artist Petr Pavlensky, renowned for his numerous acts of radical actionism against the Russian authorities, was the most anticipated culture event of the summer of 2016. No one expected the lethal violence that would conclude the talk.

Russia's best known contemporary artist arrived to deliver a lecture to an over filled hall in Odessa's Impact Hub on Friday night. He was ascetic, strikingly skeletal and possessed of an undeniable dignity and bearing. Hundreds of people excitedly packed the lecture hall, as this was widely expected to be the event of the summer. Petr Pavlensky was newly freed from a Russian prison cell in the wake of becoming a dissident cause célèbre for having set the doors of Moscow's infamous Lubyanka prison on fire. The lecture's title was a double entendre that translated roughly as the 'usage of a person' or the 'consumption of people', hinting broadly at the theme of mechanized cannibalism. However, fittingly, this electrifying lecture calling for wide scale resistance to tyranny and the everyday deployment of the mechanisms of social oppression, concluded in violence. Somewhere, one can imagine Mayakovsky smiling.

The artist spoke rapidly, in fully formed declarative sentences weighted with the moral fervor of a mystic or fanatic – and also marked by the sort of saintly simplicity that is borne of being utterly unplagued by internal doubts. As he spoke, Pavlensky quickly flipped through a power point presentation of woodcut prints of medieval tortures, gruesome pictures of Russian prison, images of his actions and documentation from his various court proceedings. He explained the connections between state methods of control and that of the bureaucratic act of naming; the 'Panopticon'; and the mobilization of modern medicine as a system whose purpose is to both name our pathologies and create pathologies out of our names. The state controls manifold resources and near limitless funds to harass the individual with the administrative, legal, political and military regimes under its control. Pavlovsky explained that his political provocations were meant to elicit a response from the system and to also forge the concrete artifacts of political documentation of its true nature. Judges, lawyers, clerks, the police are all cogs in an overlapping system of total control.

Yet, as unapologetically theoretical as the lecture had been ('the system of prisons works on the semantic level') it was also an exercise in the practical application of the discourse of Foucauldian theory to the fight against the Russian state. Pavlovsky explained that his political provocations were meant to elicit a response from the system and to forge artifacts of political documentation of its nature.

Being a Russian revolutionary, it was not more than ten minutes into the lecture before he asked the audience 'what is to be done?' Pavlensky's own uncompromising reply to a state that he views as categorically totalitarian is to literalize the usually figurative academic trope of the 'inscription of violence upon the body'. Powerless, and bereft of the usual recourses against state power enjoyed by citizens in a liberal democratic polity, "he would demonstrate the true nature of the system by committing violent acts upon his own flesh and daring the system to destroy his body in turn." The politics were unambiguously anarchist. He soon called on the audience to take responsibility for fighting the repressive state on to themselves. They should personally stand up to the cannibalism of bureaucracy.

'So what are my tools?'' he inquired majestically of the audience before showing us photos of 'ordinary and readily available weapons to be deployed against the state.' These included twine (with which he had sown shut his mouth), a blade (with which he had sliced himself), a large nail (which he had used to nail his scrotum to the cobble stones of the Red Square) and a canister of gas (it had been used in the Lubyanka performance). The men in the audience emitted a collective groan when the close up image of his genitals with a nail driven through them flashed onscreen. The Lubyanka action had been his most successful work yet, he posited, as the state had collaborated in the creation of the work by creating numerous legal texts and documentation for his trial. The audience applauded loudly after the security camera clip from the FSB building inferno was played.

An hour of discussion of aestheticised violence concluded with the question and answer period which is when the problems began in earnest.

Alexander Roytburd, one of Ukraine's best known painters and a prominent voice on the Maidan moderated the evening with probing questions about the difference between rhetorical anarchism and the proper boundaries of art. The futurist free radical who would be the one to tip the lecture over from the realm of theory into that of practice was a mutual friend of both Pavlensky and Roytburd. Vladimir Nestrenko is a well known character in Odessa's 'marginal' underground and art worlds. The question of whether he was merely a drunken lunatic or rather an inspired literal interpreter of anarchist doctrine will doubtless soon be determined by the "coercive juridico- bureaucratic" structures of the oppressive state apparatus.

A film script writer and sometime journalist, he is known to have worked on some important films and art projects in previous decades. He was visibly agitated and inebriated when he arrived at the talk. When we were first introduced by mutual acquaintance at the door, he greeted me with a handshake accompanied by aggressive and lewd gestures. He would continue to publicly consume large quantities of cognac throughout the course of the lecture.

Mr. Nestrenko waved his arms and made numerous attempts to disrupt the question and answer portion of the lecture. These efforts escalated during the portion that dealt with the difference between Pavlensky's ideas of artist political violence and that of 90's style 'Actionism' (which in its post-Soviet variant was an art movement that had roots in Odessa). Roytburd made several tactful attempts to quiet his friend down, but at a certain point, multiple incensed voices from the audience began to refer to him as a 'provocateur!'

The venue's two security guards moved in and attempted to escort the now out of control Mr. Nestrenko from the premise. At which point he initiated a melée and began to throttle them. A crowd of bearded hipsters, artists and Nestrenko's own friends knocked him to the floor. After being separated from the guards, Nestrenko stood up and produced a knife, assaulting one of the guards, who suffered cuts to his arm and hand.

Roytburd and several others then proceeded to bundle their belligerent friend out of the conference hall and to help him flee. The wounded security guard left a trail of splattered blood all along the floor and down the staircase on his way out. The police made no arrests on the premises.

In a bizarre and tragic addendum to the story, the second of the two security guards, who had not been hurt in the altercation, was reported by local television to have suffered a fatal heart attack in the back of a police vehicle immediately after the incident.

The Odessa Review 2016

Last-Minute Threat Cancels
Nobel Laureate Speech in Odessa

A long awaited reading and public appearance in Odessa by Belarusian writer Svetlana Alexievich - winner of the 2015 Nobel Prize in literature and herself of Ukrainian descent -was abruptly cancelled at the last moment in the wake of a threatening provocation. The cancellation of the reading by the most famous living Russophone writer, one who had been a staunch supporter of Ukrainian sovereignty in the midst of the ongoing conflict with Russia, was a serious blow to the city. Odessa's literati and cultural élites had fantasized for a long time about organizing an Alexievich reading in the city. This spring, after it became apparent that the Green Theater amphitheater - the venue that would host the Nobel Prize winner- would not be able to afford her customary reading fee, the entire city went about crowdfunding the sum of several thousand dollars in order to cover the honorarium and travel costs.

About four hours before Alexievich was scheduled to take the stage, an anonymous individual had added her name to the list of anti-Ukrainian activists on the controversial nationalist Mirotvorets website. The website—the name means "Peacemaker"—is run by Ukrainian nationalists and affiliated hackers, and has become internationally infamous in 2016 when it leaked the names and private contact information of more than 4,000 journalists who had reported from occupied Donbas. Those journalists all had to go through press accreditation processes with self-declared authorities in the occupied region in order to have access to the war zone. Although the site removed Alexievich's name from the list several hours later, the writer and the theater decided to cancel the event "to avoid possible risks for Alexievich and the audience in the theater."

Alexievich was born in Ukraine, and is herself half-Ukrainian on her mother's side. She has always been supportive of Ukraine in her public pronouncements over the course of the last four years. The incident that the perpetrators of this latest provocation used as their pretext seemed to be taken from comments that Alexievich had made during her 2016 public lecture in Brooklyn, during which she spoke about the involvement of Ukrainians in ethnic killings that took place in Belarus during the Second World War.

"I will tell you this as well," she said at the time. "The same sort of, the 'executioners' who worked in Belarus, they were from Ukraine, and moreover, not only in Lithuania, they themselves destroyed the Jews even before the Germans arrived. It was also the same in Ukraine."

The Myrotvorets site took down the offending material about her as quickly as it was put up, but the damage had already been done. Right before the event was scheduled to begin, Alexievich issued her own statement explaining that for the sake of public safety, she would be canceling the public appearance. The identity of the individual who had contacted the Green Theater with the information before the event remains unknown.

Aleksander Babitch, a well known Odessa tour guide and local personality, who showed the Nobel Prize winner around town during her visit, wrote on his Facebook page that he had "called all the leaders of the pro-Ukrainian groups in town and all the guys swore that they had no intention of undermining the meeting with the Nobel Prize winner, as her visit was important for both Odessa and Ukraine." They were ready to come out to the Green Theater to take Alexievich and the event under their personal protection. Babitch went on to apologize personally to Alexievich on behalf of the city for the provocation, and expressed his hopes that the planned reading would take place soon enough and that the "individuals who so grotesquely embarrassed the city would burn in hell."

While the cancellation of the public talk was surely a blow to the public and the literary spirit of the city- as well as a great disappointment to the young people who had spent months working to make it happen- it is in many ways a much bigger embarrassment for the Ukrainian nation as a whole. The Ukrainian authorities (especially some who are close to the interior ministry), had long tacitly tolerated and encouraged the Myrotvorets website and the scorn that it has heaped on journalists. They did so for the sake of shortsighted political positioning. On yet another level however, this whole sordid and unfortunate episode is part of a global cultural problem. That is of the colonizing of the separate and sacral space reserved for the arts by insidious and very crude forms of identity politics.

Tablet Magazine 2018

II. Politics and Adventure

On the Road With Bernard-Henri Lévy, the Planet's Last Superstar French Intellectual

"Incapable of talking about myself? That's not my reputation, not precisely. And when I do think about it, they reproach me with the opposite: exhibitionism, narcissism, being the type who always says 'me, me, me,' the media star and the self-promoter, king of the troublemakers, a total egocentrist, a specialist at drawing media attention ... I could go on."
—Bernard-Henri Lévy, Comédie (1997)

I.

It was a balmy Friday evening in Paris, in early March, and 500 Ukrainians had massed at the corner where rue Apollinaire meets the Saint-Germain-des-Prés Plaza to celebrate the overthrow of their country's reviled President Viktor Yanukovich. Deposed, despite his sanctioning indiscriminate fire against the crowds, he had fled the capital into Putin's frigid embrace and offer of sanctuary in the Russian border city of Rostov-on-Don. In between bouts of patriotic song and chanting ("Glory to Ukraine! Glory to the heroes!") they inquired one another's names and towns of origin. The aura of solidarity was undeniably bewitching, not least for the organizer of the event, France's most prominent public intellectual, *philosophe*, journalist, novelist, filmmaker, dandy, libertine, and sometime professional revolutionary, Bernard-Henri Lévy.

Exactly one month before, on Feb. 9, BHL, as Lévy is universally known to the French, had appeared in Kyiv to deliver a typically grandiloquent and stirring speech, studded with proclamations of fidelity to the loftiest principles of freedom and solidarity in the face of tyranny.

The apex of his oration was the declaration "France is Ukraine! Ukraine is Europe!" It was an axiom that augured the commencement of BHL's own direct involvement in the Ukrainian political crisis. It has been almost three years since the great coup of his career as a diplomatic/political operator intervening (or if one prefers, meddling) at the highest levels of the French state. With a flurry of beseeching satellite phone calls to President Nicolas Sarkozy from the desert outskirts of Benghazi, BHL helped to engineer the French military intervention in Libya that led to the ousting of the Qaddafi regime—events that confirmed BHL's unique standing as a freelance statesman who runs his own foreign policy parallel to that of the French state.

With his gifts—the intelligence and good looks, superhuman stamina, money, and connections—it would be almost criminal if BHL did not accomplish something of world historical importance, a thought that seems to animate some good part of his peripatetic engagements. His answer to questions about the oddness of one unelected intellectual pursuing his own foreign policy is that he is forced to take action when the French state fails to do so: "The real deficit is in the actions of the Quai d'Orsay." The example of his friend Bernard Kouchner's experience as French foreign minister has also doubtless made BHL cautious about accepting government posts. (Kouchner was thrown out of the Socialist party for crossing party lines, before being sacked in a cabinet reshuffle.) "I told him not to take it!" BHL confided. Sarkozy did offer BHL the culture ministry, which he duly turned down, as he habitually turns down *the Legion d'honneur.*

Still, not everyone is thrilled by the kindly policy assistance that this unelected patriot offers the French state. Sarkozy's actual foreign minister, Alain Juppé, once threatened to resign after he was looped into a critical meeting that BHL had freelanced with the Libyan rebels. The response of the current foreign minister, Laurent Fabius (the son of assimilated Jews; BHL has known him since he was 17), to BHL's meddling with his portfolio has largely been one of passive resistance: According to someone present at the cabinet meeting that BHL had set up for the Ukrainians, Fabius sat silently peering at his phone for the duration of the gathering.

***

The Ukrainian delegation had arrived in Paris that March morning aboard billionaire presidential candidate Petro Poroshenko's private plane. After BHL's intense lobbying for an official reception by the French state and cabinet—throughout the crisis, the French government had shown no interest in meeting with any representatives of Ukraine—the delegation had briefed President François Hollande on Kyiv's options in the wake of the Russian annexation of Crimea. Now they would address an auditorium filled to bursting with their countrymen, as several hundred more waited outside. Stocky Ukrainian men draped in blue-and-yellow flags fraternized with blue-eyed young men in Vyshyvankas. Pretty Slavic blondes with wreaths of flowers in their hair jostled for seats with middle-aged Soviet women with boxy haircuts. The crowd spilled out of the chairs and into the aisles clutching banners and massive flags.

On the stage, our host BHL welcomed us to "Maidan on Saint-Germain-des-Prés" and delivered a rousing speech in defense of Ukraine's natural place in Europe. BHL is tall, slim, and broad-shouldered and carries himself like a man 20 years younger. The flowing mane of famously sculpted hair is now streaked with gray, but he is still handsome in the symmetric fashion. The signature custom-made white shirt was open to his chest. The beautiful bespoke black suit from Charvet, a knightly suit of armor that has been his uniform of four decades, glittered with a soft sheen. On this occasion it was a single-button continental cut with an Italianate drape, a pinched waist, and billowing trousers. He paced the stage in fiery restiveness and thundered at the grandiose registers demanded by the revolutionary mood. His oratory that night—there are those who think that he might be France's greatest living orator—was an impassioned, astute, and morally committed denunciation of Russian imperialism. Playing to the crowd, he occasionally ventured too deeply into rhetorical plays on the theme of "Putin is the new Hitler."

The portly Poroshenko spoke next and began by informing the crowd that he had agreed to say a few words in English. The suggestion was roundly booed, and he switched into his accomplished and fluid Ukrainian to speak about the rule of law and economic reforms. Kyiv Mayor Vitali Klitschko, another presidential hopeful, addressed the gathering next. He was grim-faced and stoic, not in the least a natural politician. On the other hand, he is close to 7 feet tall and is by far the biggest person in the room; there is a primordial quality to the intuition that his leadership claim is derived from his sheer size and martial prowess in the same way that primitive tribes would choose their strongest warrior to be their chieftain. Klitschko's stiff Ukrainian hinted at his Russophone Odessa origins: He noted that "his mother is Russian and father is Ukrainian" and occasionally stumbled while trying to recall a word in Ukrainian. One did not need to be a great political scientist to see which of the two men would become president.

A minute of silence was observed in honor of the "celestial hundred" of demonstrators who had given their lives for Ukraine on and around Maidan Square. A pair of shy, teary-eyed young women, a medic and an activist, softly recounted the horror of watching their friends fall before the bullets. The shorter of the two had thick scar tissue from where a sniper's bullet had entered her neck. After they spoke, the crowd rose to its feet and cheered them with vigorous cries of *Molodzi* (good work)! The final speaker was the suave rector of the Mogilev academy, who spoke in impressive French about the need for connections between Kyiv and Paris. After the last speech, the crowd stood to sing Ukraine's mournful national anthem.

Immediately after the rally concluded, Klitschko grasped the opportunity to disappear backstage. Poroshenko dove into the crowd to shake hands, take photographs, and get into an impressive yelling match with a young activist who righteously accused the old-guard politician of not having a reformist platform. My wife and I decided to conclude the evening half a block away at the Café de Flore, where it turned out that we were not the only Champagne socialists to find themselves in Paris' plushest café at the end of the evening: The maître d' sat us at a table next to where Lévy was dining with the Ukrainian delegation, the rector of the Mogilev academy, and some of our Ukrainian acquaintances. I would learn later that he had partially planned the French intervention in Libya while hosting the Libyan rebels at the same table.

BHL was pleased with the tremendous turnout that the rally had garnered on only a few hours' notice. Earlier that day, he had convened

II. Politics and Adventure   41
On the Road With Bernard-Henri Lévy,
the Planet's Last Superstar French Intellectual

the Parisian intelligentsia and political class at his home. Reverence before the natural moral authority of the Ukrainians was the only thing that united a disparate assortment of quarrelsome politicians, journalists, and writers. President Hollande had also received the Ukrainians very warmly. He was confident that on this occasion Putin would make hubristic mistakes that would bring down his regime. "Putin will only remain stronger than us if we choose to be weak. He will lose if, and only if, we stand by our principles," he explained in his earnestly staccato style. "If we are weak, he will be strong!"

Answering my final question, as to how he saw the responsibility of France or the French intelligentsia to the Ukrainians in their darkest hour, BHL was in his element: "The merit and primary responsibility of France is to ring the bell! Europe currently has no will, no head, and no courage. In Mali, as in Libya and as in some ways also with the case of Syria, France took the lead!" Finishing his dinner, the philosophe bade the table a hasty farewell and then dashed off purposefully into the night. And so, my adventures with the world's most influential public intellectual—and maybe the last Jewish intellectual of any real global consequence—began.

II.

Several weeks after the Ukrainian rally, I was invited to lunch at the enormous duplex apartment that BHL shares with his third wife, movie star Arielle Dombasle. Ascending a circular staircase to the building's final floor, one is met at the door by a white uniformed butler. The apartment is a velvety cross between the ancient civilization wing of an art museum and an Oriental palazzo. The long divans are surrounded by extensive collections of curios: reclining golden Buddhas, coffee tables littered with knickknacks and heaps of crystals and statuettes. One can imagine it is the sort of apartment Lawrence of Arabia would have found himself ensconced in at the end of his life if he had survived his motorcycle accident. There is a view of the Palais de l'Élysée out of a window from which BHL can keep a close eye on the seat of power of the French state.

Dombasle greeted me in their dining room and, making my day, complimented my suit as *"très élégant."* Extending her smartphone with her thin elongated arm, she corralled me and BHL into a picture along with a mysterious bespectacled person named Françoise. She and Françoise then promptly disappeared, dematerializing as if by teleportation. In the movie-star fashion, the family life is both publicly exposed and carefully protected. In interview after interview, this man renowned for his self-promotion insists that the "right to privacy is one of the highest, most sacred of rights." That discretion, as well as a talent for misdirection, reveals a capacity for psychological and administrative compartmentalization of the various strands of a complex and manically busy life.

Spending any length of time with BHL, one will become cognizant of the many contradictions that shape both his private life and his public persona. His outraged sense of justice is intertwined with a brazen pursuit of an 18th-century-style world-historical greatness. Like Benjamin Disraeli, BHL is a self-fashioned Sephardic Jew who observed and masterfully replicated the manifold idiosyncrasies of the locals and climbed to the top of the greasy pole by dint of dogmatic tenacity. Like Disraeli, he had to contend with the conflicted relationship to Jews of the native ruling class, which despite its prejudices gives disproportionate power and prestige to intellectuals. Also, much like Disraeli, he accomplished everything despite the liability of an unconventional wardrobe.

An arch-romantic in the classical style, BHL is also a political operator who alternates macho bravado with delicate manners. Flitting between war zones and five-star hotels, habitually surrounded by material opulence, he is seldom caught sleeping or eating. At 65 years old, when most people are tinkering with their pension plans, he is as kinetic as a man half, even a third, his age. "Retire?" he ripostes when I broach the topic. "I am your age!" Responding to a recent query from a Parisian newspaper about the secret of his perpetual youth, his advice was, "Don't spend time with boring people." The unbuttoned white shirt—he tells interviewers that he would choke otherwise—is a form of social provocation that he doubtlessly relishes; it also constitutes a dandyish parlor trick, leading otherwise shrewd judges of character and intellectual talent to underestimate his political acumen and Puritan work habits.

Much of the anti-BHL feeling in France is clearly unabashed envy, while some of it stems from veiled anti-Semitism. It is also undeniably true that over the years his work has traded meticulousness of analysis for floridness of expression and the blunt instrumental exegeses of pure rhetorical power. If no longer the most rigorous, he remains the most widely read intellectual in France, whose stream of political journalism, commentary, and first-person participatory narratives frames and drives national political debate to a degree even his staunchest critics grudgingly acknowledge. If he were not already wealthy by virtue of his inheritance, he would have quickly become so from the sales of his books—most of which remain in print.

Born in Bén Siaf, Algeria, BHL and his family emigrated to Morocco when he was a week old; the Lévys migrated to France soon after. His father joined up and fought the Germans with the *Brigades Internationales* as part of the French Resistance, founded the timber company Becob, and accumulated one of the largest fortunes in postwar France. At 18 BHL matriculated in the exclusive *École Normale Supérieure*, which marked him as a "Normalian" and as a member of the ruling elite. He studied philosophy under the tutelage of two other Algerian philosophers: the madly rigorous deconstructionist Jacques Derrida and the rigorously mad Marxist Louis Althusser. He was 20 during the tumultuous events of 1968 but is not known to have been active on the revolutionary barricades.

After a very brief stint teaching philosophy, he traveled to Bangladesh in early 1971 to cover the civil war for Albert Camus' underground journal *Combat*. With the commencement of the Pakistani army's ethnic slaughter, André Malraux had issued a call for international intervention in Bangladesh (then known as East Pakistan) and the formation of a new international brigade of the sort that he had led in the Spanish Civil War. While BHL was only one among a hundred volunteers who signed up, he may be the only one to have actually made the trek. (A Pakistani journalist's hagiographic description of BHL's incursion as a "one-man international brigade" is not incorrect.) The trip turned into a prolonged stay as well as a stint in Bangladesh's fledgling economics ministry. It would also culminate in BHL's first book, *Bangla-Desh, Nationalisme dans la revolution* (Bangladesh: Nationalism in the Revolution—republished in the 1980s as *Les Indes Rouges*). Published when he was 24, it remains the only contemporary French account of the Bangladeshi civil war and the genocide it engendered. The book remains untranslated into English.

Returning to Paris from Dhaka, he penned three more books in quick succession that together launched his career as a public intellectual. *La Barbarie à Visage Humain* (Barbarism with a Human Face) was published to wide acclaim when he was 28. The book constituted a fraternal assault on the lingering Leninist-Stalinist tendencies of the old unreconstructed French left. *L'Idéologie Française* (1981) predicated that the French are hardwired for fascism—and the metastatic resurgence of the French right that took place soon after its publication seemed to prove the insolent young Jewish dandy correct. Not content to tangle with Marxism and the essential ontological spirit of France, he also picked a brawl with God in *Le Testament de Dieu* (1978). (BHL is an implacably atheist Jew in the "there's only one God and we don't believe in him" sense, as well as being a Zionist.) Collectively the three works managed to scandalize the French reading public, regardless of political persuasion. "I have developed a finely tuned antenna for why any given French person dislikes my work," he told me. "They will say I like all your work except this one and they will name the book. With one phrase I know if the person is a Fascist, religious, or of the old left wing."

The French ruling class to which BHL belongs is hermetic, cohesive, and centralized in Paris and also—or therefore—exceptionally incestuous. Anyone who indulges the taste for the intrigues of the French intelligentsia will know that before she married Sarkozy to become the first lady, Carla Bruni had broken up the marriage of BHL's novelist daughter Justine to the son of his close friend, Grasset publisher Jean-Paul Enthoven. In his relations with the French elite, BHL is both an outsider and consummate insider: He has been chairman of the board of the French-German culture television station ARTE for 20 years (like an oriental potentate, he jokes) as well as directing his own magazine *La Règle du Jeu*

(Rules of the Game). The confluence of politics, culture, journalism, and business relations over which he presides is controversial and unimaginable anywhere outside of France. When I inquired whether he has more or less influence under the socialists—his natural home and fratricidal "family on the left"—he shrugged thoughtfully before replying, "It's hard to say." The independence granted by his immense wealth keeps him from lapsing into the role of the court philosopher. His position in the French political firmament is akin to a secular, modern-day variation on the outsize political influence that cerebral churchmen like Cardinal Richelieu or Jean François Paul de Gondi or Cardinal de Retz once wielded over the French throne.

That said, there is also something unmistakably American about the self-fashioned transformation of an immigrant boy from North Africa into a jet-setting playboy-philosopher who advises heads of state on foreign policy. His work has smuggled Anglo-American strains of liberalism into French political thought in the same way that his friend Nicolas Sarkozy's political swagger brought the American style of brashness to French politics. Novel in a French context, the arch-individualism, swagger, work ethic, frenetic pace, and transparent ambition would all be quite normal in New York City or Washington, D.C. That he is a friend of America and of the postmodernist form of emancipation that it represents against the principled disdain of the unreconstructed old French left is a core driving force of his more recent work. In 2002, he spent a year in Pakistan and wrote a book called *Who Killed Daniel Pearl?*, about the Jewish Wall Street Journal reporter who was kidnapped and beheaded by the Taliban. It was followed by *American Vertigo*, in which he retraced, through post-Sept. 11 America, Tocqueville's bemused wanderings across the country. His 2008 book *Left in Dark Times* is a sort of sequel to *Barbarism with a Human Face* and identified obsessive anti-Americanism (and the corollary hatred of Israel) as the new totalitarian malady infecting Europe. "If you really care, are really interested in the history of ideas," he told me, "it is not a left-wing position. Historically, hatred of America is a right-wing position. We have a clear imperialism in the case of Russia and with China toward Tibet. Yet there still exists a weak left that thinks America is the real empire. It's a joke. But unfortunately it's also not a joke."

By necessity the anti-totalitarian and anti-colonialist pillars of BHL's political ontology are in continuous tension, although he denies ever uttering that piece of loveliness attributed to him by the English Jewish Chronicle: "The burqa is an invitation to rape." Still, he is very much an Arab Jew who lived in Morocco until he was 6 and now owns a palace in Marrakesh to which he flies often to relax. Of UNESCO's bowing to Arab state pressure to cancel a show about Israel being the land of the Jews, he is quite scathing: "UNESCO is the most harmful organization in the world," he said. Is that on the record? I asked. "Of course!"

BHL sees the anti-Zionism that has swept across Europe as being of a recent, confused vintage. For him, the European elites who embrace the position are "falling into a terrible trap." If the idea that "anti-Zionism is the new anti-Semitism" is not a new one, he does draw a conceptually neat armature of its modern foundations: "It is not a question of feeling, but one of mechanics." If one can't be an anti-Semite today in France using the old political vocabulary of Charles Maurras or Hitler, one can do so by synthesizing tropes from the extreme right and extreme left: "It is a denial of the Holocaust linked to the competition of victimhood coupled with the idea that Jews exaggerate their suffering in order to overshadow the martyrdom of others," he said. He sees Dieudonné's involvement in the popular mobilization of this symbolic logic as accidental rather than generative. "He is a stupid man," runs his careful dismissal, "but sometimes stupid men have intuition. He was the first person to put all the pieces together."

At the end of our lunch, he invited me to join the small and tight-knit entourage that he routinely brings along on his escapades on his upcoming return trip to Bangladesh. At the end of April he would be returning to Dhaka after a 43-year absence, on the occasion of the translation of *Bangla-Desh, Nationalisme Dans la Revolution* into Bengali. A camera crew filming a made-for-TV documentary about BHL's life for a French channel would be coming along as well. I immediately accepted.

III.

During every trip of BHL's life for the last two decades he has been accompanied by his best friend, Gilles Hertzog, whom he has referred to as *"L'homme de ma vie."* The impeccably elegant, white-haired and long-faced Hertzog is a retired book editor and an aesthete, an expert on 15th-century Venetian art; he is also the grandson of the founder of the French Communist party, Marcel Cachin. An urbane French intellectual bon-vivant in his late 60s, he says exceedingly wise and penetrating things that are also outrageously hilarious. He is as self-contained as BHL is expansive, and one gets the sense that he serves as a de facto exteriorization of BHL's conscience.

After a daylong Air France flight from Paris, the three of us arrived at the New Delhi airport at around midnight. Traveling with BHL one quickly learns that patience is not one of his many virtues. When we got to the Air India check-in counter, we saw a harried-looking young woman in a full-length orange stewardess uniform being harangued from all sides by a crowd of passengers demanding to be checked in to their connecting flights. She passed over us sternly to deal with other customers, since we were not to fly out until the morning. "You must wait, sir!" she snapped at BHL, after he impatiently asked to be checked in. He then recalculated and switched tactics into debonair older-European gentleman-of-a-certain-age flirtation mode. "You have such beautiful eyes and smile!" he cooed smoothly. "I can only say that in France or India. I am not allowed to say it in America!" Hertzog, who was standing next to him, joined in adroitly. "Yes, look at that beautiful smile!" The blushing stewardess could barely suppress her delighted giggling. She immediately ceased working on the flight registration of a large Indian family to print out our boarding passes.

After registering a room for the night at the transit hotel, BHL found that the air-conditioning in his room was not working and went to the front desk to complain. After the hotel staff fixed his AC, he went around to Hertzog's room, and then to my own, to make sure ours worked as well. It was to be the first of many glimpses of the man beneath the dandy mask: In his private relations Lévy is an exceedingly warm and considerate man who takes territorial care of his pack. He is affectionate in the Mediterranean manner: He will walk up to his friends and put an arm around their shoulders, and he picks up everyone's lunch checks and bar bills reflexively. If it were all not so matriarchal and nurturing, it would be easy to conflate all this with the controlling gestures of the monomaniacal patron. This observation would be confirmed by Marc Roussel, BHL's official photographer, whom we would meet in the Dhaka international terminal. The affable and thrice-divorced father of five daughters had filmed the 2012 Qaddafi documentary *The Oath of Tobruk* with BHL. "He inspires confidence and extreme loyalty, because he is himself very loyal, not only to people but to ideas," Roussel explained. "He could have taken any number of photographers with him, but he has always stuck with me."

Leaving my hotel room at 5:00 in the morning, I heard the soft tapping of the keyboard emanating from behind BHL's door. We boarded another Air India flight to Dhaka. Arriving in Bangladesh at 9:00 a.m., we were met at the arrival hall of the airport by the camera crew and Olivier Litvine, the director of the Dhaka Alliance Française, who was brandishing a copy of that morning's Dhaka Tribune that included a long adulatory article about BHL's return to the city. The weather was a sweltering 110 degrees, and I began to shed my jacket only to be shamed by Hertzog: "The heat has begun the decivilizational process already, my dear Vladislav?" he inquired. I slid my jacket back up. For the next three days BHL, Hertzog, and I were doubtless the only three men in the country wearing jacket and tie. BHL stared with wonder out the window of the car. The city, which had been little more than a sleepy town when he had lived here, had been transformed into a sprawling megalopolis, and he recognized almost nothing. He had returned to a different country.

While on a mission, BHL comports himself in the manner of a competent ambassador. He gazes at his interlocutor with a probing display of febrile curiosity, asking short and simple questions, and listens intently to the answer. While someone gives him new information or provides an insightful perspective, a look of unfaked curiosity crosses his eyes; he listens intensely. (This in itself admirable—the ability to stop talking and listen has escaped most intellectuals.) On the other hand, his attention and spirit lag when someone tells him something tedious or obvious. "I know, I know," he will hurry his interlocutor along, politely but firmly. He has also mastered the politician's skill of making people feel special by intimating/imputing great importance to very brief encounters. He gives strong handshakes, clasps shoulders, and gives people short bursts of attention before fluidly switching his attention to someone else.

After the rickety-looking Russian-made helicopter was readied, we flew to the dusty village of Tungipara, the home village of the nation's founder, Bangabandhu Sheikh Mujibur Rahman. After the hourlong flight over the dusty fields and stunning nature visas, flocks of children and dignitaries surrounded us at the helicopter pad. A convoy of black jeeps and police cars whisked us away to the family compound. BHL had worked under Mujibur Rahman directly before having been deported from the country, and this was the first time in 40 years that he had a chance to pay his respects to an early mentor. Hundreds of Bangladeshis gathered to watch BHL as he stood serenely motionless in front of the marble tomb, like a head of state paying public homage to his peer, with his hands clasped in front of him. We then spent half an hour looking at the photographs in the personal library, now converted into a museum, and having lunch with the village and regional elders before taking the helicopter back to Dhaka.

The afternoon was dominated by a panel discussion at the Alliance Française of the newly published Bengali translation of the *Indes Rouges* book. Before delivering a lecture or a talk, BHL will size up a crowd and retreat into a small room for around 10 minutes. There he will sketch out some notes on a piece of paper the size of a Post-it note. Upon returning he will speak extemporaneously for an hour while glancing down at it only a few times. He is particularly good at building toward a crescendo of meaning through looping digressions. One wonders if his ornate oratory perhaps comes too easily, whether his speeches and talks would be better if he had to spend more time preparing them.

Dinner that evening at the residence of the French ambassador was an intimate affair, with about a dozen men, and no women, arranged over a long table. Our small entourage was joined by some French embassy staff and a handful of Bangladeshis split evenly between intellectuals and businessmen. The French ambassador was a stern man with an oval face and round architect spectacles over a trim walrus mustache who oozed contempt for the Bangladeshis. A strident conversation about the fractional duopoly dominating Bangladeshi politics ensued; all the Bengalis agreed that a third political party would have to be formed. Throughout, the ambassador made caustic remarks about Bengalis' capacity for democratic self-governance, what he perceived as a lack of differences between the parties, and the relative merits of army rule in a country with a history of army coups.

BHL sat grim-faced without uttering a word throughout the conversation. He also ate nothing: The food was flaked with large amounts of garlic, to which he is allergic. The embassy staff and BHL's French friends likewise said nothing. The Bengalis listened glumly to this unspooling litany of their nation's political sins and their incapacity to govern themselves. Being the American free radical in the room, it fell to me to inquire about the obvious: "Would you really prefer that the army step in and take power again?" I asked the ambassador. "Yes, I would," came the contemptuous reply. Immediately after coffee was served the troubled BHL politely excused us, citing the exhaustion of travel.

In the car on the way back to the hotel, BHL fumed to his friends. To me he explained that this sort of French ambassador was a very particular type, a "cynical hater of the country he was supposed to look after. A Marquis de Norpois-type character from Proust" that he had met over and over again for 40 years "as if he was a reincarnation of Vishnu, from Cambodia to Ethiopia to Sudan."

The next morning we had all assembled in the hotel lobby at the ungodly hour of half past six. It was the one-year anniversary of the collapse of the eight-story garment factory at Rana Plaza that had buried more than a thousand garment workers under mountains of concrete. At 15 million souls, Dhaka is one of the world's most densely inhabited and haphazardly planned cities. After driving for an hour through the rickshaw-clogged roads of the city center, we arrived at a vast, desolate pile of cement studded with metal rods and flecked with pieces of cloth. Dozens of scavengers were crouching over the rubble, still digging through the debris in search of family mementos or iron fillings to sell to scrap dealers. BHL wandered around the rubble contemplatively while Roussel took pictures of him.

BHL concluded by calling for an 'enlightened Islam ... an Islam tolerant, moderate, and respectful of others—of minorities in particular.'

After tripping over a metal spoke protruding from the concrete, I spoke with Alliance Française Director Olivier Litvine, who had first come to Dhaka to do his mandatory army service in his twenties. BHL's books had been formative for him, and he had read the Bangladesh book as young man; he had organized the trip and conferences for months. He could not bear to read the Daniel Pearl book, having become acquainted with Pearl in Pakistan a week before his kidnapping. BHL's work, he said, was "Jewish in the sense of universal, of being convinced that a shared humanity is profoundly dented whenever human rights are trampled underfoot." His friend's confidence in taking such positions, he added, came from his "having satisfied very young all the ritualistic requirements of French society." Getting back into the car, we received news that one of the major credit agencies was lowering the credit rating of Russian government bonds to a status one level above junk. BHL was thrilled: "Moody's is a more efficient weapon than NATO! Fitch and Moody's might now be the greatest guarantors of Europe's honor."

Our next stop was the campus of Dhaka University, where we would be joining the French ambassador at the inauguration of a newly opened Malraux Garden—the sort of assignment that is usually entrusted to a traveling cultural or foreign minister. Standing in front of a plaque along with the university rector and a sleepy looking minister of the liberation war affairs, BHL delivered some extemporaneous exhortations to the youth of Bangladesh. This time the tone was closer to peppy than grandiloquent. He concluded by calling for an "enlightened Islam, an Islam that will advocate law and measure, an Islam tolerant, moderate, and respectful of others—of minorities in particular." It would be the same message that he would deliver in the more complex form of a policy initiative at his next meeting, with Prime Minister Sheikh Hasina, the daughter of the martyred Mujibur Rahman. He pronounced her to be "a very great lady."

On this occasion, BHL had two big ideas. First, the Bangladeshis, with their mild and ecumenical temperament and history of tolerance, should stand up and declare themselves leaders of a progressive and moderate Islam. Second, they ought to begin filling the gap of historical memory and salving the wounds of the genocide that had never been properly dealt with after the end of the war. They should, he suggested, open a Bengali version of Yad Vashem. (The Bangladeshi national museum already relates the story of the civil war genocide using the tropes of the Holocaust and compares the Bengalis to the Jews, something that is difficult to imagine in almost any other Muslim country.)

Just then, I realized that alongside his being an impeccable Frenchman, an unapologetic Jew, and an unabashed bon vivant, BHL also holds on to a deep core of Arab cultural structures. The majority of his life's political commitments, certainly the most passionate ones, from Afghanistan to Libya and Pakistan to Bangladesh, have been in Muslim countries. He was possibly the greatest champion of Bosnia-Herzegovina's Muslims and their President Alija Izetbegović inside the European Union, while his peers defended the Albanians or the Croats. He speaks about bringing together the sons of Abraham, and during the Libyan invasion he went around making sure the rebels knew he was Jewish. He is comfortable in the Muslim world, and in the east generally, in a way that most European intellectuals who talk about it, or plot to intervene in it, or make excuses for it, are not.

That week, I met with Muhammad Faruk Khan, a member of parliament from the prime minister's ruling Awami League as well as a former trade minister, in his cavernous parliament office. The Bangladeshi Parliament was out of session, and the exquisite granite halls of Louis I. Kahn's architectural masterpiece were hauntingly empty. The building was almost completely vacant other than a few guards and aides. Gigantic tropical cockroaches occasionally scurried between the granite pillars.

"We do recognize Mr. Lévy as a freedom fighter, and he did serve in our first government" as a 22-year-old, Mr. Khan told me in a truthful and slightly reverent tone. "In Bangladesh we respect everyone who took direct action in the liberation war. He is also on the shortlist of 300 foreign volunteers who came here who might receive a medal next year."

These are of course words of immaculate praise from a man who, as a 19-year-old lieutenant in the Pakistani army, crawled all night through gaps in the Indian minefield to defect to the Bengali insurrectionary forces. Lingering memory of honor earned in the liberation war will take one very far in Dhaka—the government is studded with veterans of the war. Asked for his thoughts on *Les Indes Rouges,* Lévy's book, the minister admitted that he had had time to read only the first 30 pages. Expressing his firm intention to finish the book, he thought it seemed well-balanced and like fundamental reading for a veteran. He added that "certain passages, not everyone would agree with. He [Lévy] has been quite harsh with the leftists in this book. He is quite harsh in his judgment of Mr. Rashed Khan Menon for example, who is a prominent member of our government. Mr. Menon might not agree with the book."

***

We separated for a week and a half after Dhaka. BHL landed in Paris and a few days later took a train to Geneva to argue about anti-Semitism in the works of Wagner. He made a jaunt to his Moroccan palace and gave a talk at a conference in Croatia before returning to Paris again. It was mid-May, a week before the Ukrainian elections, and we were on our way to Kyiv. BHL, Hertzog, Roussel, and I were once again boarding an Air France flight, though with a slightly different composition to the entourage: There was a different filmmaker with us as well as an elegant and high-strung woman, Le Monde's correspondent in the former Yugoslavia. BHL was scheduled to give a talk and to sit on a panel at The New Republic's "Ukraine: Thinking Together" solidarity conference. Poroshenko, with whom BHL by this time had become close—they spoke several times a week by phone and Skype—had also invited him to fly out for a pre-election campaign rally in Eastern Ukraine.

Arriving at 2:00 in the afternoon and taking an hour to get into the city by taxi, we went almost directly from the airport to the library of the National Kyiv-Mohyla Academy. In the library we were surrounded by glass-enclosed wooden bookshelves and dusty stacks of Russian and Ukrainian volumes. A ring of oil portraits of 17th-century Russian and Polish scholar-noblemen peered down from high above us menacingly. On this occasion BHL spoke in French, a tightly wound and loosely argued riff, ranging from the lessons of World War II to the intellectual composition of the new Russian fascism in its ultra-left-wing (Eduard Limonov) and ultra-right-wing (Alexander Dugin) guises. His discourse included historical comparisons of the annexation of Crimea to the Sudetenland by the Germans as well as a denunciation of the perils of appeasement (Obama would be our Neville Chamberlain). BHL was careful to note that calling Putin the new Hitler was indeed a profanation of the victims of Hitlerism. He glided smoothly from Leo Strauss to Huntington, Roman Jakobson's linguistics, and Kojeve's ideas about Hegel before circling back around to Dugin and Limonov.

Immediately before launching into the speech, BHL had texted Hollande from his phone to propose inviting the incoming Ukrainian president, irrespective of which candidate won the election, to attend the forthcoming celebrations of the 70th anniversary of the allied invasion in Normandy. Putin, who—controversially—had been invited by Hollande, would be there, so why not bring the Ukrainian president for parity sake? "It was a Ukrainian battalion that liberated Auschwitz," he wrote Hollande, reiterating a line from his speech. Arriving back at the hotel and settling in for lunch in its manicured terrace, we received Hollande's salutary response. "Sure! Good idea. Invite the Georgian and Armenian presidents as well," instructed the president of the republic.

The moral absolutism that undergirds BHL's enactment of his world-historical mission is born of an *ancien régime* conception of honor, but it is deployed using a contemporary political lexicon. The fantasy role of the hero in history is played out in a style so postmodern that it lapses seamlessly into reactionary romanticism. "My enemies say I never created a system, but philosophically speaking I have crafted some concepts for its grounding—such as *volonté de guérir*"—the desire to heal. His conceptual system "might only have been built by a Jew with the [corollary] intensity of waiting for a Messiah; we have to act as if he comes at any moment." His work might therefore be said to belong to a particularly Jewish mid-20th-century phenomenological genealogy that runs from Franz Rosenzweig and Bergson to Jean Wahl and Vladimir Jankélévich through Levinas. It is a philosophical tradition that, much like

BHL's politics of intervention, is contingent on a specific European historicity.

While the aesthetics and concerns may be purely 19th century, BHL's lone-operator's pursuit of intrastate diplomatic power is a late-18th-century fantasia, based on a system that was predicated on the division of power between cunning European generals, diplomats, and aristocrats like Napoleon, Talleyrand, and Metternich. As Baudelaire wrote, "Dandyism is the last flicker of heroism in decadent ages. ... Dandyism is a setting sun; like the declining star, it is magnificent, without heat and full of melancholy."

That this romantic fantasy has been successfully recreated by an audacious and uncommonly vital immigrant Arab Jew, long after native European elites refuted it (or became too etiolated to carry it out) is either a natural outcome of the historical dialectic, or simply comic, depending on your point of view. There is something either magnificent or bathetic in BHL's reenactment of The Last Man's stand against the end of history in the age of post-mass-democratic politics. It's an age that pins its redemptive hopes on neurobiological determinism, coercive theories of management, or algorithmic analyses of polling data. The feats of collective and historical memory and cultural literacy required for recognizing its trappings and symbols are dissipating, and so BHL will surely be the last man on earth to have played this role convincingly. And for the rest of us misanthropic intellectual misfits, who lack BHL's energy, connections, brains, and vast financial resources, there is still some pleasure to be had in living vicariously through the spectacle of BHL's noble insolence.

Tablet Magazine 2014

France's Most Divisive
Philosophical Debate Arrives in Odessa

Michel Onfray is widely acknowledged to be one of France's most prominent thinkers. A self-described 'Anarchist Hedonist' he is a prolific writer who has worked within multiple domains of Continental and French philosophy. The talk that he delivered in Odessa in 2016 was controversial because of his previous comments on the Russian annexation of the Crimean peninsula. Upon his arrival in the city, Onfray's wife was promptly robbed of her purse and so the visit to the city turned out to have been a generally unhappy one. This essay served as an introduction to a long interview with Onfray which was printed in the same issue of The Odessa Review.

It is a commonly assumed axiom that the French public loves nothing more than an adroit intellectual duel. Over the past year, attention has focused on the ongoing confrontation between French philosophical heavyweights Bernard-Henri Lévy and Michel Onfray, who are currently clashing over a range of existential issues ranging from the status of French Muslims in France to the meaning of the Maidan revolution. Onfray recently opened a new front line in the campaign when he appeared in Odessa as part of the annual French Spring cultural festival. The Odessa Review attended to see what he had to say about Ukraine's revolution, hedonism, separation of church and state, Putin's hybrid war, and France's role in the modern world.

On April 23rd, the renowned philosopher delivered a public lecture in Odessa at the Terminal 42 co-working space. Born to a family of Norman farmers, Onfray is now one of the best known, and certainly most popular, philosophers in France. A self-described 'pragmatic anarchist', he has set up a tuition free university and taught outside of the traditional university system. He routinely sells millions of books. A latter-day disciple of the work of Michel Foucault, his thought draws on a wide variety of sources: idealism, French materialism, spiritualism, Kantianism, individualist hedonism, eastern philosophy and anarchism. Having published over a hundred books, he also somehow finds the time needed for his political activism and continuous television appearances.

The anchoring subject of the talk was a recently published book that had just been translated into Ukrainian. The event was structured as a conversation between himself and his translator, and included customary references to Georges Bataille, Marquis de Sade and Sartre. Onfray's bespoke admixture of French materialism and liberationist anarchism offered a categorical mélange of categories from which he seemed to have cobbled together a taxonomy of radical individualism. He nimbly elided and roamed between ideas and concepts in a free associative and discursive style - one which will be familiar to anyone who has spent any amount of time reading contemporary French theory. Onfray also devoted a portion of the discussion to the legacy of Georges Palante, a little known, proto – existentialist – a "left-Nietzschian" - whose notion of 'social atheism' Onfray was interested in reviving.

Onfray is also well known for his commitment to the idea of hedonism, as well as for his interest in the history of the Epicurean school of thought. During his appearance he attempted to explain the distinction he saw between "vulgar" hedonism and the "authentic" variant. Afterward, an earnest student from the audience inquired about Onfray's intended meaning with his usage of the word "hedonist." The student explained that in Ukraine the concept held negative connotations and that a hedonist was actually a mirror image of the anti-social 'marginal', and so something of a social parasite. 'What is your position and what is the program that you are advocating?'' the young man reiterated.

Onfray responded to the question by proffering a slightly more expanded definition of philosophical hedonism. The concept turned out to be not very complex. The vulgar kind of hedonism was a form of consumerism, which included buying art if one did not understand it, owning an expensive car or having a very big house. As an example, he postulated Chinese mafiosi and Russian oligarchs buying their way through Europe with avaricious consumerist tastes.

'Vulgar hedonism is always connected to the desire for objects' and the sort of hedonism that Onfray practiced was rooted in the partaking in the simpler things in life. Authentic philosophical hedonism, the philosopher informed us, included sitting with a beautiful girl in a park and looking at her smile, taking pleasure in the sunlight (which, however ironically, is a definition which is somewhat more puritanical than Epicurean).

A local academic philosopher in his late fifties, who identified himself to the audience as a professor of religious studies (he humorously underlined that he had once taught the same class in the Atheism studies department) slyly told Onfray that he had just finished reading the book and that he was surprised that the book on the theme of hedonism and atheism barely mentioned Karl Marx. He inquired why this was so. Onfray responded to the question with a fluent recital of the traditional position of Feuerbach's thesis of the history of scientific atheism, but for the most part he and the professor seemed to be speaking past each other. In the middle of a former Soviet city, he did not explain why he had written a book about 'social atheism' while avoiding mentioning the historical context that the local philosopher had grown up with.

The evening did not end without overt controversy, however. Bruce Leimsidor, a professor of immigration and asylum Law at Ca' Foscari University in Venice, who is currently a guest professor at the Odessa Law Academy, and who resides in Paris, offered a criticism of the philosopher's dichotomy between atheism and religion. This was done, he explained, in view of the urgent social and legal situation in France caused by religiously inspired terrorism. Such a dichotomy avoids the institution of laïcité. Specifically, this was a response to Onfray's assertions that there exist no substantial differences between Christianity, Judaism and Islam. Leimsidor brought up the issue of laïcité while asserting that it was apriori rejected by Islamic theology. What he posited as the inability to accept secularism and the separation of religion and state in Islamic theology had become an issue of acute importance. Laïcité, it should be noted, remains a semi sacred political principle in France. Leimsidor pointed out that the ideal is defended by even the most pious French Catholics and French Jews, and is the key question facing integration of Muslims in France today. In this reading, failure of any organized religion to accept laïcité would open the door to the politicization of religion and also to religiously inspired violence.

To that question, Mr. Onfray seemed to have no answer. His response was to deflect the question by giving a long discourse on the history of religious violence in the West. He also pointed out, with questionable relevance to the discourse at hand, the distinction between ethnic and universal religions. Judaism for him was from the very beginning a nationalist religion, thus a theocracy, but one that he underlined, had had no imperialist orientation in its classical form. Onfray further maintained that there was not one Islam, but many to speak of, with the implication that to discuss the matter was to run the risk of making over generalized and even essentialist statements. Mr. Onfray also dodged a question about the terrorist situation in France. He began speaking about the place of laïcité in French society and inexplicably transitioned into a discussion of the difference between 'diasporic Judaism' and that of the form of Judaism practiced in Israel.

This was an odd direction to take as Leimsidor had posed a very specific and pertinent question about the political and cultural situation in Europe. The issue was the prevalence of organized political violence in Paris, and the question included no reference whatsoever to the history of comparative religion or to contemporary politics in the Middle East. Circling the issue, Onfray nonetheless acknowledged that he believed that from a private point of view, Muslims could accept laïcité, but it would become impossible when it became transformed into a political project. Under such circumstances, Islam would become a theocracy. He defended Islam in a roundabout way by saying that there are some Muslims who accept laïcité, but that no claim could be made of the acceptance of laïcité by major schools of Islam. It looked like he wanted to avoid any criticism of Islam and viewed such arguments as specious, and implied that this was the outcome of a possible "neo-colonialist" manifestation of French chauvinism against its Muslim minorities.

In any case, Onfray maintained that according to his world view, any assertions stipulated by French liberalism would be apriori seen as entirely false. The Catholic Church, he ventured, still holds a prominent position in French society and it does not accept laïcité. He claimed that the Church had never really been tamed in France until very recent times, and that it still plays an outsized role in French public life. From this argument followed the insinuation that there is no real Republican separation of church and state in France, which is merely a veil for religious rule by the religion held by the native majority.

Leimsidor's response to this point was that this was a completely false argument: When, two years ago, France was voting on institutionalizing same-sex marriage, no amount of fervent protestation by the Catholic Church in France had any sort of impact on the debate or its outcome. He argued that this sort of respect for Republican values is encoded in the DNA of the French nation.

No satisfactory denouement to the argument ever arrived. Onfray's answers to these difficult questions were evasive. The audience would be forgiven for being flummoxed by the hybrid interview/debate that it had just witnessed. Onfray made very little allowance for the local context or the grounding capacity needed to understand his philosophical language and positions. The final result was neither a rigorous lesson in philosophical method nor a sustained inquiry into a single issue, but rather a fairly superficial summary of a series of positions and themes that he has developed over his three decade long career. He was discussing the vulgarity of materialism in a country that had seen a 70% currency collapse over the previous two years.

Well understood by many in France, only the best-prepared Ukrainian philosophy students would have gotten very much out of the presentation of his ideas and the ensuing debate. Onfray seemed to be mechanically repeating things that he had been saying for years, without relying too much on a technical armature and he did not do very much to demonstrate the logical connections between his positions. He seemed to be directing his commentary at people who already agreed with his philosophical positions a priori. Other than offering a rare opportunity for Odessan students to observe a particularly rare bird of paradise in flight, the afternoon was disappointing in that it represented a lost opportunity for a more stimulating and thorough engagement.

The interview that follows this essay was conducted by the French novelist Sophie Schulze. The special interest of her intervention for a Ukrainian audience must surely lie with her questioning of Onfray on his views on the conflict between Russia and Ukraine, as well as his opinion of the political commitments of fellow French philosopher Bernard-Henri Lévy.

Last autumn, the French intellectual world was shaken by the frenetic public duel between the two philosophers. Onfray considers Lévy's liberal interventionism and his steering of France into taking military action in Libya, to have been a catastrophic and deadly mistake. He is also generally disdainful of Lévy's other political commitments. These include Lévy's stolid, unremitting and committed defense of Ukraine's territorial integrity and place in the European order. Lévy's muscular liberalism has been fully on the side of Ukraine's right to make its own decisions on which direction to take. Lévy has made half a dozen trips to Ukraine over the last two years, spoken at the Maidan and performed his play Hotel Europa in Odessa, Kyiv and Lviv.

Onfray is a committed member of an 'anti-Imperialist' French school of anti-Americanism which calls for Ukraine to take a non- aligned "third way" between Russia and Europe. He is skeptical of what he perceives to be a hegemonic Western narrative regarding the conflict. This is a position that is genealogically descended from anti-colonial Third-Worldism. In this interview, Onfray proclaims himself to be against what he perceives to be the authoritarianism of Russian president Putin, but also claims that the issues surrounding de-Communization and the annexation of the Crimean peninsula are "complicated." Onfray reminds us that his position is reminiscent of the principled refusal to take the side of either the Soviet Union or the United States by people like Albert Camus – himself a noted philosopher-hedonist – at the height of the cold war. Camus is, of course, the figure who insisted on charting a middle course between Raymond Aron ("since I must choose, I will choose the United States") and the Soviet Union-supporting existentialist Jean-Paul Sartre.

Lévy, on the other hand, is the author of Left in Dark Times: A Stand Against the New Barbarism, a book in which he charts the dark relationship between the anti-liberal, anti-Western, anti-American and anti-Semitic opinions held by large portions of the French left. He is clearly the liberal Raymond Aron in this story (though this is clearly a reductionist analogy; students of French intellectual history will know that relations between Aron and the young Lévy were complex). Onfray's answer to the question of whether Lévy is correct in his proclamations that Ukraine is Europe is a resounding "No." For him "this is the American thesis, and it represents an Americanized Ukraine of pauperization and McDonalds." It should be obvious to any right-thinking person that any idea or argument shared by Americans is surely malevolent and wrong. This answer evokes the "buffer zone" arguments of those who advance the great power "spheres of influence" thesis, and Onfray must surely understand that this position is very much welcome in the Kremlin. It is ironic that Onfray, a man of self-described "anti–imperialist" sympathies, would resort to the arguments of resurgent "neo-cold war rhetoric" in his opposition to (what some posit as a) new Cold War which has erupted between Russia and the West. Whether Onfray will be vindicated as a farsighted and sagacious modern version of Camus, or recalled as a well-meaning, but ultimately complicit fellow traveling Jean-Paul Sartre, is up to history – and the reader to decide.

The Odessa Review 2016

Women of the Gulag:
From Stalin to Pussy Riot

Forty years ago this week, the YMCA-Press, then based in Paris and founded by White Russian emigrants, published Aleksandr Solzhenitsyn's *Gulag Archipelago* to the collective horror of the civilized world. A moral lightning bolt, the book was a capaciously thorough investigation of the forced-labor camp system and a systematic indictment of the totalitarian force that underpinned the entire Soviet project. Reading it would quickly disabuse anyone who still harbored a lingering belief in the system's probity. Yet more than two decades after the Soviet Union's dissolution, Russia still has a Gulag problem.

Posing as a defender of a supposedly merciful church, President Vladimir Putin took a young woman away from her husband and newborn baby for years for the crime of being personally disloyal to him in the public space. Putin's ostentatious recent display of benevolence, by pardoning the ladies of Pussy Riot in much the same manner that the tzar used to amnesty bomb-tossing revolutionaries before Christmas, is certainly not a repudiation of their arrests and grotesque show trial. In fact, the pardon only further reinforced the lesson he intended to inculcate in the populace: Anyone who wishes to criticize the new tzar or his government's policies would do well to remember that concepts such as freedom and incarceration, grace and perdition, justice and retribution are held by the tzar alone.

It is the exaggerated and prolonged case of Stockholm syndrome from which Russian society suffers, as well as its state-sponsored ignorance of the recent past, that has rendered such methods of political conditioning feasible. Much of the Russian population remains willfully ignorant of the extent to which Soviet society was brutalized by the arbitrary war that the Communist Party waged against its own citizens. Sizable swaths of both the educated and uneducated public remain dubious that the Gulag was really as bad as advertised, while Stalin himself is held in wide esteem for "having won the great patriotic war"—despite the scholarly consensus that his paranoiac purging and execution of something like half the Red Army officer corps very nearly derailed the war effort. The fact that thousands of aging Communists brought carnations to Stalin's tomb earlier this year to mark the 60th anniversary of his death is one clear sign that many Russians have failed to reckon with the Soviet past. Vladimir Putin's regular references to the collapse of the Soviet Union as "the greatest geopolitical catastrophe of the 20th century" are merely the official refraction of beliefs widely held by the general population. The corollary of this intuition is a skepticism of the facts about the Gulag as spurious or worse—maliciously overexaggerated by the intrinsically seditious liberal intelligentsia.

We should of course take extreme care here to avoid the overly agitated and imprecise conflation of historical parallels: Putin is certainly not the new Stalin, and claiming that he is is an insult to millions of Stalin's victims. However, the reversion to undemocratic methods of pacifying the political opposition is essentially a grotesque form of historical farce. The Putinist reliance on popular ignorance and national awareness of Russia's terrible recent history in order to legitimize antidemocratic tendencies and tools is a deep insult to the past that does damage in the present and may have much worse consequences for Russia's political future. The deeply chauvinistic disciplining of the naughty girls of Pussy Riot for acting out in church was possible only because the general population saw such disciplining actions as normal rather than as a grotesque continuation of Soviet techniques of control.

One remedy for this shameful ignorance is to be found in recounting the stories of individual lives shattered and disfigured by the Gulag. Now, as the last witnesses and victims of the organized state violence are entering the twilight of their lives, we are presented with what may be a final opportunity to correct the widely held misconception that the vast majority of the system's inmates were "politicals" (in any sense of that term) or members of the elite. The average Gulag inmate was an ordinary worker taken into custody on spurious charges such as sabotage after the NKVD chief in Moscow had signed off on the latest directive for the month's arrest quotas from the provinces. The prisoner's wife would be taken to a women's camp, his children to a state orphanage. Both Stalin and the regime he presided over were deeply chauvinistic in the traditional sense, a quality that often manifested itself in the execution or dispatching of his henchman's wives to labor camps as a test of their loyalty. Consequently, the stories of the trials and travails that Soviet women underwent are the ones that are most seldom recounted. A recently published history, *Women of the Gulag: Stories of Five Remarkable Lives*, by the American historian Paul R. Gregory, along with what promises to be a great forthcoming documentary by the Russian-American filmmaker Mariana Yarovskya, aims to fill those gaps in our knowledge.

***

A professor of economics and a research fellow at the Hoover Institute at Stanford (from whose archives this book, as well as his previous excursions in Gulag history, are culled), Gregory has been part of a small group of stalwart historians—including Robert Service, Robert Conquest, Norman Naimark, and Anne Applebaum—who have labored assiduously to bring the horrific workings of the Gulag to the Anglophone reading public since the Soviet archives were first opened. (This November, Gregory used his own personal history to make a signal contribution to the study of the American history when he published his account in the *New York Times Magazine* of his family having taken the young Lee Harvey Oswald into its home in the early 1960s.) Gregory's monograph *The Political Economy of Stalinism* (2003) may be the definitive macroeconomic study of the command structure and economic policy of the Soviet Union in the English language. A volume that followed, *Terror by Quota* (2009), detailed the fashion in which the Soviet economy was suborned to a shadow superstructure of systematic political repression. Even when taking the availability of the slave labor that built such marvels of engineering as the Moscow metro into the economic calculus, running a vast network of prison camps to incarcerate a significant chunk of the population turned out to be an economic disaster for the Soviet Union.

"When the Soviet Union collapsed and Russia was born," Gregory explained to me, "the archives opened up and we started to get a mother lode of information to process. This was 10 years of work." A natural storyteller, if not a natural stylist, he has a talent for illuminating complex systems with flourishes of revelatory archival finds. My own favorite of his books is his quirky chronicle of the archetypal romantic and doomed Bolshevik marriage in *Politics, Murder, and Love in Stalin's Kremlin: The Story of Nikolai Bukharin and Anna Larin*. At the conclusion of that book, Gregory wonders whether it was inevitable that Stalin would emerge as general secretary of the party against seemingly better-organized, more charismatic, and stronger adversaries like Trotsky, Bukharin, or Lev Kamenev—all of whom were outmaneuvered and liquidated. His answer was, "most probably."

In brief alternating chapters, *Women of the Gulag* tells the fascinating stories of five representative Soviet women—Agnessa, Maria, Evgenia, Adile, and Fekla—drawn from across the class and geographic spectrums of the Soviet empire. Three of these women were connected to the highest echelons of the nomenclatura by marriage, though the common denominator is that all were arrested for the actions of their husbands or fathers. Agnessa, the wife of the ambitious Jewish NKVD officer Sergei Mironov, was in some ways the most representative of the quick trajectory of ascension and tumble that constituted the implicit risk of working for the intelligence agencies. The capable Mironov took himself and his wife from Western Siberia to Moscow before being arrested and sentenced to 10 years of hard labor by his successors. His hostess wife was cast out of Kremlin balls into the Karlag labor camp in Kazakhstan and forced to acquire a new set of skills on the black market.

Adile was a 15-year-old Abkhazian beauty who was married into the family of the dashing communist leader Nestor Lakoba. When her new brother-in-law lost his struggle for control over the Transcaucasian Communist Party to his archival, Lavrenti Beria, he was poisoned and his entire extended family and a thousand clan members arrested: Adile was deported to an austere camp in Kazakhstan.

Eugenia, the vivacious and ambitious daughter of a rabbi from provincial Gomel in modern day Belarus, made her way to Odessa. There she traded up husbands, from a Jewish journalist, to a second secretary in the Soviet embassy in London, and finally to the utterly ruthless NKVD head Nikolai Ezhov. Her marriage catapulted her to artistic heights as an editor of the legendary Soviet glossy art mag *USSR in Construction*. During her third marriage to the debauched alcoholic Ezhov, who was legendary for his cruelty (the book reveals that he kept photo albums of the tortured bodies of his enemies' children), she found herself entangled with Isaac Babel before the great writer's own arrest and shooting over his ill-judged but entirely correct observation that "arresting and executing people had become as regular as weather reports." Ezhov was himself soon engulfed by the inferno he had tended and was succeeded by Beria: His execution took place in the basement of the Lyubanka prison, where he had presided over the executions of thousands of others, including his own predecessor, Genrikh Yagoda, and where Beria himself would be shot several decades later. After penning a series of unanswered personal letters to Stalin begging for clemency, Eugenia took her own life before the system could do it for her.

Maria's husband, a railway engineer named Alexander Ignatkin, was arrested by the NKVD, which had been instructed to unearth phantom saboteurs operating along the Chinese/Russian border. After Ignatkin was executed for his supposed role in minor railway accidents that he had dutifully reported, Maria was sentenced to eight years imprisonment. It was only after years of searching for her husband that she learned of his torture and execution. She would be forced to wait years for the Khrushchev thaw before her husband's name could be rehabilitated and would afterwards devote her energies to founding a memorial organization for the victims.

Fekla came from a religious family of Russian Orthodox landed peasants—kulaks, or "fists"—who were dispossessed of their small farm and meagre private property by a Soviet campaign of "dekulakalization." A frenzied mob broke into their house and "socialized" their pots and linen. After the family patriarch was executed for absurd and nonexistent economic crimes, the rest of the family was sent to a barbed-wire-enclosed "special settlement" in the Urals. The deracinated kulaks lived in pits that they had dug out of the frozen earth. They were unable to grow anything and their considerable farming skills were utterly squandered on the barren wasteland.

These testimonies are of course a mere handful of millions; they are also deeply personal for all involved, including Gregory, whose grandfather, a Russian refugee from Harbin, worked as an engineer on the Trans-Siberian railroad and thus would have been shot if he had heeded Stalin's call for the Harbinite diaspora to return. He and Maria's husband would have known each other. Yarovskaya, the daughter of a Soviet actress and playwright and the granddaughter of a well-known Soviet actor, grew up with the specter of repression hanging over her household: After receiving accusations of straying from party line and being banned from some of the leading roles at the Moscow Art Theater and Lenfilm, her grandfather suicidally volunteered for the front and was almost immediately killed in action. In the film, she visits a relative who moved next door to the prison that had held her arrested husband and lived next door to it every day for the rest of her life after he died. "I grew up with it, and I feel that our generation is sort of paying for what was happening back then. I think that the lack of historical memory is what produces governments like [that of] Putin, who simply don't care," Yarovskaya explained.

That some of the book's protagonists, like Fekla, are still with us into their late 90s is a remarkable testament to human endurance and resilience. "The most touching thing is to see how tough these Russian women are," Gregory marveled. "When we got to them they would invariably ask us: 'Where have you been all these years? I have been waiting to tell my story.'" It is hard not to feel that the inability of contemporary Russian society to remember its repressed and mangled kin is directly related to the authoritarian direction it is now taking.

Tablet Magazine 2014

Ukraine Tells Depardieu to Get Lost

After cavorting with Vladimir Putin in Moscow, Ramzan Kadyrov in Chechnya, and Aleksander Lukashenko in Minsk, French actor Gérard Depardieu, who had previously been a guest of the Ukrainian president Viktor Yushchenko, finally pushed Ukraine's patience to the limit. President Yushchenko chose not to publicly comment on this ban when I reached out to him, but his press secretary did inform me that the whole incident "made him very sad".

Earlier today, the Ukrainian authorities banned French film star Gérard Depardieu from entering the country for five years. A government spokeswoman confirmed that Depardieu had been placed on an official blacklist of public figures deemed hostile to Ukrainian sovereignty.

The decision didn't come as a complete surprise. Depardieu has been drawing attention with his pro-Russian antics for some time. Last year, during an appearance at an event in Latvia, he declared, "I love Russia and Ukraine, which is part of Russia." And then, of course, there's his much-publicized friendship with Russian President Vladimir Putin, which probably didn't help. A few weeks ago, at the Cannes Film Festival, he assured reporters of his continuing fondness for Putin ("I like him a lot") and cryptically downplayed the Russian annexation of Crimea ("if Crimea had been American it would have been a different matter").

The ban is the latest twist in a bizarre saga that began two years ago, when Depardieu proclaimed his plan to establish tax residency in the Belgian border town of Néchin as a protest against a proposed French wealth tax on high earners. Vladimir Putin, who had already hosted the French film star on his multiple visits to Moscow, seized upon the opening to offer Depardieu citizenship in Russia (which, it should be noted, boasts a flat tax rate of 13 percent).

Depardieu thereupon embarked on a madcap odyssey across the former Soviet Union. In Moscow he rubbed elbows with Putin and assorted Kremlin court celebrities, and even starred in a Russian sitcom. He attended a well-lubricated birthday party for brutal Chechen strongman Ramzan Kadyrov. He recorded a soppy duet with Gulnara Karimova, daughter of Uzbekistan's dictator (who has since, in effect, been declared persona non grata by her own father). He also made a trip to Baku, where he hobnobbed with local leaders and appeared in a commercial for Azeri cuisine.

Earlier this month, in what may have been the oddest encounter yet, he turned up in Minsk, where he took to the fields and scythed grass together with Belarusian President Alexander Lukashenko". On Sunday, Depardieu gave an interview in which he generously gave his stamp of approval to Minsk's role as the site of negotiations to end the war in eastern Ukraine. (This was also a rather odd move, considering that the widely criticized Minsk II agreement, signed by Ukraine, Russia, France, and Germany, was concluded there five months ago.) Just for good measure, Depardieu also seized the opportunity to hail a recent Belarusian law aimed at penalizing the unemployed. He referred to Lukashenko's reinstatement of the gruesome Soviet era "tax for a parasitic lifestyle" as a "sign of a democratic society."

Paradoxical as this may now seem, given his current penchant for the company of dictators, Depardieu had once embraced democratic Ukraine: He toured the Carpathians and took part in a failed scheme to open a restaurant in Kyiv. Long before Kadyrov proffered him the gift of a free apartment in Chechnya, Depardieu even spent a pair of vacations with ex-Ukrainian President Viktor Yushchenko at his country house. (A spokesman for Yushchenko declined to comment when contacted for this piece.) The French star once floated a plan to make a movie, set in medieval times, celebrating a Ukrainian nationalist hero. Now he's talking instead of a joint Franco-Russian film project set in World War II, featuring French fighter pilots who fought with the Soviets against Nazi Germany.

The Kyiv government's latest move appears to mark the final break in Depardieu's long romance with Ukraine. It's sad to think that the French star once courted democratic Ukraine as fervently as he now woos autocrats. But then, consistency was never his strong suit.

Foreign Policy 2015

European Parliament Hosts Conference on Crimean Tatars in Fourth Year of Occupation

On January 31, 2018 the European Parliament in Brussels hosted a conference devoted to the issue of "4 Years of Occupation: Ways to support Crimea and Crimean Tatars".

The speakers relayed the extreme difficulty of the situation faced by the Crimean Tatar people in the 4th year of the occupation of their ancestral homeland, the Crimean peninsula. The conference was organized by Green Party parliamentarian Rebecca Harms, a steadfast ally of the Ukrainian and Crimean Tatar causes within the European Parliament, and was co-hosted by Lithuanian MP Petras Auštrevičius and the Czech parliamentarian and former journalist Jaromír Štětina.

The conference focused on technical issues related to the de-occupation of Crimea in Brussels, and featured the undisputed leader of the Crimean Tatar people, Mustafa Dzhemilev. Two deputy Chairmen of the Mejlis, the elected deliberative assembly of the Crimean Tatar people, Akhtem Chiygoz and Ilmi Umerov — who were freed from Russian captivity in October — and other political activists also took part in the discussions. The Crimea SOS organization was represented by its founder, Tamila Tasheva, whose own family had been exiled by Stalin in 1944 to Uzbekistan and only later returned to Crimea.

The half dozen Crimean leaders, politicians and lawyers spoke of the importance of documenting and archiving the actions of the Russian authorities. Indeed, the repression faced by the Crimean Tatars is severe. Some kidnappings and coercive searches in which the Russian authorities on the peninsula have engaged have even ended with high-profile deaths — such as when Vedzhie Kashka, a renowned, eighty-three-year-old activist died of a heart attack in the midst of a security service raid on her home.

The systematic repression faced by pro-Ukrainian residents of Crimea and the Crimean Tatar community include the systematic kidnapping and torture of civic activists, enforced passportization (without which life in Crimea and access to government services is functionally impossible), a ban on freedom of expression and a prolonged process of economic and ecological degradation in the Crimean peninsula. The Crimean Tatars in particular are being targeted by Russian security forces, and have suffered more than 95 percent of the 1000 searches that have taken place in the last four years.

At the conference in Brussels, the Crimean Tatars reiterated the illegitimacy of the referendum that preceded Russia's annexation of Ukrainian territory in March 2014. Of the 280,000 Crimean Tatars who had the right to participate in the internationally unrecognized referendum on Crimean independence, only 900 (less than 1% of the eligible population) showed up to vote, according to the internal numbers available to the community leadership. (Only 30 to 35 percent of the Ukrainian and Russian population of the territory took part in the vote.)

Czech MEP Štětina underlined that this year marked the 50th anniversary of the Soviet occupation of Czechoslovakia. Ironically enough, much of the dialogue took place in Russian, with Štětina switching to Russian from English at the end of the panel to point out that Dzhemilev spoke out against the Soviet occupation of Prague and that he was now returning the favor. With pro-Kremlin Czech President Miloš Zeman recently re-elected to office with a comfortable margin, Štětina publicly apologized to Dzhemilev for Zeman's statements in support of legitimizing the Russian annexation of Crimea.

Dzhemilev spoke about the effect of Russian propaganda and compared the new regime unfavorably to the Soviets.

"During Soviet times, there was at least a procedure to the killings; with the 'troikas' (the hastily assembled military tribunals of three that were empowered to prescribe summary military justice) ordering the shootings, but it was nothing like the disappearances and killings that are taking place now," he said.

Chiygoz stated that it was the second time the Russians had exiled the Crimean people from their own homeland and that the Russian authorities routinely refused to provide responses to official requests from Crimean Tatar lawyers.

The conference participants also addressed the role of Turkey — a country with its own complex human rights situation — in Tatar affairs. The Turkish government has been intimately involved in lobbying on behalf of the Crimean Tatars with Moscow. However, in detailing his post-occupation meeting with President Recep Tayyip Erdogan, Dzhemilev expressed his disappointment that the Turks did not blockade the Dardanelles or the Bosporus for transit by Russian ships and did not join the international sanctions against Russia.

"To be honest, we expected more sharp condemnation from the Turks, who did not do more because of economic reasons," he explained to the audience.

The Turkish government has actively engaged with the Russians to push for hostage exchanges — Erdogan even lobbied Russian President Vladimir Putin to secure the release of former political prisoners Umerov and Chiygoz. However, Harms stressed that there are still many cases of extralegal detention in Crimea that must be addressed.

The Russian authorities have engaged in the systematic purging of teachers, university instructors and doctors who have publicly spoken out against the occupation. The speakers underlined that the majority of the judicial processes being levied against Crimean Tatars are illegal according to the norms of the Russian Federation itself, as well as the international requirements of human rights law. Perhaps as many as 200 people are being held under administrative detention, they noted. The occupying authorities' repression and their total ban on traditional Tatar media in Crimea have necessitated the emergence of "civic" journalism to provide information about events on the peninsula.

The conference participants' practical recommendations for accountability included an exhortation to work closely with the exiled office of the Crimean Prosecutor, which is now based in Kyiv, and to maintain sanctions pressure on the Russian government. All the speakers were in agreement on the importance of maintaining a united front on sanctions in order to preserve the rules-based international order set up in the wake of the Second World War.

Dozens of cases are ongoing against Crimean Tatars in Russian courts, in the same fashion that previous generations of political prisoners have attracted international attention, contemporary Tatars should also enjoy that level of support, the conference participants stated. They also encouraged national parliaments to create Magnitsky-style legislation, as well as to provide moral and political support to the Crimean Tatar activists who remain in Crimea and those who have crossed the newly imposed border into the Ukrainian mainland.

Several speakers, including the MEPs present, called for conditionality to be imposed on the upcoming World Cup tournament in Russia, although several of the Crimean Tatar speakers voiced understanding of how difficult it would be to call for a total international boycott of the football tournament.

The conference concluded with a screening of 'Mustafa,' a meditative mixture of documentary and fictionalized biopic depicting Dzhemilev's life, in the iconic Brussels art house Cinéma Vendôme. The 2016 film, produced by CrimeaSOS's Tasheva through piecemeal donations made by the Crimean Tatar diaspora and activists, caused a minor international incident last year after the Russian government banned its screening at a Russian film festival.

The film juxtaposes historical archival material and long pans of the lush Crimean countryside with acted scenes dramatizing Dzhemilev's titanic struggle against the Soviet regime, including scenes from his 303-day-long hunger strike in the gulag and interrogations by Soviet psychiatrists.

The film frames the stoic Dzhemilev as an elderly Soviet pensioner who is called out of his hard-earned retirement when his Moses-like life's work of leading his people back to their ancestral homeland is cruelly snatched away in his old age.

After the screening, Dzhemilev spoke movingly about his life's struggle and the plight of the Tatar people to a film theater full of Belgian youth and members of the Ukrainian diaspora. It was the 1,432nd day of the occupation and each new day involved harassment as well as new instances of humiliation against the dignity of the indigenous people of the Crimean peninsula.

An impassioned Dzhemilev pleaded with the Belgian youth to not accept Russian state arguments for the continued occupation of Crimea: "If you accept those arguments and give into appeasement now, soon enough, you may see Russian tanks in the streets of Brussels!"

The Odessa Review 2018

The Death of Ukraine's Liberals

This analysis of the 2019 Ukrainian snap parliamentary elections was published as the Western-oriented reformers, who were never unified as a bloc and were distributed throughout numerous political parties - looked set to get decimated. President Volodymyr Zelensky's Servant of The People Party would go on to take half of the parliament in the election.

On the morning of his presidential inauguration speech in front of the tribunal in parliament, Ukraine's newly elected president, the former television actor Volodymyr Zelensky, announced his first act would be to dissolve the very parliament that he was addressing and to hold snap elections. The 41-year-old's victory over the incumbent president, Petro Poroshenko, amid widespread dissatisfaction with the pace of economic and political reforms marked a political rupture for Ukraine. But the parliamentary elections promise a bigger rupture yet—and perhaps the demise of the previous generation of Ukraine's Western-oriented liberal reformers.

Facing electoral annihilation, several dozen members of parliament challenged the legality of the dissolution of the legislature in front of Ukraine's Constitutional Court. The televised judicial process that followed was a media circus, with Ukrainian political insiders speculating openly on the political loyalties of the presiding judges. But the result felt like a fait accompli: the court ruled in favor of the president. The snap parliamentary elections are set to take place on July 21.

According to polls, Zelensky's Servant of the People party— named after the television show that propelled him to power, in which he played, appropriately enough, a disgruntled everyman unexpectedly elevated to the presidency—stands ready to receive up to half of all cast ballots. The process is strongly reminiscent of the swift and total parliamentary victory of French President Emmanuel Macron's En

Marche! movement shortly after he had similarly decapitated the structure of the previous political regime. If the president's party does not underperform most expectations, the only serious question is whether it will need any other coalition partners to govern. It would be the first time since Ukrainian independence that one party took sole control of the government.

Several major parties are set to be wiped out electorally after failing to clear the 5 percent threshold necessary to join parliament. The ranks of liberal lawmakers who had been the backbone of the reform process over the last five years will be especially hard-hit. Former Prime Minister Arseniy Yatsenyuk's People's Front, and the western Ukraine-based Samopomich ("Self-reliance") party are two major parties with distinct platforms formed in the wake of the 2014 Maidan revolution, but even their critics acknowledge that both have been home to many of the most creative and reform-oriented members of parliament. Both parties are currently represented by dozens of MPs; both seem set to be eliminated entirely from representation in the next parliament.

One way for the liberals to preserve their reform agenda would have been for them to join parties that have not become as thoroughly discredited with the public. The newly formed Holos ("Voice") party, founded by rock singer Svyatoslav Vakarchuk, is gaining in the polls. It is in competition with Poroshenko's party to present a viable reform alternative to Zelensky. Holos would seem to offer one viable option, and polls suggest it will be one of five parties to join the next parliament. But, like Servant of the People, it has declared it wants to bring all new faces into parliament; both parties have decided to play up their "change" credibility by refusing to accept sitting members of parliament onto their party lists.

Prominent liberal representatives of the 2014 revolution are beginning to reckon with the end of their movement. Mustafa Nayyem, the investigative journalist whose thunderous clarion call over social media for Kyiv to rise up in revolution against the kleptocracy of pro-Russian President Viktor Yanukovych, recently announced over Facebook that he would not be running to retain the seat in parliament that he originally took on Poroshenko's party list in 2014. "I do not need a mandate at any price," he wrote. Several other prominent and widely respected Ukrainian lawmakers from the class of 2014—including Foreign Affairs Committee Chairwoman Hanna Hopko—have joined Nayyem in stepping down. Other prominent reformers such as Alex Ryabchyn, who is a member of former Prime Minister Yulia Tymoshenko's Fatherland party, were allocated party list numbers that are much lower than the parties' projected polling, thus ensuring that they effectively have no chance of reelection.

Several reformers have taken their names off of party lists, hoping instead for direct election in single-mandate districts, but most will be running against opponents who are better funded and organized and have access to powerful oligarch-backed media. Some of those opponents will have the advantage of being attached to the new president's party, which a quarter of Ukrainians are inclined to vote for, regardless of the candidate.

Nayyem's friend Svitlana Zalishchuk, a journalist-turned-reformist politician, is one of many prominent MPs who did not find a place on a party list. She has returned to her native village in the Cherkasy region to contest an individual mandate seat on a bare-bones budget along with flyers and billboards paid for by her Kyiv-based friends. Zalishchuk told FP that only a handful of the previous generation of reformers were likely to reappear in the next parliament. She characterized the rejection of liberals as an indiscriminate purge by the public of post-Maidan politicians—even members of the opposition and reformers who had initiated the Maidan revolution (and, in some cases, the previous 2004 Orange Revolution) and made such political expression possible in the first place. "This is a kind of de facto lustration of the post-Maidan reformers," she said.

There are many reasons for Ukrainians' dissatisfaction with the reformers they entrusted in 2014 to help change the country, but the irony is that the liberals inadvertently contributed to the atmosphere that has led to their own political demise. The reformists' harsh criticism of the corruption of former President Poroshenko's government didn't just create an atmosphere of impatience for gains that by any objective measure would take decades to take hold. It also helped produce public disenchantment with the entire political class, convincing the public that all the parties in parliament were corrupt, including the reformers themselves. Ukrainians are in no longer in any mood to make nuanced distinctions between insiders and the principled opposition.

The Ukrainian Maidan reformers also did not help their case with their incessant infighting. Squabbling among competing factions of pro-Western reformers increased in the past year, and liberals were unable to agree on basic strategic and operational questions, including the question of who should lead their movement. Unfortunately, the Ukrainian public will now decide on their behalf. It's unlikely to be an answer that any of them will find satisfactory.

Foreign Policy 2019

III. Ukrainegate:
Donald Trump and Paul Manafort

Breaking Manafort Scandals Reveal the Rot at the Heart of the Trump Campaign; Russia Wins

This long essay was published in March of 2017, a month after the inauguration of Donald Trump as President of the United States. It constituted the first of many articles that I would publish over the next several years regarding the role that Paul Manafort had played in Ukrainian and American politics. Manafort`s decision to become Donald Trump`s 2016 campaign manager was ultimately a tremendous act of hubris which would lead to his being imprisoned. The essay was published with the subheader: "Rival Ukrainian government factions also have their reasons for dropping dirt on the former campaign manager and consultant to the underbelly of world governance".

Nine months after Paul Manafort's ouster as Donald Trump's campaign chief and almost a half year after the elections, Kyiv is once again the locus of accusations and suspicions in the evolving scandal over the Trump administration's possible collusion with Russian authorities. A pair of newly minted and linked scandals involving Manafort broke out this week, exponentially compounding the Trump administration's Russia-related problems and further complicating relations between Washington, Kyiv, and Moscow. White House spokesman Sean Spicer was forced to deny that Manafort had ever done anything important or had much to do with Trump's presidential campaign, which he headed in the run-up to the Republican National Convention.

On Friday, Manafort volunteered to be interviewed by the House Intelligence Committee's inquiry into allegations of connections between members of the Trump campaign team and Russia. He was likely cornered into having done so by the threat of a subpoena, which would have compelled him to testify. His testimony will come in the wake of FBI Director James Comey's submission to Congress that the FBI had found evidence of contacts between the Trump campaign and individuals linked to the Russian state. Comey has declined to specify whether Manafort was a target of the FBI's investigation.

Much of the information now being revealed to Congress and causing so much excitement on social media was, in fact, made public in whole or in part during the final weeks of last year's presidential campaign. The Manafort revelations are no exception. Last summer, it emerged that Manafort's name had appeared next to an entry for a $12.7 million cash payment from former Ukrainian President Viktor Yanukovych's Party of the Regions' slush fund. The infamous "Black Ledger" had allegedly been left behind in a bank vault after Yanukovych, a majority of his ministers and his political circle had fled to Russia in the wake of the successful Maidan "revolution of dignity." The ledger detailed the secret cash payments that knit Yanukovych's corrupt political regime together, and it cost Manafort the chairmanship of Trump's campaign.

The latest accusations from the Ukrainian side are an extension of last year's revelations. The story was reported by *The New York Times*' Andrew E. Kramer. Last Monday, Sergii Leshchenko, a dogged anti-corruption activist and rock-star journalist, who had entered parliament as a member of President Petro Poroshenko's faction (and since left it to become a harsh critic of the president), released documents that purported to demonstrate that Manafort had taken steps to hide secret payments from Yanukovych.

As *The New York Times* reported:

A handwritten accounting document for the fund, known in Ukraine as the Black Ledger, showed entries for Mr. Manafort's advisory work. Mr. Manafort has dismissed the ledger as fraudulent.

On Monday, Sergii Leshchenko released an invoice that he said was recovered from a safe in Mr. Manafort's former office in Kyiv, the

III. Ukrainegate: Donald Trump and Paul Manafort   85
Breaking Manafort Scandals Reveal the Rot at the Heart
of the Trump Campaign; Russia Wins

Ukrainian capital, that seems to corroborate one of the 22 entries in the ledger from 2009. The invoice billed a shell company in Belize, Neocom Systems Limited, for $750,000 for the sale of 501 computers which were tied to Mr. Manafort's work for former President Viktor F. Yanukovych. The documents included an invoice that appeared to show $750,000 funneled through an offshore account and disguised as payment for computers.

Manafort has denied the allegations and last month hit back at Leshchenko with allegations of attempted blackmail, which were also detailed in *The New York Times* piece. Leshchenko vigorously denied these accusations in the press and in his Ukrainian Facebook posts, which appear to have been launched to discredit his own accusations.

Though a panicked Ukrainian government initially dropped the investigations against Manafort two days after Trump's election, the authorities have since requested that Manafort respond to multiple depositions. And while no charges have been filed—and it's unlikely that they would come after Manafort personally—the American government would certainly not extradite him, even if Kyiv chose to proceed with a trial in absentia.

Unlike the authoritarian Russian state, the democratic Ukrainian state has often been weak, fragmented and historically suffered from a byzantine political culture, and is made up of competing independent actors. At the same time, it is critically important to understand the sources and internal context of the accusations and documents now being leaked, as well as the role that internecine Ukrainian politics has had in shaping the timing of their appearance. To accept these documents at face value because they support a larger narrative about Trump that was fashioned by his opponents in both parties for overtly political purposes, and which may contain many elements of falsehood mixed in with truth, is likely to further inflame the political mess that Trump helped to create, rather than to heal it.

***

Ukraine's General Prosecutor's Office (GPO) is in the midst of waging a war against the National Anti-Corruption Bureau of Ukraine (NABU), a recently created and ostensibly independent anti-corruption body formed under the auspices of Western technical assistance to Ukraine. NABU had been created as a special anti-corruption investigative force to get the job done when the prosecutor's office would not touch certain politicized cases or powerful individuals. There has been concerted friction between the two bodies as elements of the political old regime in Ukraine's entrenched political elites have resisted allowing the new structure to have full independence, lest they and their allies find themselves to be the ones being investigated next. Having failed to get rid of NABU or to neuter its independent chief prosecutor, the Ukrainian parliament is now in the midst of a bruising battle to determine the composition of its auditing board - thus deciding who will control it.

Within the Ukrainian political context, the newest leaks of details of Manafort's work in the country is almost certainly a sideshow to the political skirmishing that is now taking place between representatives of the younger pro-Western reformers and the political old guard, which does not wish to relinquish its power. Leschenko was one conduit of the documents handed over to *The New York Times* (wether he likewise was also last summer, with the cache that cost Manafort his leadership role in the Trump campaign is an unresolved question): The deeper question is whether or not the latest batch of documents was handed over at the instigation of the government or elements of the intelligence agencies. It is most likely (but not certain) that the leaker to Leschenko was a senior source within NABU, which might mean that this was not done at the instigation of the Poroshenko government.

The ever-expanding litany of scandals connecting Trump and his team to Russia has great strategic value for Ukraine, as it has made forging a deal deleterious to the Ukrainians almost impossible in the current climate. Still, the Ukrainian state remains hypersensitive about relations with Washington after having backed the wrong candidate in November's elections. (They sent a delegation of almost 50 MPs to Trump's inauguration.) Going after Manafort to preempt Russian machinations is, from the standpoint of Ukrainian strategy, risky enough to warrant being referred to as "suicidal." The backlash from an enraged Trump might very well be catastrophic.

III. Ukrainegate: Donald Trump and Paul Manafort   87
Breaking Manafort Scandals Reveal the Rot at the Heart
of the Trump Campaign; Russia Wins

However, the set of allegations against Manafort that came from Kyiv this week may turn out to be an even bigger deal than the similar accusations last summer, as they appear to show a money trail that in the current climate may prompt accusations of treason. An incendiary AP investigation revealed that, in addition to his work for Yanukovych, Manafort had also secretly worked a decade ago for the Russian billionaire Oleg Deripaska, who is considered to be personally closely linked to Russian President Vladimir Putin. The accusation, which sounds like something from a bad spy novel, is that, in the summer of 2005, Manafort had proposed a concerted political strategy to undermine anti-Russian opposition across the former Soviet republics in which he would influence "politics, business dealings, and news coverage inside the United States, Europe, and the former Soviet republics to benefit the Putin government" in favor of Russian policy. Having engaged in that sort of work would mean that Manafort had lied in the many instances that he insisted that he had never worked directly for Russian interests. A $10 million annual contract was eventually signed between the two parties at the beginning of 2006.

The 2008 lawsuit that Deripaska filed against Manafort in the Cayman Islands, asking Manafort and an associate to account for $19 million intended for "investments" (and which may have been a concerted payoff for services rendered), remains a subject of mirth in Ukrainian political and business circles.

The open question here is how much Manafort actually did for either the Russians or for Yanukovych—and how much of his representations and proposals were the hot air of a consultant-for-hire. In Kyiv, most political and journalistic insiders remain highly skeptical of the idea that Manafort was the all-powerful puppet master of Ukrainian politics during the Yanukovych era. Peter Dickinson, who edits the *Business Ukraine* magazine, explained that he "found all these attempts to portray Manafort the evil genius behind the Yanukovych regime a bit far-fetched. He may well have been useful to Yanukovych for his contacts within the American establishment, but in terms of his role in Ukraine, most people regarded him as mere window-dresser whose chief accomplishments were teaching Yanukovych to wear a shirt and tie and encouraging him to stop scowling in public—[Yanukovych] used to dress like a Mafia don. Claims that Manafort was the brains behind Yanukovych's efforts to use language and history to divide Ukraine are particularly absurd—these have been textbook Kremlin tactics since Stalin's time and hardly needed any prompting from an American spin doctor."

So what actually motivated the release of the new Manafort documents? A well-connected political operative in Ukrainian intelligence circles, who asked to remain anonymous, explained that "there is talk in Kyiv that some of the new accusations had been planted by Russian FSB officers to discredit the Ukraine reformers and thus to destabilize Kyiv's position by setting Trump up against the Ukrainian Government. But I doubt that theory," he continued, pointing out that all the proceedings laid out in the documents seemed odd. "The Russians were holding huge amounts of money offshore, so why would they not just pay Manafort directly" instead of using complex cutouts?

Off the record, several figures pointed out that the idea that Manafort would leave compromising documents in a safe to be slightly ridiculous. Skepticism is called for, as both the FSB and the Ukrainian intelligence apparatus have been known to plant fake stories for the consumption of the Western press. One should not forget, for example, the infamous—and preposterous—2015 "dirty bomb" story that appeared in *Newsweek* of a nuclear weapon purportedly being assembled with homemade radioactive isotopes in a Donetsk bunker by Russian-backed separatists who were being aided by Russian nuclear scientists.

It is also true that we are now applying the standards of 2017 to what Deripaska, Trump, Manafort and many others were doing 10 years ago, when the Russian regime existed in an entirely different form, and it was hardly a crime to meet with the Russian Ambassador or to do business with oligarchs tied to the Kremlin.

Perhaps what is most shocking in these stories is Manafort's lack of political self-awareness in accepting the position of Trump's campaign chairman after decades of taking cash payouts from some of the world's most unsavory characters. Did Manafort think that his decades of political work on behalf of African and Asian dictators, Russian oligarchs, and

III. Ukrainegate: Donald Trump and Paul Manafort   89
Breaking Manafort Scandals Reveal the Rot at the Heart
of the Trump Campaign; Russia Wins

Moscow's Ukrainian political proxies would be overlooked when he took over a Presidential campaign? Perhaps he took the candidate himself as his model: Trump had likewise spent those same decades leading a dissolute life, having done hundreds of unseemly, semi-legal, and utterly vulgar things, any of which would have disqualified him from the Presidency under normal circumstances. Indeed, Trump had also done business with shady Russians and Ukrainian oligarchs and Kazakh billionaires, who all lived together in perfect post-Soviet harmony with Manafort in Trump's gilded gold tower in the middle of Manhattan.

In the *Atlantic*, Julia Ioffe's interpretation of the Manafort story is that nothing he did was particularly special within the context of the outrageous behavior typical in Russia in that time and place. Having spent years living in Moscow, she is underwhelmed. It also seems likely that most of his lobbying activities were borderline legal because he was and remains a very savvy operator who was careful to not leave tracks. If Manafort ever broke the law, he certainly never would have expected any of this to come out into the public sphere.

An American journalist in Kyiv told me that "among political consultants in the former Soviet Union there exists a persistent attitude of 'what happens in Vegas, or Ukraine, or Kazakhstan stays in Kazakhstan.' Even if Manafort was the most corrupt bastard who had ever come through Kyiv and broke a lot of rules, which is not to say that I am saying that he was, he is up against some very stiff competition in that department."

So was Paul Manafort really a Russian agent? Well, he certainly overpromised his clients and told them what they had wanted to hear. It is certain that his great skills, myriad relationships, total lack of ethics and unique willingness to work for cash made him a figure of primary interest to Russia and its intelligence agencies. After he became a senior Trump adviser, all of those machinations and promises and relationships became issues of national security that were serious enough to get him kicked off the campaign, and now to plunge the administration into a morass of scandal.

The democratic mechanisms, traditional norms of political propriety and institutional checks and balances did in fact work in keeping Manafort away from the White House. Yet they did nothing to stop the even more reckless and flagrant Trump from himself taking political power: if indeed Manafort broke the Foreign Agents Registration Act, the man who is now president of the United States may be guilty of the same crimes or worse.

This is the soul of today's crisis: The social and business decisions that Manafort, Trump, and the various figures that had accreted around them had taken many years before the 2016 campaign, to forge associations with Russian authorities, oligarchs, and intelligence agents will continue to haunt them, because they were dirty to begin with. The president and his staff behave as if they were guilty even if they are not—which, as everyone knows, in the realm of politics only exacerbates and amplifies the original crime, prompting all the more speculation based on evidence that is often circumstantial or sketchy.

The Trump administration is quickly taking all of us into new realms of specialized civics by teaching us skills that we never had before—like knowing how to tell the outrageously sordid from the totally illegal and teasing out the lies from the half-truths of anonymous intelligence sources, who are playing their own power games. The new administration is inculcating in its constituents the ability to tell which of our many different political norms and traditions are breakable, and which can be flirted with if one has enough impudence. It is teaching us the technical specifications by which one might separate improper communication from outright collusion.

The Russian scandals—real and imagined—will doubtless continue to reverberate and build upon themselves. Even if they do not bring down the Trump government, they will have essentially tarnished it beyond any possibility of repair, if not also crippling its legislative capacity. Even if none of the specific accusations is of impeachment grade, the cumulative effect of all these accusations will be to further the Trump administration's systematic de-legitimization, which rests on its own actions and is being fueled by partisan political operatives who hand weaponized "scoops" to their pet members of the press. One undoubted result of these ongoing scandals is the further decay of democratic norms and safeguards that Americans formerly took for granted. Another consequence is that Trump's hands have been shackled in dealing with the

III. Ukrainegate: Donald Trump and Paul Manafort 91
Breaking Manafort Scandals Reveal the Rot at the Heart
of the Trump Campaign; Russia Wins

main geopolitical issue facing the United States of America at this moment in history: Russia.

Tablet Magazine 2017

Did Tony Podesta and Paul Manafort Know They Were Taking Dirty Money in Ukraine?

On Monday, special counsel Robert S. Mueller III, who is leading the special investigation of the Donald Trump presidential campaign's possible collusion with Russia, indicted former Trump Campaign chief Paul Manafort along with his associate Rick Gates on charges related to Manafort's foreign lobbying activities before the Trump campaign began. Surprisingly, Mueller has also begun a related federal investigation into the Podesta Group, a Washington D.C. lobbying firm run by Tony Podesta—the brother of Hilary Clinton's campaign chief John Podesta—who was working with Manafort to represent interests in Ukraine. Specifically, both lobbyists were representing the European Centre for a Modern Ukraine (ECMU), a Brussels-based NGO. Podesta has since announced that he would be leaving his lobbying firm, which will change its name from The Podesta Group.

In Ukraine, the ECMU was widely understood to be a "Trojan Horse" NGO for Viktor Yanukovych's Kremlin aligned Party of Regions. The ECMU's agenda was to pursue the Yanukovych party line in Brussels and Washington D.C. through the actions of a seemingly independent civil society actor—which was actually a front for Yanukovych and his cronies. It should be remembered that the Washington D.C. lobbying competition between rival political factions in Ukraine escalated along with the developments of the Maidan protests, so the involvement of big-time D.C. lobbyists in this fight was hardly unnoted or uncontroversial at the time.

The infamously venal Manafort, who ran political campaigns for the highest bidder, had worked on Yanukovych's election campaigns, and directed the work for ECMU on behalf of Yanukovych. He is alleged to have received tens of millions of dollars that he channeled through various central Asian dictatorships and offshore islands.

Podesta's work on behalf of ECMU was alleged back then to be undisclosed influence peddling on behalf of Yanukovych. In early 2014, The Ukrainian-American diaspora actively protested Podesta's accepting cash from the ECMU, as the desperate Yanukovich government turned to brutal methods to disrupt the EuroMaidan protests. The anti-Moscow Ukrainian opposition denounced the payments as "blood money from the regime fronted by and funneled" through the ECMU. Podesta's work for ECMU ended only when Yanukovich and his government fled at the conclusion of the 2014 EuroMaidan protests.

But were Manafort and Podesta's actions criminal? Though their lobbying work began in 2012, both Podesta and Manafort registered as foreign lobbyists with the Justice Department under the Foreign Agents Registration Act (FARA) only in April of 2017. The issue now is whether members of the lobbying firm understood at the time that they were working for a government backed institution rather than a conventional think tank. That is, whether it is indeed true, as Mueller charges, that the firm "deliberately filed a less-detailed LDA disclosure knowing a FARA registration would have been more appropriate." Numerous accounts now seem to corroborate that was indeed the case.

The ECMU was first registered in Brussels by then Foreign Minister Leonid Kozhara; Evgeny Hiellier, head of the parliamentary Budget Committee; and Vitaliy Kahlyushnyy, who was at the time the head of the Foreign Affairs Committee of the Rada. With a stated annual budget of about $15,000, the institution nonetheless spent almost $2 million on lobbying efforts. The lobbying money was split between Podesta and the Republican-linked Mercury lobbying firm, with the Podesta Group accruing the lion's share of the money.

Western Intelligence sources active in Ukraine at the time tell *Tablet* that "no doubt those on the Hill and within the Beltway knew all of this very well at the time, as that is why you have a Political Attache in the Kyiv Embassy and a Ukraine desk in the State Dept." Any suggestions that Podesta personally did not know that the payments were coming directly from the Yanukovich government and such payments were personally directed by Manafort, and represented the sort of high level government lobbying that needed to be reported, would clearly be farcical.

Some of the most astute observers of American politics have noted that the proceedings represent the "most significant prosecution of a Foreign Agents Registration Act violation ever." Another way of making the same point would be that FARA violations are commonplace in Washington, and are rarely punished.

Yet it is still fairly remarkable that both the Trump and Clinton campaigns are now linked to the same Russian-connected source of corrupt lobbying cash. That Trump's sometime campaign manager and the Clinton campaign manager's well-connected lobbyist brother were both brazenly accepting bundles of dirty money through off-shore banking accounts from the same Russian political proxies indicates that American politics has something deeper in common with the famously corrupt, oligarchical politics of Ukraine.

Tablet Magazine 2017

In Ukraine, Speculations About the Manafort Investigation Continue

In what will doubtless be remembered by historians as a terrible political miscalculation, the Ukrainian government did not take Donald Trump's presidential campaign seriously enough in 2016. The Poroshenko administration had made transparent overtures to Hilary Clinton, and when the campaign was coming down to its final frenzied weeks, they doubled down on that tacit support. At the very least, Kyiv did nothing to dispel the impression of having taken sides. Admittedly, they were very far from being the only ones to have made that costly mistake. When Trump ultimately ascended to power, those overtures were not forgotten or forgiven. As is now well known by anyone who keeps track of Kyiv politics, the Ukrainians have since paid for their lack of foresight with months of anxiety and the necessity of having to engage in bouts of hectic lobbying during the first months of the Trump presidency.

Last Wednesday, Andrew Kramer of *The New York Times* published a stunning article in the exact aftermath of the official Ukrainian confirmation that advanced American Javelin anti-tank missiles had been delivered to Ukrainian warehouses. Kyiv had long campaigned to receive the symbolic and lethal aide which had been denied to them by the outgoing Obama administration, with the final decision to sell them having been made last December. Kramer alleged a direct causal link between the final sale of the missiles and Ukrainian legal action in relation to Paul Manafort, Trump's former campaign manager. Manafort, who had made millions of dollars in consulting for Viktor Yanukovych, the pro-Russian president of Ukraine, before he was deposed at the conclusion of the 2014 Maidan revolution, is now widely viewed as a pivotal figure in the ongoing Russian collusion probe being led by special prosecutor Robert Mueller.

Kramer's *Times* piece boldly posited that Ukraine had brokered at the presidential level a transparent political deal with Trump, releasing the prized missiles in exchange for Ukraine dropping pursuit of Manafort in the numerous cases opened against him. The allegations were quickly seized upon in many circles as a logical continuation of the Russia collusion story. In that purview, President Trump is seen as one more pliant oligarch for President Poroshenko to strike a deal with. The allegation was received with naked partisan glee despite being, at this juncture in time, a tendentious claim that remains to be proven definitively.

The Political commentator Matthew Yglesias laid out the American domestic implications of the piece quite cogently:

> "It's also a country that's at the center of Mueller's legal case against Paul Manafort, and scoring legal wins against Manafort may be an important step in trying to turn him into a cooperating witness against President Trump or other members of his family. Naturally, then, Mueller and his team are interested in securing the Ukrainian government's cooperation with his investigation since financial records and business dealings in Ukraine are critical to some of the charges. Conveniently for Trump, there's no indication that US officials directly told the Ukrainians that shutting down cooperation with Mueller was a condition of getting the anti-tank missiles."

Kramer's article is certainly a useful contribution, and his core assumptions and framework are undeniably correct in positing that president Petro Poroshenko has largely succeeded in framing a transactional relationship with Trump based on commonality of practical interests rather than appeals to geopolitical values or any other sort of values. It is the sort of pragmatic business relationship that one would expect to blossom between two billionaire business executives turned heads of state.

In the days after the publication of this important piece, a lively debate broke out over it among journalists, analysts, and political operatives who work on Ukrainian issues. Many in my circle questioned the subtext of the article as well as its possible implications. Yet the *Times* investigation was neither airtight in terms of legal procedure in proving a quid pro quo, nor did Kramer go far enough in asking Ukrainian officials the difficult and embarrassing questions. There are also multiple interpretations of the details that emerged in Kramer's story, as well as issues that have been questioned by critics. Notably, Volodymyr Ariev, the influential Poroshenko bloc member of Parliament who is quoted in the article as having readily acknowledged that Kyiv put the investigation of Manafort's activities "in the long-term box," took to Facebook after the piece was published to insist that he had been quoted out of context. Ariev insisted that his lengthy and nuanced quote about his own assumptions about possible issues had in fact been shortened.

Granted, the Ukrainians are incredibly sensitive to international criticism, and their first impulse in light of damaging press would be to deny everything. Yet Kramer's article does conclusively demonstrate a previous lack of an official American request for Ukrainian bilateral cooperation with the Mueller investigation. Serhiy Horbatyuk, the special investigations head of the General Prosecutor's office, explicitly states in the article that his January missive had gone unanswered. Horbatyuk also claims that he has no authority to continue his investigation, having recently been blocked from continuing to do so (though, of course, questions of jurisdiction arise). Whether the prosecutor is a trustworthy and reliable narrator is a question that we shall return to later.

Likely disquieted by the international furor that was created by the story, Ukrainian Prosecutor General Yuri Lutsenko (who is very much a Poroshenko loyalist) quickly signaled his willingness to coordinate with the US on the Manafort case, and complained of not having gotten results previously. "The ball is on the U.S. side... (we) can't finish our investigation without their results," he is quoted as saying.

Special prosecutors Horbatyuk and Mueller can only engage with law enforcement agencies in other countries on the ministerial level, operating along well defined international protocols. They cannot just call each other, even as both would likely want to. The deep and sensational conclusion of Kramer's story for various seasoned Ukraine analysts and journalists was exactly the stunning implication that Lutsenko's counterpart, Attorney General Jeff Sessions, was blocking official requests for Manafort-related investigations from either Mueller, the Ukrainian authorities, or both.

Ukrainian-American lawyers familiar with legal procedures in both countries have informed me that the US Attorney General is explicitly designated as the receiving authority of any such requests on the American side, according to the bilateral treaty obligations. They also further wondered about the issue of the attorney general having designated a deputy for dealing with any Ukrainian-Mueller related issues after he had recused himself from the Russian investigation. If an official request had indeed been blocked, that would certainly constitute a scandal and a significant story. It would also point to a deal having been struck between the Bankova (the seat of Kyiv's presidential administration and the White House), but such a deal is at this point purely speculative. If the Ukrainian authorities had (reasonably) decided of their own accord to avoid antagonizing Trump, and no official requests had come from the Americans, well who could blame them for downgrading the importance of the Manafort probe?

There is however a great deal of insider politics on the Ukrainian side that needs to be taken into account in ascertaining the deeper meaning of what might very well be targeted planting of information by elements within the Ukrainian government. As I reported for *Tablet* a year ago in my interview with the reformist opposition MP Serhiy Leshchenko (he spoke about this to multiple other outlets as well), all the Manafort material that we have was leaked by the NABU (National Anti-Corruption Bureau), the anti-corruption prosecutors who compete with the General Prosecutor's office. Those people are not Horbatyuk's friends, and having been created to be independent of the GPO, they are not under the political control of the Ukrainian president either.

Horbatyuk is chiefly known in Ukraine for having — depending on your politics and allegiance — either failed dismally in his mandate to bring cases of the Maidan killings to trial after four years or, conversely, for having tried to do so heroically despite institutional roadblocks in his path. Some Ukrainians that I spoke with view his comments as being transparent attempts to deflect attention from a perceived lack of effectiveness in his role. Others, including a prominent Maidan activist and journalist, informed me that he is widely respected, especially by human rights activists. Horbatyuk's intentions to prosecute as they are outlined in the *Times* piece are, under another view, rather inconsequential because of the obvious jurisdiction issues. That is with the exception of the intentions of prosecuting any Manafort-related cases that took place on Ukrainian territory (rather than say in Cyprus or America).

One logical question that Kramer might have asked his interlocutors is what additional information is there for Mueller to have received from the Ukrainian side? The particulars of Manafort's financial dealings with Yanukovych and the massive cash payouts that he took are by now well known by everyone, though of course hard evidence of the financial operations that took place on Ukrainian soil would need to be provided to complete the circle for Mueller's investigation. The ledger of illegal payments left behind by fleeing pro-Russian politicians is embarrassing for sure, but it is weak tea in terms of evidence proving collusion. Paul Manafort's widely reported connection to the Kremlin-linked oligarch Oleg Deripaska is the most obvious likely connection that Mueller would have to attempt to leverage in proving possible collusion between the Trump administration and the Russian government.

Kramer's article concludes with speculations that veer off in the wrong direction, including the infamous "black ledger" payments. If what the Ukrainian intelligence agencies have—I have been informed by people involved in the intelligence world that they have been observing Manafort carefully since at least 2005—is a serious threat to Trump, it is certainly not the black ledger. David Sakvarelidze, a former deputy prosecutor general, is quoted at the very end of the article, but he was sacked two years ago by Lutsenko's predecessor. There is no reason for him to have details of government deliberations. Was the cooperation of various Ukrainian authorities with the *Times* part of an exceedingly clever gambit to telegraph their intentions to the Trump administration? Some of my more cynical colleagues certainly seem to think so. Or, was it an even more guileful attempt to plague the administration by revealing to anyone who is seriously paying attention that attorney General Jeff Sessions is stonewalling Mueller's investigation in Ukraine? For Kyiv, a Trump administration reset with Russia must be avoided at all costs, and Ukrainian elites may very well have calculated that Trump should be conditioned by a mutual destruction pact to fear Ukrainian revelations as much as some now think he fears Russian ones.

On a grander level of course, all this points to the larger problem for countries that wish to be allied with the United States on a foundation of shared interests and values, but instead find themselves forced into alliances with one American political party or the other, making an enemy of the other party. American partisan warfare now engulfs the entire planet, harming both American interests and the interests of our prospective allies. The Ukrainians in many ways charted their course years ago, and are now ensnared in having to engage in internecine American party politics in order to continue receiving security guarantees. For years, both sides in the Washington political class have been taking Ukrainian money. The Ukrainians now find themselves locked into that relationship to the detriment of what they actually need: stability, political neutrality, and the experience of having to make formal arrangements with rule-based political systems and depersonalized institutions rather than individuals. Ukraine is now deeply entrenched in American party politics in a way that is fairly bizarre, and the Ukrainianization of American politics continues apace. We have only ourselves to blame.

Tablet Magazine 2018

A Ukrainian Insider on Manafort, Man About Town in Kyiv

By the conclusion of the trial of Paul Manafort in August of 2018, a tremendous amount of information that Ukrainian muckrakers and activists had merely speculated about was made public. Ironically, Manafort's trial was useful in revealing that he was, in fact, instrumental in creating the very 'swamp' that his candidate Donald Trump had vowed to clean up.

Government prosecutors rested their case yesterday in the high-profile tax- and bank-fraud trial of former Trump presidential campaign chief Paul Manafort. To an outside observer, it may have looked like the prosecution's argument rested on Manafort's failure to file taxes for millions in income, or the misleading statements he made applying for bank loans. But this is only part of the story. Looming large in the background is Manafort's work on behalf of pro-Kremlin Ukrainian political elites in the now defunct Party of Regions and his business and lobbying relationship with Putin's close associate, the Russian oligarch Oleg Deripaska.

In the first case brought by special counsel Robert Mueller as part of his mandate in the wide-ranging probe into Russian interference in the 2016 presidential election, testimony from more than two dozen witnesses depicts Manafort leading an extraordinary lifestyle. Most incredibly, Manafort managed to keep up his man-about-town habits even after the consulting fees collected from his client and former Ukrainan President Viktor Yanukovych evaporated when Yanukovych fled to Rostov in the wake of the Maidan revolution.

Manafort, you may recall, famously declined to take a salary for his role running the Trump campaign. But that act, once posited as a public demonstration of apparent civic-mindedness, must now be seen in light of the trial's revelations about the campaign chief's serious cash flow issues. In this context, Manafort's willingness to run the campaign for free looks more like an attempt to monetize his position within the campaign, as many have long alleged, rather than an act of selfless service or political commitment. It was a brazen risk taken by a man who had spent decades taking brazen risks, and so, it mirrored the extreme appetites for risk of the man whose campaign he was now running.

Most of all, what the trial revealed is that Manafort had been instrumental in creating the very "swamp" that his candidate, Donald Trump, vowed to clean up while campaigning in front of crowds roaring with outraged approval.

Yet as the Manafort trial winds down to a conclusion, we might take a moment to look back at the figure the former Trump campaign chief cut in Kyiv.

The portrait of Manafort that has emerged from the trial is unerringly familiar to those of us Ukraine hands, journalists and political analysts who have observed his machinations in Kyiv. Myriad articles have been written about his swaggering and self-confident affectation during the proceedings, his telltale tics, and the part in his hair. In my conversations with his former colleagues and employees around Kyiv, Manafort continues to be widely respected and admired, with many of them still claiming that he was the greatest political operator of his generation.

Manafort spent quite a bit of time in Kyiv, typically at the city's high-end hotels and their immediate environs. There, he would have room service brought to his presidential suite while he churned out memos and conducted detailed polling surveys into the wee hours of the morning. As much as Manafort helped to "Ukrainianize" American politics, he brought the cutting edge tools of American political consulting to Ukraine. It started after Donbas oligarch Rinat Akhmetov contracted the services of Davis Manafort Partners to rehabilitate Ukraine's corrupt former president Yanukovych and his Party of the Regions. In the wake of Yanukovych's first electoral defeat, Manafort introduced professional polling and sampling techniques to Ukraine and in the process professionalized the craft of political consulting in the country. He and his cadres would transform into something between a serious business and a racket.

Canny observers of the Manafort case have understood it for what it really is: a symbolic trial against a form of American kleptocracy that had formerly been relegated to the regions of Eastern Europe where a character like Manafort could operate with impunity.

Tablet Magazine 2018

Will the Manafort Trial Turn Trump Against Ukraine?

The answer to the question posed by the title of this article, as we would all learn during the 2020 impeachment trial, was "absolutely yes". Donald Trump did indeed come to despise Ukraine and the Ukrainians and held aid to Ukraine hostage, leading to the impeachment process in the Spring of 2020.

On Tuesday, a federal court convicted Paul Manafort, President Donald Trump's former campaign manager, of eight out of 18 charges leveled against him by special counsel, Robert S. Mueller III. The successful case was the first trial brought by Mueller as part of his wide-ranging mandate to investigate crimes related to collusion and the 2016 Trump presidential campaign. It revealed, in addition to Manafort's criminal activities, his profligacy — buying $15,000 ostrich jackets for instance — a testament to his experience maneuvering in Eastern Europe for more than a decade. It is perhaps no surprise then that in Kyiv, where the corruption of the former government led the country to revolution only a few years ago, Manafort's prosecution has been savored by many as a long delayed act of justice.

Despite the trial taking place in Virginia, the echoes of Eastern Europe's political and business culture were clear. The presiding judge had to instruct the prosecution to elide the word "oligarch" so as to not prejudice the jury. The case exposed the offshore banking practices that Manafort had utilized to avoid paying taxes, and crucially, revealed the identities of Ukrainian oligarchs and politicians who funneled the funds to accounts in the Cayman Islands.

Manafort's comfort in doing shady and shadowy financial dealings comes after he spent over a decade hustling for cash working in Eastern Europe. He first began consulting for Russian interests on behalf of Kremlin linked Russian oligarch Oleg Deripaska in 2005. The case revealed that over several years Manafort accepted more than $65 million in consulting fees from the pro-Kremlin Party of the Regions, whose 2010 presidential candidate, Viktor Yanukovych, he had ushered into power with his first-rate skills as a political consultant.

Manafort's downfall as Trump's campaign manager came after the revelations of the Party of Regions "Black Ledger" book of payments first uncovered the extent of Manafort's corrupt dealings with Yanukovych and his oligarchic clan. Serhiy Leshchenko, a reformist member of the Ukrainian parliament, was instrumental in getting that news out as part of an internal Ukrainian conflict between competing Ukrainian prosecutorial organs. Leshchenko spoke to Tablet about the ledger last year. Whether the ledger was directly leaked by Ukrainian intelligence in the summer of 2016 remains a point of contention among journalists and analysts who work on Ukraine, but it is certainly believed to be the case in conservative circles in Washington, D.C.

Next month Manafort will have to stand in a second criminal trial on seven additional charges stemming from the investigation. These include obstruction of justice, conspiracy to launder money and failing to register as a foreign agent (a violation of the rules of the Foreign Agents Registration Act, or FARA). As much as anything else, the Manafort saga has demonstrated that FARA violations, which were almost never prosecuted, constituted a commonplace form of corruption among the Washington, D.C. lobbyist class. Already, though, the repercussions of Mueller's case are proving to be quite radical back in Kyiv.

Four and a half years after Manafort's kleptocratic client, former Ukrainian president Yanukovych fled the Ukrainian capital for asylum in Russia, Kyiv has yet to convict a single high-ranking member of his administration for their part in any of the numerous crimes of corruption in which they were implicated. It was the many crimes of the political establishment that led to the massive street protests in Maidan that caused Yanukovych to flee his presidency and the country.

Many members of Yanukovych's government followed him into Russian exile. Of those who remained, some escaped prosecution through timely defections or resignations before the killings of protesters took place, while others stayed active in Ukrainian politics. The current Ukrainian government has chosen to take a gentle, conciliatory approach to maintaining consensus within the governing class, striking opaque deals and foregoing corruption prosecution.

The Ukrainian prosecutor's endless deferral of that process, depending on one's viewpoint, has either kept the wagons of an interlinked and codependent elite tightly circled or kept a fragile political system from imploding. Regardless, for many Ukrainians, the American trial of Manafort on charges related to his work in Ukraine constituted the first time that a criminal court had made any serious inquiry into Yanukovych-era corruption. Even if Manafort had not stolen all those billions from the state budget himself, his prosecution was deeply satisfying to many Ukrainians familiar with his role in the plunder of their country. The outcome in the U.S. federal courthouse has been widely seen as a belated and very satisfying victory for the rule of law.

The verdict will also push the Ukrainian state to make difficult decisions it has so far avoided out of political considerations. Last May, a widely read and controversial *New York Times* article by Andrew Kramer alleged a direct causal link between the finalization of the long planned Javelin missile sales to Kyiv in a quid pro quo exchange for foregoing Ukrainian legal action against Manafort in Ukrainian jurisdiction. Any additional revelations from the Ukrainian side can only serve as further irritants to a famously mercurial President Trump and are thus likely to be avoided.

As I wrote at the time:

"Kramer's *Times* piece boldly posited that Ukraine had brokered at the presidential level a transparent political deal with Trump, releasing the prized missiles in exchange for Ukraine dropping pursuit of Manafort in the numerous cases opened against him. The allegations were quickly seized upon in many circles as a logical continuation of the Russia collusion story. In that purview, President Trump is seen as one more pliant oligarch for President Poroshenko to strike a deal with. The allegation was received with naked partisan glee despite being, at this juncture in time, a tendentious claim that remains to be proven definitively."

While numerous journalists have speculated about a possible deal having been made between Presidents Poroshenko and Trump, none have been able to prove its existence. President Trump has done little to hide his lingering resentment toward Kyiv for what he views as Ukrainian machinations in the summer of 2016 to help the Hillary Clinton Presidential campaign. Though nothing was conclusively proven, the Ukrainians, much like everyone else, never believed in the possibility of a Trump victory and placed their bet on Clinton. Kyiv's political class then scampered and lobbied frantically for at least the first half-year of Trump's presidency to repair the damage that had been done.

The continued existence of an independent Ukrainian state depends on American economic, military and diplomatic backing, and Kyiv officials have been understandably anxious about further jeopardizing the relationship. In *Politico*, my colleague and friend David Stern described the newest round of anxiety that the Manafort trial has fostered in government and intelligence circles around Kyiv as renewed pressure builds to prosecute oligarchs and officials connected to Mueller's probe. "Some politicians and anti-corruption advocates believe new information disclosed in Manafort's trial on bank and tax fraud charges should trigger new criminal action in Ukraine against officials and oligarchs who lavished Manafort with cash," Stern wrote. Manafort himself remains a person of interest in three open case files of the Ukrainian general prosecutor's office, yet systematic impediments had been placed by the government in front of efforts to prosecute, with some of the cases having been effectively frozen until recently.

Kyiv's civil society has called on Ukrainian prosecutorial bodies to act on the evidence made public in Virginia by the Mueller probe. And finally, a few days ago, Ukrainian prosecutor General Lutsenko held a press conference to announce that a case had indeed been opened against several high profile members of the Yanukovych government.

RFE/RL has reported on the testimony of Manafort's former partner and protégé Rick Gates, who accepted a deal and cooperated with the prosecution:

Gates has testified in court that those who transferred millions of dollars to a Manafort account in Cyprus included Yanukovych's former chief of staff, Serhiy Lyovochkin; ex-Infrastructure Minister Borys Kolesnikov; former National Security Council Secretary Andriy Klyuyev; and lawmaker Serhiy Tihipko.

In another little-noticed revelation, yesterday an investigation by a pair of Ukrainian journalists into Manafort's longtime Kyiv fixer Konstantin Kilimnik concluded that Manafort had previously worked in Kyrgyzstan on behalf of Russian interests during the 2005 "Tulip" revolution.

As the trial continues in America, one important side story being revealed by the Mueller drama are the further revelations of Manafort's dealings across the former Soviet Union. The question remains how far the prosecutions will go, and how close to the top they might reach in both Washington D.C. and in Kyiv.

Tablet Magazine 2018

Trump is our first
Central Asian-Soviet President

This is one of my very few interventions in interpreting the events surrounding former New York City mayor Rudy Giuliani and his attempts to either procure a Ukrainian political investigation of the activities of Joe Biden's son in Ukraine. This article was published during the last week of September 2019. I became a cooperating witness in a United States law enforcement investigation in regards to these matters in October and so ceased reporting and publicly commenting on impeachment related issues. CNN publicly reported my role in "Ukrainegate" in March 2020.

The transcript of the July 25 phone call that took place between television star-turned-president Donald Trump and comedian turned president Volodymyr Zelensky overshadowed the long-awaited meeting between the two on the sidelines of the United Nations General Assembly. Let us assume until proven otherwise that the transcript, produced from notes taken by members of the NSC, was not doctored or falsified. What does the record of that phone conversation tell us?

For starters, it reveals to the entire world what everyone in Kyiv had known for six months: Trump's personal lawyer Rudy Giuliani has been on the warpath in Ukraine on a quest for kompromat to be deployed against Joe Biden in the American presidential campaign.

Trump is, of course, America's first Central Asian president: our own Nazarbayev or Aliyev, born in the New York City "stan" of Queens. Anyone who spends a great deal of time in Kyiv, as I do, will have known about the machinations of Trump's colorful band of emissaries for at least half a year. One diplomat stationed in Kyiv that I know once referred to it as "bizarro-world track three diplomacy."

In the transcript, the linkage of aid and military assistance to the investigation into Biden and his wayward son Hunter, who really was profiteering off the family name, is intimated rather than stated outright. We were promised a hostage situation, but what emerges is something more darkly interesting and based on mutual understanding.

I'd expected Trump to make the request directly. He turns out to be capable of more sophisticated maneuvering than I would have imagined. The linkage is brought up so delicately that, rather than swaggering threats straight out of *Goodfellas*, we hear something closer to the laconic and understated mutual understandings of *The Godfather* trilogy. (Enterprising Ukrainians quickly overlaid the text of the phone call onto a *Godfather* gif.)

In many ways, this is also the sort of conditional transaction that every American president engages in to secure policy goals, perhaps less crassly. That this is considered to be an impeachable offense is honestly stupefying. This is election-time stuff and so doubtless of a different order, but the great irony of the scandal is its core: Biden has bragged of withholding a billion dollars in aid in order to get Ukraine's prosecutor-general fired. There should be no mistake: Biden was, of course, executing a policy that was collectively decided upon by the European Union, America and Canada and every responsible adult wanted PG Shokin sacked.

Trump on several occasions directs Zelensky to speak with his personal lawyer Rudy Giuliani as well as attorney general William Barr. (And what, by the way, are we to make of this Crowdstrike business?)

The instant rapport and chemistry between Zelensky and Trump was not surprising. There are many similarities between the two and capacity to operate on the register of bluster is shared by both. Soothing a mercurial personality on whose emotional whims rests your country's national security is an act of basic survival and patriotism. Anyone who reproaches Zelensky for his approach is simply wrong. Zelensky's starting position was that Trump already resented the Ukrainians, thinking that they intervened against him in favor of the Clinton Campaign in 2016. This was founded in the existence of the so-called 'black ledger', a handwritten document which was found in the burned out remains of the headquarters of Yanukovich's 'Party of Regions' and which included information on all the off-the-books payments made to various Ukrainian elites. The ledger's publication resulted in Paul Manafort's ouster from the Trump campaign and was made public in the summer of 2016.

The black ledger, with its revelations of Paul Manafort's off-the-book payments, quickly led to his resignation from the Trump campaign after an article about them appeared in The *New York Times*, and led eventually to a seven-and-a-half year long prison sentence. A running debate about the ledger's authenticity continues in Kyiv, with skepticism of its veracity typically distributed along partisan lines. Some people speculate that either the entire thing or the entries related to Manafort could have been falsified.

The three individuals who were responsible for passing the Black Ledger to Americans were the National Anti-Corruption Bureau of Ukraine (NABU) head Artem Sytnyk, former SBU deputy head Victor Trepak and the muckraking parliamentarian Serhiy Leshchenko. That at least some parts of the Ukrainian political elite had played a dangerous game in 2016 is an incontrovertible and uncomfortable fact, and one that has gone mostly unremarked in the flurry of news reports about what is already being referred to as "Ukrainegate." It needs to be underlined that they were independent actors, or members of the opposition who were engaged in conflict with the Poroshenko administration. To the best of our knowledge, the Ukrainian presidential administration was not involved in the handing over of those documents. Explaining the nuances of Ukrainian internal political factional in-fighting to Trump is not an easy assignment however.

The chorus of denunciations of Zelesnky as 'obsequious' is categorically objectionable. Conversations between world leaders are also meant to stay private for this very reason. Likewise, bonding over beating up on the Europeans, and Berlin especially, is no great metaphysical crime.

For their myriad sins (pontificating and posturing as if they were multilateralists while doing what is good for Berlin, being a weak link on Iran sanctions, cutting a gas deal with Putin on the Nord Stream 2 pipeline) the Germans especially deserve to get this sort of thing in private. Whether this backbiting will cool relations between Kyiv and Berlin remains to be seen. All of it is, of course, destructive and vulgar, but that is par for the course for Trump. On Thursday, Zelensky, who was not thrilled, publicly stated to Ukrainian newspapers that no one consulted him about his portion of the conversation being made public.

In my personal interactions with President Zelensky, I've found him to be emotionally intelligent and a shrewd calculator of psychological profiles. Like Trump, Zelensky himself can be a macho and prickly character, though I have experienced him to be a highly skilled courtesan and flatterer. Here, he did what he had to do for the good of his country.

Having compared my experiences with half a dozen others who have had private conversations with Zelensky, I have come to the conclusion that, in such interactions, he tends to mirror to the tone and register of his audience – the expert deployment of a comic stage skill.

Ironically, even as Kyiv has become the center of the political universe, Ukrainians are mostly uninterested in the news coming out of Washington and New York. If they bother to read the transcript of the phone call however, the only part that might surprise them is where Zelensky assures Trump that the new prosecutor general is 100 percent his man.

Neither president seems very gentlemanly when discussing Marie Yovanovitch, the former American ambassador to Ukraine. She comes off sounding almost like a witch in the transcript. Whether you think that she was indeed out of her depth during wartime, or was personally too brittle, or stood stolidly in the way of a malignant conspiracy, or bad-mouthed the president, or championed anti-corruption activists who were hostile to Trump, or simply overstepped her institutional bounds in a personalized political environment depends on one's politics. Still, she was a hard-working, patriotic professional and listened attentively when she took me out for dinner in Odessa. The way that she is treated by the president in the phone call — like the way she was humiliatingly recalled a few months before the conclusion of her tenure — debases everyone involved.

In his television show *Servant Of the People*, Zelensky played an everyman history teacher, Vasyl Holoborodko. Zelensky characterized him as striving to continuously demonstrate that despite all the corruption around him, he was not owned by anyone, and that he was above all beyond reproach in his own personal morality. This phone call, two months into the real-life drama of Zelensky's presidency, reminds us yet again not to believe what we see on television.

The Spectator (US) 2019

What Mueller Taught Ukraine

Empowered to investigate Russian interference in the United States' 2016 election, Special Counsel Robert Mueller's team undertook a thorough discovery process. The team uncovered, and made public, a trove of information about Donald Trump's former campaign manager, Paul Manafort, and his machinations in Ukraine. Fascinated Ukrainians gained insight into the way the Ukrainian political elite deals with the Americans. More importantly, we learned that irrespective of Manafort's guilt under United States law, he had clearly broken *Ukrainian* laws.

Ukrainians are dejected that Manafort has been sprung. But we have no right to be. We relied on Americans to prosecute him instead of doing it ourselves. Watching Manafort leave prison and return, triumphant, to his lobbying efforts may disconcert many in Kyiv, but we should draw a lesson from this prolonged farce. If you want the law enforced in your country, prosecute your own criminals. That is what sovereignty is about.

Ukrainian politics, as Americans were forced to learn, are boisterous and lively. Ukraine's elections are ferociously competitive. The country's surreal, wild, and often sociopathic politics devolve, in part, from regional social cleavages. Different parts of the country are *radically* different. Western commentators focus on Ukraine's linguistic divisions, but they're not a genuine problem. The genuine problem is this: From the Holodomor to the ongoing war in the east, Ukraine is a traumatized country, and the cursed process of coming to terms with the Soviet legacy has been geographically, socially, and psychologically uneven.

Different regions of Ukraine have achieved radically different levels of economic development and thus have radically different visions of the future. Ukraine's infrastructure remains primitive. It has taken me 18 hours to get from one city to another. Most people have never spent time outside their region. Older people, pensioners, often lack the money to go to cafés, or travel; they spend their time at home watching propaganda television. Ukrainian politicians routinely ratchet up these social tensions to serve their own ends. Meanwhile, Westerners looking to make a quick buck are attracted to the mountains of cash stockpiled in the Ukrainian black and grey economies.

Western political consultants have long been deeply involved in Ukrainian politics. In the 2010 election, for example, Manafort and his crew—many of them alumni of the International Republican Institute—helped Viktor Yanukovych win the Presidency. The skills foreign consultants bring, such as their mastery of modern polling and campaigning techniques, can swing an election.

The documents unveiled during Trump's impeachment trial featured blow-by-blow accounts of the way Ukrainians lobby D.C. These fascinated us: The American investigation revealed more about Ukrainian politics than Ukrainian investigative journalism ever could.

We also learned that American journalists are vacuous, partisan, and credulous. Text dumps in the US media showed us that the Giuliani conspiracy was an intricate and very silly feedback loop. Ambitious schmucks like Andriy Telizhenko (a former low-ranking diplomat and political operative), General Yuriy Lutsenko (a lame-duck prosecutor), and Andrei Derkach (a now-sanctioned Russian agent and Ukrainian MP) produced nuggets of partly-true but torqued-up information, or just made up something deranged—or maybe not—and fed it to the gullible American media. Two days ago, the US Treasury sanctioned most of these figures for attempting to influence the 2020 US presidential election.

Some of these people were working with Russian intelligence, which we know because the US Treasury said so—and sanctioned them. They provided much of the nonsense; mercenary personalities in Kyiv packaged their own *kompromat* with tantalizing tidbits for American consumption. Some of it was nonsense and some of it was real and it was hard to tell which was which. Giuliani read these revelations and instructed his minions in Ukraine to search for more evidence of this seemingly plausible (or insane) thing.

The minions found a host of opportunists: Some were malicious Russian operatives, assets, or fellow-travelers; but many in Kyiv were only too happy to make up anything their American visitors wanted to hear—be they Democratic Americans or GOP Americans—because now they were being *paid* to spout nonsense, not only in dollars (though that too, of course) but in important-sounding meetings, connections, television coverage, and fame, all emanating from Washington, D.C.—the whole game calling to mind nothing so much as Auden's lines:

> God bless the lot of them, although
> I don't remember which was which:
> God bless the U.S.A., so large,
> So friendly, and so rich.

Any new material they found was then repackaged by partisan American journalists who so clearly knew nothing about Ukrainian politics that they retailed it without asking any questions.

Giuliani instructed the hapless Ukrainian government, essentially held hostage by these repackaged stories, to find more like them. Or to hold meetings it had no interest in holding with odd and disreputable characters. This gave semi-sidelined and discredited schmucks like Lutsenko an incentive to unearth more self-serving nonsense, which was then fed directly back to Giuliani. The former prosecutor—who back in his glory days took down the New York City mafia—was now doddering and credulous; he eagerly believed everything these notorious scoundrels fed him; and they used him to serve their own personal and political ends.

The other side of the American partisan divide was no more shrewd. CNN, for example, gave extensive airtime to Serhiy Leshchenko, presenting him as a neutral observer who could explain the complexities of Ukrainian politics to mystified Americans. They failed to notice that the former MP and investigative journalist was up to his neck in complex court intrigues; they presented him as someone perfectly qualified to explain this story to befuddled Americans who, understandably, couldn't quite follow all the intersecting plot lines.

Thanks to the Mueller investigation and Trump's first impeachment, Ukrainians learned how all of this works. Many were startled to discover that much like the Wizard of Oz, the mighty United States was just an old man with a megaphone and a smoke machine, frantically pulling at levers.

We learned so much more, though. We learned that Manafort had kept tens of millions of dollars in 31 bank accounts spread across more than a half a dozen countries. We learned that the former presidential administration kept Manafort's services off the books, making payments through intermediary companies owned by Ukrainian oligarchs and regional officials, including Rinat Akhmetov, Borys Kolesnikov, Serhiy Lyovochkin, and Dmytro Firtash.

Ordinary Ukrainians always had their suspicions, of course. But we wouldn't have known *precisely* how it worked if Manafort's right-hand man, Rick Gates, hadn't laid it out, in detail, at Manafort's trial. Gates explained the web of some fifteen connected Cypriot shell companies and another dozen offshore entities: Ukrainian oligarchs paid Manafort and Gates millions for their services; the money then got wired back and forth among these entities—many of them controlled by Ukrainian oligarchs— to disguise these illicit payments as internal loans and conceal the income from American authorities.

And what were those services? Manafort advised Ukrainian president Viktor Yanukovych and his Russophone, Donbas-based political party, the Party of Regions. *Nota bene*: the Party was politically and culturally aligned with Moscow, but not quite the slavish proxy of Russian geopolitical interests that numerous American accounts have suggested. The party never had much interest in seeing Ukraine's national interests totally subsumed or assimilated by Moscow; it represented the interests of the region and its political clans above all else.

Manafort spent nearly a decade in Ukraine as a consultant to the Party of the Regions and to Yanukovych personally, crafting policy and inculcating in party members proper manners and dress habits. He was part of a generation of consultants who taught Ukrainians how to hold elections and win them. The tools he brought with him, such as precise and modern polling, gave the Party of Regions winning campaign themes. Later, he pivoted; he planned to help Ukraine integrate—eventually—into the European Union under his "Engage Ukraine" plan. He brought in heavyweight European politicians such as former Polish president Aleksander Kwaśniewski—lobbying guns for hire.

Most of this falls under the penumbra of "What lobbyists do." Lobbying isn't illegal in Ukraine. What *is* illegal, under Ukrainian law, is breaking the laws governing the behavior of political parties—and the entire illicit financing scheme.

So why wasn't he prosecuted for these crimes *in Ukraine*? Because Ukraine, for the most part, still lacks an independent judiciary. So long as Manafort's client was Ukraine's president, Manafort was too big to fail.

After Yanukovych absconded to Russia, his extravagant Mezhyhirya Residence was thrown open to the public. Ukrainians marveled at the private zoo, the peacocks and ostriches, the personal golf course and vintage car collection, the kitschy handmade galleon floating on a private, man-made lake.

Manafort offered his services to the administration of the new president, Petro Poroshenko, but he didn't get the account. The regional oligarchs who used to pay his invoices—an informal tax or tithe levied on them by Kyiv—ceased making payments. Manafort was in debt to Kremlin-proxy and oligarch Oleg Deripaska (a proposed joint investment in real estate went awry), and he was accustomed to a profligate lifestyle. He needed a new source of income.

Famously, though, he refused payment for running the Trump Presidential campaign. His subordinates and colleagues told me that his goal was to use Trump's victory to create the ultimate D.C. lobbying shop: He meant to become the biggest lobbyist in town.

In the summer of 2016, Poroshenko's domestic opponents miscalculated terribly. Believing Hillary Clinton would win, and hoping to guarantee this, they provided the so-called Black Ledger to the media and the DNC. The Black Ledger, discovered in the charred remains of the headquarters of the Party of the Regions—which had been burnt down in the final days of the Maidan revolution—contained handwritten records indicating, among other things, that the Party had illegally funneled $12.7 million to Manafort, in cash. These records were conspicuously displayed at a Kyiv news conference and simultaneously published by British and American newspapers, forcing Manafort to resign from Trump's campaign.

Trump, it seems, blamed all of Ukraine for the imbroglio. Kurt Volker, the former special envoy to Ukraine, testified under oath during the first impeachment trial that in White House meetings, Trump had ranted, "Ukraine is a terrible place, they're all corrupt, they're terrible people, they tried to take me down." Trump's paranoid response to the Russia investigation, combined with what he viewed as an illicit Ukrainian effort to sway the 2016 Presidential elections, led him to blackmail Kyiv and thus to Ukrainegate.

But Ukrainians should not be interested in this widely misunderstood story, nor in the bizarre, cinematic drama that ensued. What should interest Ukraine is that it took an American prosecutor to expose Manafort's crimes and put him behind bars. Furthermore, the prosecution that put him behind bars devolved from an American *political* scandal, not from the United States' principled and consistent stance against kleptocracy—and certainly not from a campaign against kleptocracy in Ukraine.

It remains unclear whether Manafort knew anything that could incriminate Trump. A jury in Northern Virginia convicted Manafort of eight counts of financial fraud and deadlocked on ten other charges. Facing another trial, on related charges, in the District of Columbia, Manafort accepted a bargain: He would plead guilty to several felony counts, including financial fraud and conspiracy to obstruct justice, in exchange for answering "fully, truthfully, completely and forthrightly" questions about "any and all matters" of interest to the government.

In November 2018, however, federal prosecutors announced that Manafort had lied to them, violating the terms of the deal and thus rendering it void. They announced their intention to try him—and nail him—on all of the charges. Manafort, who habitually thought that he was smarter than everyone else, entered a guilty plea; and Trump, meanwhile, showed his hand with a typically impertinent tweet:

"I feel very badly for Paul Manafort and his wonderful family. 'Justice' took a 12 year-old tax case, among other things, applied tremendous pressure on him, and unlike Michael Cohen, he refused to 'break' - make up stories in order to get a 'deal.' Such respect for a brave man!"

The lead prosecutor in the Mueller investigation says the investigation team simply assumed that Trump had—by means of this tweet and perhaps otherwise—offered Manafort a pardon in exchange for his silence. Perhaps. Or perhaps there was no grand conspiracy with Moscow in the first place—or if there was, Manafort didn't know about it.

Everyone has noticed, and derided, Trump's odd and obsequious behavior around Vladimir Putin. Many of Trump's enemies are absolutely persuaded that he's the Kremlin's Manchurian candidate. Figures in the legacy media who should have known better have given themselves over to elaborate conspiracy theories to this effect. Yet despite the frenzied searching, no one has come up with the smoking gun or the *kompromat*.

I would posit that Manafort didn't have it, either. Maybe Manafort didn't provide the testimony Mueller wanted because he was counting on a pardon from Trump. But Occam's Razor says he *couldn't* provide the testimony. Rachel Maddow's theory—that Trump is an out-and-out controlled secret asset of the Russian intelligence services, Putin's marionette—was always far-fetched, and she squandered the institutional credibility of the legacy media in suggesting so. While Putin no doubt rejoices in every bit of destruction Trump has unleashed, Trump doesn't have the discipline to be a professional Russian asset. He couldn't organize a piss-up in a brewery. His narcissism and bad memory militate against the hypothesis that he's capable of being involved in the kind of complex conspiracy that many American journalists posited. It is *much* more plausible that Trump is what Russians would call a useful idiot.

Assume that Trump has no moral compass. Assume he still has no idea why his behavior toward Russia alarmed the American establishment. Assume he sincerely believes the Mueller investigation was, as he continues to insist, a witch-hunt—a *personal* attempt to destroy him. Assume Trump genuinely believes a cabal of deep-state spies and bureaucrats is out to get him. All of this seems plausible. If so, we should conclude that Trump pardoned Manafort because he sincerely believes Manafort was politically persecuted. In this case, Trump may be half-right: Disagreeable though he may be, Manafort was politically prosecuted, if not politically persecuted.

Was Manafort's pardon a grave injustice, as many in the US media have passionately declared? Yes and no. If American journalists believe Manafort was prosecuted as part of a principled fight against kleptocracy, they're kidding themselves. Manafort has already spent two years in prison. The pardon means he won't serve the next seven years of his sentence, which was increased when he formally ceased cooperating with the Mueller investigation. He lost millions of dollars in the civil forfeiture; Trump's pardon won't bring any of that back.

Manafort is not a sympathetic character. Leave out of the moral equation the inherently *louche* nature of his work: He was undeniably guilty of tax evasion, money laundering, and failing to register as a foreign agent.

But in truth, there never was a principled fight against corruption and violations of the Foreign Agents Registration Act in Washington. You'd know if there had been: They'd put half the city away in a single day. Manafort helped create the Swamp; Trump made it even Swampier.

Manafort was prosecuted because he was close to Trump. He was an idiot to expose himself that way, given the cemetery's worth of skeletons in his closet. He was foolish and he was hubristic. Taking the reins of the Trump campaign was *obviously* going to end badly.

Manafort behaved as if he was untouchable. Why did he think so? Americans and Ukrainians alike would profit from asking that question.

Manafort figured he was untouchable because he'd grown accustomed to the sensation—after all, he'd enjoyed decades of tacit protection; or at least, sustained indifference, from one after another American government. He was untouchable in Ukraine because he was a valued legate to the Ukrainian political establishment—and that establishment has, for decades, protected its own. No major political figure ever goes to prison in Ukraine for crimes committed at the top of the Ukrainian power vertical.

When Poroshenko first came to power, in 2014, he *de facto* ratified this understanding by making a series of deals with his peers in the political elite that crossed every political and economic red line. No senior figure but Yanukovych, who by then was safely in Russia, was ever prosecuted. To be fair to Poroshenko, this allowed him to govern, rather than spend precious political capital fighting ultra-powerful oligarchs who possess both parliamentary proxies and vast media holdings.

Ukraine's current president, the former television actor and comedian Volodymyr Zelensky, ran a populist campaign against corruption. He attacked Poroshenko's compact on the campaign trail. But once in office, he likewise failed to prosecute a single senior member of the oligarch class. Perhaps Zelensky, like his predecessor, concluded that taking down an oligarch, or a major political figure who owns a television network, would just get in the way of governing and implementing his agenda for reform. Zelensky, unlike his predecessors, owns no television networks. He is reliant on good relations with the oligarchs to convey his political message.

Whatever Ukraine's leaders are thinking, the fact is that only Americans have succeeded in putting senior Ukrainian miscreants behind bars. This was true of the massively corrupt former prime minister, Pavlo Lazarenko, too: He was prosecuted and jailed in California for money-laundering, corruption, and fraud. If Manafort saw justice—however briefly—in a Virginia courtroom, it was not because Ukrainians themselves had the balls to take him on.

Manafort operated at the highest levels of government in Kyiv. He committed serious crimes in multiple jurisdictions. It is a criminal offense in Ukraine for a political party to make off-the-books payments. Manafort was both the accessory and the beneficiary of that crime. Yanukovych illicitly transferred state funds to Manafort by means of a system everyone concerned knew damned well was illegal under Ukrainian law. Manafort was both an accessory and beneficiary of that crime, too.

Yet he would never have been prosecuted by Ukrainians or tried in a Ukrainian court. Even if the prosecutors had the will, they wouldn't have dreamt of taking on someone with that kind of political protection. Only American prosecutors and judges could bring him to justice. When they did, there was an outbreak of joy among reformers in Kyiv, who celebrated in cafes, on television talk shows, and in their social media posts.

Their vicarious pleasure was misplaced. Americans nabbed Manafort for violating *American* laws, not Ukrainian ones. Why should

Ukrainians care about that? *Our* system remains corrupt and incapable of prosecuting all the other Manaforts.

The American system remains corrupt, too. Foreign lobbyists continue to defy the Foreign Agents Registration Act. There are no common ethical or legal norms governing foreign lobbying in the United States. Any hope that Trump might drain the swamp—even if inadvertently, or through the power of his counter-example—has long since evaporated.

After many long conversations and interviews with Manafort's associates and subordinates in Kyiv, I have concluded that he was a world-class sociopath. I've also concluded he enjoyed the tacit protection of sectors of the American government for decades. He was a campaign adviser to Ford, Reagan, Bush, and Dole. In the 1980 presidential campaign, he worked under the man who was to become Reagan's CIA Chief. He then founded a lobbying firm and represented clients significantly more distasteful and violent than Yanukovych. He didn't scruple against lobbying for Mobutu Sese Seko or Jonas Savimbi. It's reasonable to think many in the US government viewed him as a useful tool of Cold War US foreign policy—or at least, "basically on our side."

Several former American ambassadors to Kyiv confirmed to me, in detail, that Manafort had been very useful to the State Department: He had advanced the US agenda and passed the right signals and messages on to the brutish Yanukovych. He was always a useful backchannel.

Manafort's defenders have claimed that he pushed Yanukovych toward engaging and eventually integrating with Europe. Manafort discovered though his polling (no one had really done it in Ukraine before) that a majority of voters wanted to be part of the EU—even if a solid majority, at the time, did not want to be in NATO. This was the strategy that created the bidding war for Kyiv's loyalty.

Manafort went afoul of American interests in his money-making schemes with Oleg Deripaska. Because of this, and because he undertook assignments in the Balkans to lobby *against* NATO and American foreign policy interests, Americans grew sick of him. But he only became radioactive after joining the Trump campaign. And he didn't become radioactive because of his crimes overseas, which were hardly a shock to the US government.

The US clearly did not undertake to prosecute Manafort because we'd had it with the rot in Ukraine. Or the United States. Manafort's prosecution was political, not part of an independent judiciary's principled assault on kleptocracy. The latter has not yet happened—not in Ukraine, and not in America; both political cultures are more similar by the day.

> ... *Twelve voices were shouting in anger, and they were all alike. No question, now, what had happened to the faces of the pigs. The creatures outside looked from pig to man, and from man to pig, and from pig to man again; but already it was impossible to say which was which.*

The Globalist Cosmopolitan 2021

IV. Mikheil Saakashvili in Odessa

In June of 2015, Mikhail Saakashvili, the extraordinarily colorful, charismatic and chaotic former President of Georgia entered Ukrainian politics. He had spoken out in defense of Ukrainian liberty on the Maidan and had been offering his advice to the government in Kyiv. He was brought into the Ukrainian government and the Cabinet by President Petro Poroshenko, who had been his classmate in Kyiv. It was a heady time of political promise and Poroshenko signaled his intentions to reform the country by bringing in multiple experienced reformists into his government from Lithuania, Canada, Georgia and Russia. This period of internationalist led reformist zeal would ultimately prove to be short lived. The results would be prove to be uneven.

Saakashvili was granted Ukrainian citizenship to great public acclaim. Amid tremendous expectation and expectation he was entrusted with the governorship of the critically important Odessa region. The region was similar in size to Georgia and it was hoped that the buccaneering former President would be able to replicate his Georgian successes by transforming the crime ridden and mafia captured region. It was also hoped that he would be able to bring in much needed foreign investment as he had done in Georgia. Whatever one's ultimate opinion of Saakashvili, he had undeniably left behind a checkered record in Georgia. That is despite his many remarkable successes in reform and his political survival after Russian invasion of his country. His overriding political ambition ultimately convinced many observers that he was not a stable or reliable political partner who was prone to engaging in endless feuds. He turned out to be very much more of a wrecking ball than a builder.

It was always obvious to those of us covering Odessan politics that Saakasvhilli had itchy feet and was most interested in using the Odessa governorship as a springboard to launching a political party and taking power on the national level. He also joined the Poroshenko cabinet, having been given the anti-corruption portfolio. Memorably, Saakashvili would become embroiled in loud arguments with Interior Minister Arsen Avakov in the midst of cabinet discussions. Avakov once threw a glass of water at Saakashvili in the wake of a very amusing screaming match.

Poroshenko toyed with idea of offering Saakashvili the position of Prime Minister, but this eventually turned out to look like a political gambit. Poroshenko had wanted to use Saakashvili as a sort of "battering ram" to undermine Arseniy Yatsenyuk, who was the Prime Minister of Ukraine between February 2014 and April 2016 and with whom the President had had a tumultuous relationship. Poroshenko was successful in his machinations to replace Yatsenyuk with a political ally. After about a year in the job as governor Saakashvili himself came into concerted conflict with the President. This quickly degenerated into a very nasty feud. In November of 2016, Saakashvili resigned and began to focus his energies on taking power through popular protests and tent camps erected outside of parliament. He hoped to cause popular insurrection.

The enraged Poroshenko eventually had the troublesome Georgian expelled from the country, going so far as to strip Saakashvili of his Ukrainian citizenship. Saakashvili ultimately returned in cinematic fashion crashing through the Polish border illegally and returning to Ukrainian politics as a gadfly — only to be banished yet again to Amsterdam. When the actor/comedian-turned-politician Volodymyr Zelensky defeated Poroshenko in the 2019 Ukrainian presidential elections, he returned to Saakashvili his Ukrainian citizenship and allowed him to reenter Ukrainian political life.

For better or for worse, the saga of Saakashvili`s Ukrainian political adventures — which have at times been hilarious, sordid, sad and bizarre — never seem to end.

Can Saakashvili Do It?

My first dispatch – hopeful and idealistic – on Saakashvili's tenure in Odessa was published in July 2015, a month after his arrival in the port city. The general sense of optimism would prove to be unfounded.

Odessans living in the city's center were shocked awake by the sounds of a bomb exploding at the Angelovyh Cafe in the early hours on a Wednesday morning in early July. The bombing campaign which had reached a near weekly peak this spring had commenced mysteriously at around the time of the second Minsk accords. Terrorists, widely assumed to be agents provocateurs run by Russian special services, carried out such attacks across most of the major cities in southern Ukraine all spring.

What made this incident particularly noteworthy was that it was the first to occur on the watch of Mikheil Saakashvili, Georgia's former President, whom Ukraine's President Petro Poroshenko appointed as governor of Odessa oblast (or province) last month. While the bombings had tapered off over the spring, many assumed they would begin again in earnest, especially when Saakashvili began to do what he does best: root out corruption in his own frenetic, hyper-focused fashion. His appointment in Odessa reflected hopes that he might be able to emulate his relative success in reforming corruption in the judicial and political arenas of decrepit post-Soviet Georgia.

The cafe that the bombers targeted is operated by the eponymous Angelovyh family, who are fixtures of Odessa social life and well known for their nationalist politics and fundraising for the Ukrainian army. (The cafe serves a pastry in the form of the red and black flag that the ultra-nationalist militia Right Sector has appropriated from the World War II-era Ukrainian Provisional Army.) A bomb left on the cafe's doorstep had been defused earlier in the year. This second attack bore the hallmarks of a direct challenge to Saakashvili's capacity to deliver on his lofty promises of restoring security, fighting corruption, and bringing investment to the region.

If the purpose was to rattle the Governor and his supporters, then they soon let it be known they would not be so easily intimidated. The next night, the windows swiftly replaced but the doors still blown wide open, the cafe`s operators defiantly re-opened to serve customers in time for the evening shift. At around 10:30 p.m. Saakashvili and his loyal police chief Giya Lortkipanidze arrived for a chat over tea and cake with shaken family matriarch Irina, as well as Odessa's Mayor Gennadiy Trukhanov. Trukhanov, a trim and muscular fifty-year old former Soviet artillery officer and Thai boxer, hails from Odessa's sleepy suburbs. His constituency encompasses shady business clans connected to organized crime. Long used to dominating the city council and city politics, Trukhanov didn't look especially comfortable playing second fiddle to the voluble Saakashvili. Saakashvili finished every bite of his opera cake; Trukhanov did not touch his own.

Saakashvili used the opportunity to browbeat the Mayor and the city authorities for not having illuminated the city properly, and called for a host of improvements to the city center. In a pointed exchange, he demanded that the city, which is mostly dark at night, should be better lit. "The city feels like Tbilisi in 1995, with shady types hanging around in dark alleys," Saakashvili observed several times that "it should be safe to walk at night in this gem of a resort town." Trukhanov mumbled some self-exculpatory excuses about the bureaucracy and the burdensome expense of procuring new light bulbs. With mayoral elections slated for this autumn, he didn't look pleased addressing such thinly veiled allegations of incompetence, if not outright embezzlement, in a public setting.

The Mayor is just one name on a long list of local figures Saakashvili will need to bring to heel. Former President Viktor Yanukovych's Party of Regions (now reconstituted as the Opposition Bloc) has a firm electoral base in Odessa oblast. It has reconstituted and reenergized itself as a formidable opposition bloc in the regional legislature. Not having a natural power base or any elected allies, Saakashvili won't be able to rely on an overwhelming parliamentary majority of the sort that undergirded his reforms in Georgia. His friends and powerful allies in Kyiv (and the world over) may be too far away to be of any use in the day-to-day legislative infighting that is clearly ahead.

And the task at hand is undeniably daunting: to cut the gangrene out of a single limb while the rest of the nation's body politic writhes from the malignant infection of rampant corruption. Nurturing a healthy region in a deeply sick country may be a Sisyphean task. Despite calls to fight corruption emanating from seemingly every sector of society, Ukraine slipped to 142nd place last year on Transparency International's Corruption Perceptions Index. And the problems of Odessa are a microcosm of the nation in miniature. The widespread assumption is that Saakashvili's work in Odessa is a preliminary run for tackling the country's issues from the post of Prime Minister, currently held by President Poroshenko's uneasy rival Arseniy Yatsenyuk.

The morning after the nighttime meeting with the Mayor, I joined the Governor and several journalists aboard a minibus on an impromptu tour of a decaying resort town in the outskirts of Odessa oblast. The locals, initially shocked by the governor's presence on the bus (accompanied by a token security detail), were soon complaining of the lack of gas and plumbing in their villages. Alternating between Ukrainian, Russian and English Saakashvili briskly insisted to both the journalists and the passengers that improving infrastructure is among his highest priorities. He also addressed the oft-levied charge that this sort of trip was pure PR demagoguery. He insisted that he also took helicopters as needed, but that this sort of travel gleaned excellent information and insights. An assembled crowd met us at the depopulated seaside town and fought for the governor's attention. They cursed their oligarchic mayor and complained bitterly of disputes over resources with the more than 300 refugees relocated from fighting in the East. Saakashvili promised to follow up by sending aides to deal with their problems and election monitors in the autumn.

The roads around Odessa truly are in ghastly shape. What should be a critical transport corridor linking Moldovan, Romanian, and Turkish markets to Ukraine's core and industrial eastern regions is all but impassable. No dedicated artery to Romania even exists, which beggars belief considering that it represents a direct link for the region to Europe. European visitors to Odessa have no option but to drive down from the north, using the (also quite dilapidated) Kyiv highway.

Odessa is a critically important region for Ukraine's economy, and it should by all rights be a hub of global foreign investment rather than an underdeveloped regional backwoods that it is, given its magnificent location as a deep-water port on the Black Sea. Yet the region's roads are in such an abominable state that they serve as an active deterrent to regional trade. Cavernous potholes all too frequently rip tires off of axles. The funds earmarked for the roads are without fail embezzled by local and regional authorities.

As our bus rocked as it swerved to avoid a barely filled pothole, Saakashvili seethed. "What the hell? Don't they know that I can see that they filled in the potholes just a few days ago? After they found out that I would be coming here?" Many of the roads leading to the region's small towns and villages have not seen a road crew since the time of Perestroika. Until now, that is. Some roads are being patched up, albeit in a slapdash manner, and in efforts that appear to be financed directly out of the pockets of local administrators, terrified of the new governor's reputation for mercurial wrath.

When I proposed that he solve the road problem by scheduling such impromptu jaunts to every single town in the region, the Governor's response was amused resignation. That method would have diminishing returns he pointed out, smiling wryly. One had the sense that the thought had crossed his mind, however. His estimate for the total cost of repairing the region's roads is $100 million, which unfortunately seems like a wildly optimistic figure.

It is the criminally underpaid and thus thoroughly corrupt mid-level bureaucracy populated by intransigent Soviet era apparatchiks that will constitute the greatest threat to Saakashvili's reform program. Upon arriving back to Odessa from the resort, our group of journalists followed the Governor back to his office for a meeting with his department heads. In what would have seemed like a well-choreographed stunt had Saakashvili not told us on the bus that he was uncertain if he would bash heads together at the meeting, he went around the table demanding progress reports on the status of the various officials' efforts at fighting corruption, while television cameras filmed away. It was a tense and uncomfortable interrogation, with terrified officials proffering up unconvincing reasons for why there had been so little progress. When the head of Odessa's anti-corruption agency admitted under questioning that no one had yet been put in prison for corruption in the region this year, the assembled journalists began laughing out loud. It was likely the moment had made his decision. Starting in a low mournful voice that built up into a crescendo pitch, Saakashvili informed his cabinet that outside of the building people were not laughing. He then promptly fired all twenty of the officials and called for the region's young people to file applications for the newly opened positions with his administration.

Such effusive and effective displays of political theater—as well as the crowd-pleasing gestures like his unilateral move to open up unlawfully privatized beaches to the public—seem to be resonating with much of Odessa's population. Political theater will only go so far, however. Simplifying the cumbersome multi-step process to attract foreign investment will be critical. Paring down the thicket of rules governing foreign investment is paramount, and, to this end Saakashvili, has announced the opening of a dedicated foreign investment service center to help guide potential investors. He is a proponent of a libertarian ideal of helping to "get government out of people's way" so that they can nurture their business.

Saakashvili has called for many of the top administrative spots to be opened up to young people, free of tainted practices, often Western-educated, entrepreneurial and honest—and Odessans are answering his call in droves. The administration has announced that it has already been inundated with thousands of applications.

Whether the obstacles in the path of Saakashvili's gargantuan ambitions and undeniable skills are surmountable remains to be answered. Beyond fixing regional infrastructure, simplifying the land registry, modernizing privatization laws, reforming the police, and bringing transparency and accountability to government, Saakashvili is working on opening up Odessa's airport to low cost and foreign carriers. His own time as a conscript in the Soviet army was spent serving with the border control guards in Kyiv's Boryspil Airport. On this he faces opposition from both inside Ukraine International Airlines and among regulators (many of them former employees of UIA), and has enlisted Poroshenko's help in cleaning up the aviation board in Kyiv. He is also looking to clamp down on customs fraud by implementing some of the reforms he championed in Georgia: Odessa's port is notorious for its smuggling and evaporating custom's fees. Stanching the bleeding of those fees from the region's coffers would provide the needed capital for his program of capital investment and infrastructure repairs.

Asked how long he intends to stay in the job, the Governor habitually proffers the reply one would expect from any competent politician: he will serve as long as is necessary. He followed this declaration up, however, with a rather more realistic estimate of a year and a half to get the reforms going. With some luck, that could be enough, though the administrative gears in Odessa move slowly.

Poroshenko has taken a huge gamble in entrusting Saakashvili with both the region and his political credibility. On the one hand, the move ensured that Saakashvili has more political firepower backing up his reform program than anyone else here has ever had—and most likely ever will. This is undeniably helpful. Conversely, it also ensures that the entrenched political interests and oligarchic forces fighting threats to their livelihood and title to expropriated public assets will be equally energized. If they manage to thwart Saakashvili, they will have struck a significant blow for the debilitated *status quo*: his failure will constitute an unmistakable signal to the entire world that large-scale reform of the Odessa oblast, and by extension of Ukraine, is functionally impossible.

The outright threat of armed separatism in the region has been greatly diminished, as the Kremlin has sent out peace feelers (genuine or not) over the course of the summer, placing lesser emphasis on, and even intimating the unwinding of, the "Novorossiya project." The death of almost fifty of Odessa's citizens in street fighting last March has inoculated the city and deprived the separatist campaign of its potential leadership. The city's middle and professional classes have also taken careful stock of the banditry and lawlessness endemic in the cities administered by the so-called Lughansk and Donetsk People's Republics.

Yet, Saakashvili's proximity to Moldova's breakaway statelet of Transdnistria is a recurrence of the grandest sort of historical irony: as he once did in South Ossetia, he is yet again administering a boundary with a pro-Russian separatist region occupied by Russian peacekeepers. Somewhere between a quarter and half of the population of the city itself harbors latent pro-Russian sentiments, and those figures are probably much higher in the depressed region itself. Having failed spectacularly to subsume Odessa under the aegis of the embryonic Novorossiya project, the Kremlin's consolation offer to the city is a glamorous one: Hong Kong-like autonomous status. Pro-Russian separatists and pro-Russian media have adroitly taken to referencing the city's 19th-century economic glory under its status as "Porto Franco"—a free port where, symbolically enough, one did not need to pay taxes. Proud, anarchic, and perpetually independent, the city that haughtily refers to itself as "the southern capital" will need to be corralled into the ongoing project of the construction of Ukrainian national identity.

As the sweltering first summer of Saakashvili's quixotic, theatrical reign begins, the reaction of the populace to his appointment has mostly shifted from an initial befuddled distrust to approval of his frenetic style. He and the entourage of technocratic Georgian friends that he has brought along are competent and dashing. They can be found drinking at the bar of the Bristol, Odessa's chicest hotel several nights each week. The city is a raucous port town where criminal maneuvering, cosmopolitan self-reinvention, and theatrically have always gone hand in hand. Odessans have always been practical and entrepreneurial, and their values mesh with his ambitions to remake the port town in the image of a modern start-up. Most everyone I spoke with is optimistic in a way that they have not been in a very, very long time.

As Saakashvili is fond of pointing out, the city already has 50,000 Georgians calling Odessa their home. Why not one more? And in any case, if all he accomplishes is to rehabilitate the roads and do something about the decrepit airport, that will be more progress than anyone else has delivered in a generation.

Arriving at a beach club owned by a friend late one night, I observed a drunk woman attempting to get past the security guards at the door.

"Let me in!" she bellowed at the men who blocked her entrance. Finally acknowledging her case as hopeless she deployed a last, desperate gambit to gain entry.

"I am going to tell Saakashvili if you don't let me in, you bastards!" she bellowed.

Alas, she would not be drinking on the beach that night. One can only hope her other expectations for reform will not be similarly dashed.

The American Interest 2015

Odessa on Edge

In May of 2016, the city almost degenerated into chaos and political violence.

In a quirk of the calendar, the somewhat ideologically divergent holidays of May Day and Orthodox Easter fell on the same Sunday this year. In Odessa, the Easter Sunday festivities took place on an afternoon so lovely that the citizens of the city could be forgiven for forgetting the generalized sense of dread that had taken hold of the town for more than a week. Still, anyone who did manage to forget would be quickly reminded by the sight of armed men, many decked out in full camouflage attire and sporting baklavas, holding down almost every block of the city.

You can taste the tension in the air. Several weeks ago, the April 10th commemorations of the emancipation of Odessa from the Romanian occupation had concluded with massive brawls between those who celebrate the holiday as moment of triumph, and those who identify it as toxic Soviet nostalgia. Protesters from both sides fought the armed police, who used tear gas to disperse the mob, and arrested one member from each side. The day after Easter this year, May 2nd, is the second anniversary of the tragic events at Kulikova Field, where almost fifty Odessans—mostly pro-Russian activists—lost their lives in fighting and a subsequent conflagration at the trade union house. May 9th, just around the corner, is also the day that the Soviet Union traditionally celebrated its victory over the Nazis, and thus represents another potential flashpoint for possible violence between pro-Russian and pro-Ukrainian activists.

The tensions, of course, have been present since the Maidan protests deposed President Viktor Yanukovych in 2014 in one form or another. On top of that, top officials in the city's government, both pro-Ukrainian and both pro-Russian in sympathies, have dragged their feet on completing an inquiry into the events of two years ago, leaving a suppurating wound in the public psyche. And finally, Odessa's famously complex and bitter local politics have been playing their part, especially in the last six months.

Mayor Gennadiy Trukhanov, long alleged to have strong ties to Moscow (as well as a history of working with underworld figures in the 1990s), vanquished Odessa Governor Mikheil Saakashhvili's aide, Sasha Borovik, in the closely contested and ultimately compromised mayoral elections in October of last year (I was among the international election observers and we witnessed ample systematic "irregularities"). The enmity between the Saakashvili camp and the mayor has been accruing ever since, and recently threatened to spill out into open war.

The proximate cause of the latest crescendo was the sacking of Saakashvili loyalist and noted reformer David Sakvarelidze, who had been fired as Deputy Prosecutor General by Poroshenko's notoriously obstructionist Prosecutor General Viktor Shokin just hours before he himself was dismissed by parliament. Nikolai Stoyanov (who had held the job from 2012 to 2014, at the height of the Yanukovych government) was returned to his old job, which gave him jurisdiction over Odessa Oblast. With Saakashvili's emphatic blessing, an "Odessa Prosecutor's Maidan" sprung up in front of the regional prosecutor's office. Blockades were set up, and the newly reappointed prosecutor was denied access to his office. After a seventeen day standoff, the Justice ministry in Kyiv ruled that Stoyanov had fallen afoul of national lustration laws, and thus could not stay in the post.

The Prosecutor General's office had blinked, and emboldened by their easy victory, the motley bunch of nationalist and civil society activists moved their tents and barricades a hundred meters up Pushkinskaya street, onto Primorski Boulevard and the "Dumskaya" Square facing city hall. The "Prosecutor's Maidan" quickly morphed into the "Anti-Trukhanov Maidan," though, in its new incarnation, it was much less peaceful.

On the night of April 25th, fifteen activists spending the night in front of city hall were attacked and severely beaten with bats and chains by more than forty masked assailants. Four of the assailants were later identified, arrested and released with 50 Hrivna fines (less than $2) for charges of aggravated hooliganism. The next night, an RPG was fired at the headquarters of the Pivdennyi Bank. The Trukhanov's office immediately accused Saakashvili's team of being behind the explosion, claiming it was a false flag operation meant to terrify the population and drum up support for the swashbuckling Governor ahead of the May 15th anniversary of his appointment.

Last Tuesday, Saakashvili publicly asked for assistance and reinforcements from Kyiv, which the capital grudgingly sent (though not before the Interior Ministry pooh-poohed the request to the media). Even the possibility of another round of bloodletting, or worse, a repeat of the operations that led to captured government buildings in Eastern Ukraine, could prove to be politically too costly for the new government. Poroshenko ordered a thousand policemen from other regions around the country to join the more than 1300 local police officers already on high alert. Interior Minister Arsen Avakov, who had recently thrown a glass of water at Saakashvili in the middle of a cabinet meeting, was now throwing the weight of his support behind the governor. He ordered some 500 National Guard troops to the city, made up mostly of members of the notorious and controversial Azov Battalion. Even Azov's commander and MP Andriy Belitsky made the trip to Odessa. "The First 300 Azov men have arrived, we are waiting for the rest!" a jubilantly giddy Saakashvili posted on his Facebook page on Wednesday as the troops rolled in.

Speaking on Sunday, the Governor seemed to be girding for war. "Based on the experience that I have with Putin's Russia, I have no doubt that they are preparing a provocation, they will try to use the anniversary of the tragedy [May 2] to undermine the situation in Odessa and Ukraine. There is specific information, we received it from the Security service and other services. It's quite alarming."

The Mayor's speech on Sunday was less shrill. Dressed in jeans and a shirt, as fit at fifty as most men are at twenty, Trukhanov, a former artillery officer, stood ramrod straight in the middle of the city park gazebo. A choir of shy school girls from the local music school, wearing blue Sunday dresses and white frocks, sang Eastern hymnals. A black-robed Orthodox priest appeared (I had never seen one in public in the seven years I have called this city my home) to chant some half-felt homilies about the need for spiritual values and a belief in authority. The Mayor proceeded to take the microphone and echoed the priest's downbeat remarks, gravely inveighing on the need for spirituality, the omnipotence of God and the importance of not lying.

"I cannot help myself but speak about this today," he finally said. "We must be against spiritual filth and degradation, and also against the scourge of separatism and the manipulation of events," he went on, seemingly criticizing the pro-Russian activists.

He paused before adding somberly: "I take responsibility for everything that happens in this city today and tomorrow."

What happens next is anyone's guess.

The American Interest 2016

Ukraine's Best-Known Reformer Succumbs to the Lure of Populism

"In his inflammatory response to a brutal and shocking crime, governor Mikheil Saakashvili reveals his dark side," read the Foreign Policy subtitle. Saakashvili's response to my article took that revelation much further. When he learned of my article Saakashvili personally posted a long ranting attack against me on his Facebook account. Afterwards, his press secretary, a young Georgian woman who had been educated in Georgetown, called me to threaten me. Racist stickers attacking the "Roma mafia" suddenly appeared all over the block of my apartment building and were also posted on the door of my office.

The article was published a month before Saakashvili resigned from the office of governor of Odessa in order to fully devote his time to his fervent one man war against the Ukrainian government. A week later I ran into the governor at the annual Pinchuk YES conference in Kyiv.

A Vice President of the head of the Soros Foundation, whom I had told about the stickers, took me by the hand and walked me over to him in order that I might confront Saakashvili at the conference. Enraged, Saakashvili looked as if he wanted to fight me and yelled in my face that he was not a racist.

Incidentally, Odessa was passed over as the host of the Eurovision song contest. Five year later, Mayor Trukhanov and Saakashvili are still full of rage at one another.

Last Saturday, in the final week of what is usually a sedate period of summer vacation for almost everybody in Ukraine, the country's bucolic southern Odessa region experienced an ominous and unusual bout of ethnic violence.

The episode had nothing to do with the simmering war between Ukrainians and pro-Russian separatists. It had the air of something more ancient, and perhaps even more sinister: a pogrom against a small community of Roma.

The violence was triggered by the discovery on August 27 of the body of a young girl, variously described as 8 or 9 years old, whom police said had been raped before her murder. A day later, a 21-year-old Roma man from Loshchynivka, a village of ethnic Russians and Bulgarians that also has a tiny Roma community, was taken into custody and charged with the horrendous crime. In response, last Saturday evening, an enraged mob of young men went on an anti-Roma rampage, throwing stones, smashing windows, burning down a house, and desecrating property. Thankfully, there were no injuries, as the Roma had already fled — but the widely shared videos of the episode led multiple Ukrainian observers to describe the situation as a pogrom, implying violence motivated by ethnic hatred.

The authorities responded quickly. After locals demanded the permanent removal of the Roma — about six families comprising about 50 individuals — the village council provided buses to take them away. Immediately after the violence, the governor of the Odessa region, former Georgian president Mikheil Saakashvili, dispatched special police units and paramilitaries to the village under the personal command of his police chief.

But it was another element of the governor's reaction that most troubled domestic and international observers. In comments directly after the incident and again after the girl's funeral on Wednesday, Saakashvili made public statements which, in a tense situation, are hard to see as anything but inflammatory. "I fully share the outrage of the residents of Loshchynivka," he said, adding that in the village there was "a real den of iniquity, there is massive drug-dealing in which the anti-social elements that live there are engaged. We should have fundamentally dealt with this problem earlier — and now it's simply obligatory."

Saakashvili's appointment to the governorship of the Odessa region just over a year ago was met with great excitement and engendered hopes that he could emulate his earlier success as a democratic reformer in his native Georgia. The governor is often viewed as modern, progressive, and even hip.

Prior to his return to the post-Soviet world in May 2015, the *New York Times* published an amusing portrayal of his hipster-like exile in Brooklyn. He is almost universally characterized as a principled anti-corruption crusader who is attempting to make Ukraine's Euromaidan Revolution produce results in the south of the country. But, in the face of stonewalling by local and national authorities, his results have been mixed. And after wasting time and political capital this spring crisscrossing the country and forging a movement for reform in misplaced expectations of early elections (these did not happen), he has now refocused his energies on creating local infrastructure. His projects include championing a new highway to Romania and finalizing construction of a long-stalled second terminal for the local airport.

Yet Saakashvili's ungracious and even dangerous response to last weekend's tragic incident in a region with fresh historical memory of ethnic strife highlights a different side of his character. His inflammatory rhetoric in a delicate moment was not befitting of a Westernizing reformer.

Comments offered by Saakashvili's officials were no less revealing. "We must respect the presumption of innocence," said Zurab Hvistani, a spokesman for the Odessa region's interior ministry, "but it is merely the constitution of a fact that every Ukrainian and Odessan on the level of ordinary life understands that members of the Roma community are involved in the drug trade." Local villagers have indeed been quoted complaining about a rise in crime since the arrival of the Roma families — which, of course, can offer no justification for vigilante violence.

Hvistani was insistent that the Roma were not being forced to leave the village against their will. He described their voluntary departure as an implicit admission of the reality that further peaceful coexistence with their Ukrainian neighbors would be impossible. He also declined to provide the location where the Roma families would be moving.

Meanwhile, Roma organizations have filed direct appeals to interior minister Arsen Avakov, a staunch Saakashvili opponent, decrying the violence and noting that the state's failure to protect the Roma stands in direct contradiction with its stated goals of building the rule of law in Ukraine.

The episode couldn't come at a worse moment for the city and regional government. Odessa is widely viewed as the favorite candidate city to host the 2017 Eurovision song contest, for which it is competing with Kyiv and Dnipro. The winner is expected to be announced in the coming weeks, and the prospect is seen as so important to the city's future that, just a day after the killing, Saakashvili and his sworn local enemy, Odessa mayor Gennady Trukhanov (whom he has repeatedly referred to as a separatist, bandit, and thief) hosted a joint press conference in support of the bid. It was the first time that the two had appeared together in public in almost 15 months, though Odessa's elites have since become accustomed to seeing the two men milling about at opposite sides of banquet halls and official gatherings.

The two men's unlikely truce is evidence that this episode of sectarian violence might endanger the city's bid for Eurovision glory. And that, in combination with his frustration by the slow pace of his attempted reforms, is what may have prompted Saakashvili to adopt a strikingly populist tone in response. Though the incident may be viewed as random, it is, in fact, a demonstration of the relative fragility of the social compact in the ethnically diverse region. Saakashvili's response offers an unflattering picture of a governor many had hoped would help Odessa — and is particularly troubling since he remains the only force likely to offer the region any meaningful reforms for years to come.

Foreign Policy 2016

Saakashvili in Odessa and Ukraine: Anatomy of a Failure

This article was co-written with another editor and appeared as an unsigned editorial in the February 2017 issue of The Odessa Review after Saakashvili stepped down from his post as Governor of Odessa region.

Appointed by President Petro Poroshenko in what was viewed as a test to see what kind of progress could be made in one of the most notoriously corrupt regions of Ukraine, Saakashvili had thrown himself into his job with relish. At the time, it looked like the only plausible threat to Poroshenko would be the credibility hit that his party would take if the country's various squabbling oligarchs and assorted mafiosi managed to thwart the swashbuckling anti-corruption fighter from Tbilisi.

In the beginning of last November, Saakashvili went on television and gave a typically fiery speech resigning the governorship. He also accused Poroshenko-the man who had rescued him from political wilderness- of being complicit in highest levels of corruption.

Living in Odessa, we are continuously asked about Saakashvili's results in the city; whether he had managed to get anything done in the relatively brief time that he had spent here. Our tentative answers always seem to leave our interlocutor unsatisfied. His results were decidedly 'mixed' and hard to quantify, we typically respond, and they left many in Odessa unsatisfied.

On the one hand, his arrival created a ferment of energy and high expectations. On the other, he was from the very beginning stymied by structural issues to getting anything done in Odessa.

He greatly undervalued the skill of the feudal local elites in settling issues and creating impediments to his rule.

The pivotal event that may have pushed Saakashvili to shed any scruples about turning on his erstwhile boss was likely the October 25,

2015 local elections—an event that was widely seen as a setback for reformers and a victory for wily oligarchs across the country.

Saakashvili's plan for implementing reform in Odessa had been to replicate the same sort of "power vertical" that he had managed to establish in Georgia: control over the various branches of government that had allowed him to clean house and push through his aggressive reformist agenda. He had already managed to get two of his former Georgian cabinet ministers appointed as regional prosecutor and chief of police, and he had gotten his 26-year-old aide appointed to head the Odessa port customs while his own Georgian team ran the technical operations behind the scenes. He thus had three out of the five key pillars of power in the region under his thumb. However, as the judges presiding over Odessa's regional courts were said to be loyal to local political parties, and could not be swayed, he was unable to exercise authority over the courts.

The final pillar, the Mayorship of the city of Odessa, however, was up for grabs in the elections and Saakashvili made a decision to contest it vigorously.

Saakashvili chose his aide, Sasha Borovik, to run for the spot. Borovik had always been a long-shot candidate against Gennady Truhanov, the candidate favored by the entrenched local interests. At the start of the campaign, he had around 7 percent name recognition among likely voters in Odessa. Many of Odessa's political insiders told us that they suspected that Truhanov's local patrons and Saakashvili's backers in Kyiv had reached some kind of deal, allowing for fair elections in the city. The deal, which was said to have been negotiated as high up as at the level of President Poroshenko himself, was reportedly struck when the chances of Saakashvili's proxy advancing to the second round were still low.

Then came the anarchic month-long campaign. A man dressed as Darth Vader ran for office, as did a 30-year-old representing a pensioner coalition. Another, who had legally changed his name to "Emperor Palpantine" was elected to the city council. Several vote-siphoning "technical candidates" were up for election as well. One candidate withdrew when a hand grenade was thrown into his garden. Despite all of this, Borovik ended up coming just a few percentage points shy of forcing a second round run-off, something that exit polls showed that he probably was due. Regardless, there was never much of a chance of his winning the second round based on all the polling.

Video evidence of ballots being mishandled, and of votes being bought for cash, food or even building materials, quickly surfaced. The Chief Editor of the Odessa Review, was embedded with an international delegation observing the elections, and what he saw more closely resembled the proceedings at the Queen of Hearts' court in Alice in Wonderland than any kind of proceeding adhering to normal standards of fairness and transparency. The city election territorial commission, which was stacked with appointees of the old city elites (the city election commission head, whom he went to see during the evening of the elections, was a Darth Vader bloc appointee) quickly declared the elections legitimate in favor of the incumbent mayor.

Having been promised a clean election by Poroshenko, immediately after the elections, Saakashvili went on the warpath. He publicly accused the incumbent mayor of complicity with various local mafiosi, including the reputed Odessa kingpin Alexander "Angel" Angert. He convoked town hall meetings and beseeched Odessans to rise up in massive Maidan-style demonstrations against what he described as a stolen election. All of Saakashvili's exertions came to naught, alas. The final decisions closing the door on Borovik's appeal came down only after Poroshenko himself appeared to send a definitive signal on how to proceed in a TV interview: he said he considered the Odessan elections flawed, but legitimate.

Having lost his battle for the Mayorship, Saakshvili was fundamentally unable to implement the model of reform that he had employed in Georgia. He found his anti-corruption crusade frustrated again and again by his limited powers, as well as by the well-established networks of local politicians with greater regional familiarity.

In late December of 2015, Saakashvili announced the birth of a new anti-corruption movement—not quite yet a full-fledged party, but something with all the trappings of one. His initiative largely focused on naming "leading corruptioneers," and implying the involvement of then-Prime Minister Yatsenyuk. Saakashvili's increasing engagement in national politics led to considerable friction, including his now-infamous confrontation with Minister of Internal Affairs Arsen Avakov. Throughout 2016, the relationship between Poroshenko and Saakshvili became increasingly strained, as the latter stepped up his populist rhetoric and began criticizing the President himself.

Tensions came to a head in early November of 2016, as Saakashvili resigned his post, delivering a characteristically fiery speech accusing Poroshenko as well as the highest figures in government of having betrayed the principles of the Maidan revolution as well as the sacrifice of the soldiers fighting in the East. He pointed to the recent disclosure of the hidden wealth of high-ranking officials in justifying his resignation. Nonetheless, despite his promise that he would not give up on his anti-corruption campaign, many observers of local Odessa politics concluded that he was spending too much time outside of the city on a nationwide campaign, and that this was contributing to his relative ineffectiveness in running the Odessa region.

Several days following his November resignation, Saakashvili appeared in Kyiv, evidently to make good on his promise. He laid out his plan to establish a "platform of new forces," a populist political party that seeks to fill its ranks with young, reform-oriented politicians. Saakashvili declared that the party's goals were to "remove the current political elite" and "force early parliamentary elections as soon as possible." To these ends, the party would deny membership to any politician who had served in parliament for more than one term, or who had links to prominent businesses. Saakashvili directed his ire at his critics and made direct reference to his personal acquaintance with Donald Trump.

Saakashvili's new party has thus far been unsuccessful in demanding early elections, and it is unclear in what capacity Saakashvili himself might participate. The most evident achievement of his "new forces" has been to divide the opposition, driving a wedge between young reformist politicians who are wary of Saakashvili's leadership style and those that are encouraged by his vehement populist message.

Meanwhile, Saakashvili has continued to remain involved in the affairs of the party he once led in Georgia, the United National Movement (UNM). This has been met with dismay by many members of the UNM, who feel that his identification with the party is detrimental to their political objectives. His public engagement with the party prior to the 2016 parliamentary elections led twenty of the twenty-seven MPs representing the UNM to defect, forming their own party, the Movement for Liberty–European Georgia. With the split in his party, the chance for a UNM victory and Saakashvili's hopes for a return to Georgia were dashed. His intervention in Georgian politics seems to have turned off many voters in Georgia.

The legacy of Saakashvili's tenure in Odessa is as contentious as that of his presidency in Georgia. Many locals have the impression that bribery – especially in the port – decreased significantly under his anti-corruption campaign. Many others, however, feel that this was less to do with effective policy and more closely related to the fear among local elites of being openly criticized by Saakshvili. In any case, measuring the opaque maneuvering at the port is notoriously difficult. His numerous public pronouncements and abrasive personality characterized his time in Odessa, and his team suffered from a lack of organization and poor staff cohesion. Saakashvili sought to compensate for this through his highly personal approach, consistent public engagement, and his signature impassioned delivery – a combination which may have intimidated some local politicians, but which is unlikely to produce long-term results. Populist methods appear to have won Saakashvili the greatest support in his early days as Governor, and to have done the most damage to his reputation in the latter half of his time in Odessa. As he turns again to this approach and his rhetoric aggressively targets Ukraine's current political elite, he may find that he strikes a chord with Ukraine's opposition, or that he weakens them and entrenches the very elites whose power he wishes to supplant.

The Odessa Review 2017

Is the Odessa Mafia's
Angel of Death Actually Dead?

Isaac Babel's *Odessa Tales*—1920s stories following the misadventures of the fictional Jewish gangster Benya Krik—codified the lifeblood of Odessa's famous criminality into literature. The gangster funeral has always been an important set piece in that mythic world. Babel's story "How Things Were Done in Odessa" charts the entrée of the man who would become the king of the Odessa gangsters on his climb to the top of the pyramid. In the tale, a robbery gone awry concludes with one of Benya's henchmen shooting a clerk and revolves around the machinations over who pays for—and profits from—the clerk's funeral. Now, in a tale straight out of Babel, the possible passing of Odessa's main underworld mafia boss, Aleksandr Anatolevich Angert, universally known as "the Angel," has launched a thousand conspiracy theories and thrown both legitimate and illegitimate political arrangements in the city and in the nation into turmoil.

Angert is (or was) considered to be the "don of dons" of the Odessa mafia, a position that placed him at the center of multiple concentric circles of organized crime, the oil business, shipping, banking, drug- and gun-running, and political influence. It also offered control over assets and financial flows spanning the length of Europe from Moscow to London, whose total valuation runs into the billions of dollars. The compulsively secretive Angert, who is known to hold various European passports as well as Venezuelan and Israeli citizenship, has spent the last few years living quietly in London with the full knowledge of the British authorities and intelligence agencies. Significantly, one of Angert's major business partners is the reputed mafioso Alexander Zhukov, the father of Moscow's Garage Museum of Contemporary Art Director Dasha Zhukova, the current wife of London-based Russian-Jewish billionaire

Roman Abramovich. Zhukov and Angert have both been implicated in crimes in Italy, but neither has ever been convicted.

In 1979, while he was still in his mid-20s, Angert was convicted of premeditated murder and sentenced to a 15-year prison sentence. Serving ten, he was paroled and, upon his release in 1990, he began his ascent of the ladder of the Odessa crime syndicates. The dissolution of the Soviet Union saw the same sort of bloody street fighting between armed thugs in Odessa and the same sort of gangland-style executions in broad daylight as happened in other post-Soviet cities. Within several years and after a struggle, "the Angel" had, according to reported conversations with those active at the time, bested men with sobriquets such as "Karabas" and "Katsap." Odessa's mafia wars concluded as a hierarchy was instituted and spoils were distributed.

Angert swiftly expanded his underworld mastery into political influence and diversified into any number of businesses. In the mid-1990s he came into concerted conflict with Odessa's legendary and colorful Jewish mayor Eduard Gurvits (Hurvits), who served from 1994–1998 and 2005–2010, and was cheated out of a third term.

Though it is well known that Angert has been battling an illness, perhaps cancer, for at least a year, the rumors of his demise have set off preparations for the bloody battles that are likely to split the Ukrainian underworld. Yet while numerous obituaries have already appeared in local Odessa and national Ukrainian media, the question of whether the man who has sat atop Odessa organized crime since the early 1990s has actually died remains unanswered as of press time. Ukrainian intelligence operatives and political sources have yet to provide a definitive answer on whether the shadowy figure, of whom there allegedly exists only one known public photograph, has actually expired.

The current mayor of Odessa, Gennadiy Trukhanov, is widely considered to be a protégé of Angert, and the mayor has never denied the intimate relationship between the two men. A bald and chiseled former army officer in his fifties, Trukhanov is the patron of a chain of kickboxing clubs all over the city. Mayor Trukhanov has been widely implicated in a variety of legal and illegal businesses. Bank accounts of offshore companies connected to him as well as photocopies of his Russian passport were the most prominent Ukrainian revelations to have come out of the publication of the Panama Papers.

According to Ukrainian and several foreign-intelligence officials, Angert relied on the young sporty men that Trukhanov's kickboxing clubs produced, as well as veterans of the Afghanistan war, as enforcers. Though they are skeptical of Trukhanov and view him as a potential separatist and a front man for figures connected to Russian intelligence agencies, the Ukrainian presidential administration seemed to have come to an arrangement with the mayor, thus ensuring that he remain on the Ukrainian side in exchange for being allowed to remain in power, a deal that played out within the context of widespread latent separatist feeling present in the majority Russian-speaking region.

Over the past two years Angert, Trukhanov, and the old Odessa regime essentially broke former Georgian President Mikheil Saakashvili's attempts to reform and root out corruption in the city.

Saakashvili had been the appointed governor of the Odessa region for 18 months from May 2015 until his flamboyant resignation from the post in order to move to Kyiv to continue his assault on entrenched political forces and his quest for political power. Saakashvili was sent to the region in the context of latent pro-Russian and separatists feelings held by many Odessans and a year after fighting at and conflagration at Trade Union Houses killed about 50 citizens of the city. During the September 2015 mayoral elections, Saakashvili attempted quixotically to wrest control of the mayoralty from the mafia clans by running one of his deputies, Sasha Borovik in the mayoral election. In his fiery populist speeches aimed at mobilizing the progressive elements in the city for a frontal assault, Saakashvili had held rallies in which he publicly denounced both mayor Trukhanov and Angert as bandits.

"This Angert! … Only in Odessa do they refer to the devil as an angel!" Saakashvili would thunder to the ecstatic crowds.

Still, Saakashvili's attempts to replicate a Euromaidan-style revolution in Odessa would invariably founder. Pragmatic, mercantile, and essentially apolitical, Odessa was simply interested in business as usual. The 2015 elections would turn out to be among the most dishonest in the history of the Ukrainian state. The projected second round of the elections, to which the pro-West/progressive camp was projected to advance, never took place, in the wake of widespread voting irregularities. I was a member of The Committee for Open Democracy's international election monitoring mission during the election, which was led by the Kyiv-based American political operative and analyst Brian Mefford.

Instead, the international media filled up with news that a candidate named Darth Vader was running for office under the aegis of his own political party (this was done to disrupt and split the vote, and in fact Darth Vader's man had been appointed to be the head of the city electoral commission) and that Chewbacca had been arrested while illegally campaigning.

Trukhanov's bodyguard, a 25-year-old kickboxing champion who had legally changed his name to "Emperor Palpantine," was elected to the city council. "You must inform the Americans, and the international public of the plight of Chewbacca!" the muscular goon instructed me impudently, as we watched his votes being tallied at 2 in the morning.

Mefford, the premiere non-Ukrainian expert on Ukrainian electoral policy, penned the definitive summarization of that criminally-flawed election in which he aptly predicted that it would be viewed by historians as Saakashvili's Waterloo:

Smelling victory close at hand, Trukhanov's team went for the jugular with the blessing of Odessa's top criminal authority Aleksandr "the Angel" Angert. Trukhanov, the Angel, and Russian businessman Aleksandr Zhukov are business partners on multiple ventures. By stealing a first round victory and breaking the "deal" with Saakashvili, the Georgian team was caught flat-footed. Thus, as a key Saakashvili ally said the day after the election, "war has begun."

Indeed, after the elections, an enraged Saakashvili would mostly lose all interest in governing Odessa and began spending ever more time in Kyiv and building a political movement around the country. Hereto having concentrated his fire on Prime Minister Arseniy Yatsenyuk, he now began openly attacking the presidential administration. He essentially declared total war against almost every political player in Ukrainian politics. "Bankova," named for the street in Kyiv on which the presidential administration is located, was understandably wary of allowing

Saakashvili to grasp too much power in the region, which he would inevitably use as his regional power base for seizing power in Kyiv. Though he would continue on as governor for another year before stepping down from the post, Saakashvili accused President Poroshenko's administration of collusion with Trukhanov.

Saakashvili would eventually begin accusing the president's loyalists and the president himself of corruption. By the end of his tenure, a clearly frustrated Saakashvili began to succumb to his populist impulses, and a month before his resignation, his press secretary threatened me with a lawsuit, with him himself lashing out at me with a defensive post on Facebook after I pointed out his troubling behavior in relation to a scandal involving Roma in *Foreign Policy* magazine.

I interviewed Saakashvili in his Odessa Regional administration office in early November of 2015—he served me tea with lemon as we sat on low couches under a bust of President Ronald Reagan that he had installed in the office. As Saakashvili had by that point earned a reputation for stamping deals with various shady Odessa characters to advance his agenda, I inquired whether he had ever met with Angert personally. Saakashvili assured me that he had not. Hinting at Angert's nebulous nature, he also claimed that he did not even know what the mafioso looked like.

> When I asked him point-blank if he thought that there had been a deal brokered by the (then acting) powerful head of the presidential administration Boris Lozhkin and the Odessa mafia clan to allow Trukhanov to take the elections in the first round, Saakashvili said, "I do not know of any such deal in particular."

Yet any deal struck between the local elites and the presidential administration is now likely to have been called off, as President Poroshenko's loyal enforcer and fixer Igor Kononenko has, according to intelligence sources, engaged in direct conflict with Angert. Kononenko has been accused by both Ukrainian officials and foreign experts of continuing to generate money in an illicit manner with utter impunity under the cover of his legal immunity as an MP from Poroshenko's "Solidarity" fraction. Kononenko is a deputy chief of the president's party, known as a "gray cardinal," and was also mentioned in the Panama Papers.

Over the last few months, Oleksandr Onyshchenko, a Ukrainian parliamentarian who is now a fugitive in London as well as in other parts of Europe, has publicly accused Kononenko of being part of a scheme to bribe lawmakers as well as extort from state companies. The presidential administration has vigorously denied those allegations. It should be noted that President Poroshenko, has, according to the commentary of multiple American and European diplomatic sources who have spoken to Tablet on condition of anonymity, refused innumerable Western entreaties and threats to sack his army buddy Kononenko.

The well-known English language blogger on Ukrainian security matters Nick Holmov has explained that "a weak or dead Angel naturally makes Trukhanov weaker, and opens up a succession issue which would create questions over the ownership of some prime assets and their future."

According to a highly-placed intelligence source who tracks these connections, Angert, through his control of the Odessagaz company, had spent years to get to the point where he could decide to file for bankruptcy of the Odessa CHP—the Odessa regional thermal power plant. A large portion of the debt of Odessa CHP is owned by Odessagaz—which would proceed to take over Odessa CHP as part of any debt settlement. Taken in conjunction with Odessa CHP control by the Odessagaz company (another unresolved issue in the wake of Angert leaving the scene), ownership of both utilities would have constituted a regional energy monopoly and would provide its owners with considerable political clout within both the city and the region.

The individual or entity that controls the majority of the Odessa CHP debt will be in a position to control its future when it inevitably declares bankruptcy. That individual was supposed to be Angert. However, in December of last year, Kononenko stepped in to purchase a majority of the Odessa CHP debts, and thus placed himself in the position of arbitrating the future of the CHP. These were the same debts that Angert had been accumulating in order to seize the plant as payment for his debts, according to the intelligence source.

In January, Igor Kononenko was diagnosed with acute mercury poisoning. More than 50 times the normative amount of mercury was found present in his bloodstream. Any insight on whether the poisoning of

Kononenko constituted an act of retribution can only be speculative in nature.

Holmov added that "if Angert is still alive and aware that this loss to Kononenko may be viewed as the Don losing his grip, then a loyalty test may have been decided upon. If this was indeed a "barium meal" to flush out disloyal elements within his organization, floating the rumor of his early demise would identify those that would make associated plays for assets."

If indeed Angert is with the other sorts of angels, and thus actually no longer with us, and the announcement of his death is not merely a stratagem to flush out disloyal members of his coterie, the death augurs a wholesale realignment within Ukrainian (and also Russian) mafia hierarchies. Conflicts will now most likely erupt over the control of arms smuggling, black market counterfeiting, skimmed port duties, as well as over the contraband that flows through the port and control over billions of dollars in business assets.

Tablet Magazine 2017

In Ukrainian Politics,
It's Fear, Loathing, and Chaos

The weeklong commemorative events honoring the fourth anniversary of the Ukrainian Maidan revolution wound down late last month in Kyiv. Between February 18th and 21st, 2014, the "Berkut" special security services killed almost a hundred protesters in the center of city, precipitating the collapse of the presidency of Viktor Yanukovich. Four years later, any semblance of legal redress for the killing continues to stall, withholding emotional closure for both the society and the families of the murdered. On Ukrainska Forum, one of Ukraine's freewheeling political debate shows, a group of a half-dozen Ukrainian MPs engaged in the annual ritual of rehashing the final days of the Maidan revolution with arguments about responsibility and which side began shooting first. Last week, the authorities unveiled plans for a new museum to be dedicated to the memory of the martyred "heavenly hundred," thus committing to the construction of a historical memorial before the actual facts of history have been thoroughly settled.

At the Munich Security Conference, which took place a week before the anniversary of the revolution, the idea of deploying an international peacekeeping operation to Eastern Ukraine was gaining traction. Diplomats representing Germany, Russia, Ukraine, and France, the four nations of the so-called "Normandy Format" tasked with resolving the situation, discussed the latest possible ceasefire deal on the conference sidelines, though at least one Ukrainian MP who attended later told me in private that the Americans were skeptical of implementing a peacekeeping operation out of fear of creating a de facto frozen conflict zone. Blasting the Russian "world hybrid war effort," Ukraine's president Petro Poroshenko continued his recent trend of delivering ever more rhetorically slashing speeches to audiences of international elites. His comments at Davos—where a Ukrainian house opened up for the first time to great acclaim across the street from Russia House—a few weeks prior had been equally ferocious, with him casting himself as the indispensable shining paladin of the fight against corruption.

Not everyone seemed to be convinced by the performance.

The new International Monetary Fund resident representative in Ukraine, a square jawed and bespectacled former Swedish Finance Ministry official straight out of central casting, began his tenure with the demand that the recalcitrant Ukrainian government make headway on the creation of an independent anti-corruption court. President Poroshenko remains anxious about giving up power to a legal body outside of the control of the presidential administration. He has long rebuffed Western pressure by countering with an offer of a "chamber" instead of a full-fledged court. Yet the Ukrainian elites understand that international and local demands for the creation of an anti-corruption court will have to be met sooner rather than later.

While progress on the campaign against corruption is certainly taking place, frustration with the pace of change is endemic, and Western diplomats have recently become much less patient and polite in their public utterances. Ukrainians, along with their often-derided political class, have in fact made tremendous efforts to transform their country. Yet the results of often complex or technical reforms that have long-term effects (the sorts of success stories such as the banishment of dozens of under-capitalized "zombie" banks, some of whose primary purpose seemed to be making loans to their board of directors) are often difficult to explain to outsiders, let alone to voters. While parliament has recently implemented new health care and education bills, electricity prices are up and pensions do buy less than they used to.

That the Ukrainians continue to grit their teeth and soldier on despite a general distaste for their political leadership is a testament to national cohesion and to their perseverance, demonstrating perhaps that they are the only people in Europe more stubborn than the Russians.

"It is indeed difficult for ordinary people to understand the substantive accomplishments of parliamentary reform as no one really explains the 'why' or the 'what' of those reforms, how they are made or implemented, as well as the manner in which they will benefit people eventually," Victoria Voytsitska, a reformist MP who chairs the energy committee in parliament, explained to me last month.

The fateful phrase "Ukraine Fatigue" began to spring ever more easily from the mouths of senior European diplomats charged with the Ukrainian portfolio. Pointedly, the European Union scrapped a much hyped border project in the midst of the Maidan commemorations.

Speaking with ordinary Ukrainians, especially less educated ones, one might notice a marked uptick in the conspiracy theory idea that president Poroshenko and his circle have a vested interest in keeping the war going and actually do not want a peace settlement.

"Given the various info war campaigns, I am weary of so much of what I read these days" Ariana Gic, an independent political analyst, told me. "Unfortunately, it appears that some are easily manipulated by false narratives from various sources including disinformation campaigns from political actors (some of whom are suspected of having Russian backing) with the aim of undermining Ukraine's government."

The Ukrainian political class has turned its attention to the 2019 presidential race, which, with more than a year to go before voting begins, seems to be locked into an underwhelming campaign between the incumbent president and populist former Prime Minister Yulia Tymoshenko. Her luster has faded, and the entire political class is unpopular, but a populist swing is certainly not impossible, and polls this week showed her overshadowing the president for the first time. And then there's Mikheil Saakashvili, the former Georigan president and Odessa regional governor whose sweeping denunciations of the government in Kiyv have caused the most trouble to the sitting government. Saakashvili, who has been appointed by Poroshenko to the governorship of Odessa, had resigned from his post, and soon began to attack the government.

In fact, the deportation of Saakashvili in the days leading up to the commemoration events WAS widely seen as the opening salvo in the 2019 presidential campaign. The deportation of Saakashvili, who had forced his way over the Polish border in September after having been stripped of his Ukrainian citizenship by presidential decree, had been long coming and was the conclusion of an ignoble saga that made all involved look bad.

Saakashvili was taken by force in broad daylight. Having exhausted his legal appeals, the presidential administration would take no chances after Saakashvili had previously (and often comically) resisted arrest. A group of commandos in balaclavas swooped into a Georgian restaurant where the former Georgian president was having lunch to drag him by the hair onto a private plane chartered for Warsaw. A photo of the unpaid lunch bill began circulating over social media along with inevitable jokes about "Misha's last supper."

Appearing in Holland, where the local government granted him a visa as he is married to a Dutch citizen, Saakashvili was reduced to filming Facebook videos of himself sitting in front of an Amsterdam canal to rally his troops into battle from afar. In any case, The long planned grand protest, which coincided with the anniversary of the commencement of the killings on February 18th, surely did not realize his expectations of a mass revolutionary uprising. No more than five thousand protesters showed up for the revolution. Either out of fear, prudence, or a dash of rigging the game, the Kyiv authorities took no chances, with most of the major metro stations in central Kyiv closed down for the duration of the protests. They likely could have avoided the effort. The regional protests, organized across the regional capitals were no more impressive. No one seemed especially surprised when the Ukrainian Border Guard announced a ban on Saakashvili reentering the country until February 2021. That is long after the election.

The last time I spoke with Saakashvili was on a Sunday afternoon in late December when we were both attending the same play in Kyiv. He was in an uncharacteristically subdued mood. It was obvious that the clock was running down on his appeals of the deportation notice but he swore to fight on. He assured me that he would return again

Over social media, the journalist/political analyst class broke into jocular debate over the odds of Saakashvili staging another triumphantly illegal return before the Presidential election. It would be an impressively cavalier gesture as the next deportation would most likely be back to face the legal music in Georgian courts controlled by his political enemies rather than to the side of an Amsterdam canal.

Not all was bitter news for the former Georgian president, as he concluded his canal video by jeering at the misfortunes of his great enemy, Odessa's Mayor Gennady Trukhanov. The alleged death last year of the Odessa underworld mafia boss, Aleksandr Angert, known as "the Angel," continues to play out within Ukrainian politics. The Ukrainian underworld is currently in the midst of a flux. The National Anti-Corruption Bureau of Ukraine (NABU), which was created to be an independent anti-corruption body, arrested Saakashvili's arch nemesis, Mayor Trukhanov, at Kyiv's Borispyl airport two days after the Georgian president had been deported from it. Trukhanov, whose ties to organized mafia structures date back decades, had been under investigation by the NABU for corrupt sale of a building.

Mayor Turkhanov had not appeared at work in City Hall for more than two months, hiding out abroad, allegedly while a deal for his political future was being worked out with the government. As Odessa is no longer under separatist threat and Saakashvili was no longer gathering political forces to use the region as a base for taking over Ukrainian politics, Turkhanov is now much less useful to Kyiv than he had been in 2014 or 2015. A day after being detained at the airport he was released by the judge, with outraged ultra-right wing nationalists and the Kyiv police engaging in a massive brawl outside of the court house.

The mafioso mayor was released under a personal guarantee of good character by the Odessa parliamentarian Dmitry Golubov, a professional hacker, libertarian activist, and Bitcoin investor, who is thought to be wanted for questioning by American intelligence (he cannot be prosecuted as he currently holds Ukrainian parliamentary immunity), and has often appeared in public dressed as Darth Vader. As an American political operative quipped to me at a party once, "When Darth Vader comes to court to attest for you as a character witness, welcome to the dark side my friend…"

Tablet Magazine 2018

V. Influence Operations and Kleptocracy

In Attempt at Fiscal Transparency, Ukrainian MPs Publicly Open Their Coffers

Tens of thousands of Ukraine's elected officials had until the end of the last weekend to declare their 2015 income and assets to an open access public database. A part of the International Monetary Fund's efforts to increase fiscal transparency in the severely corrupt and oligarchic dominated economy, the archly resented law was essentially imposed on the political system and on the Ukrainian parliament by its Western partners.

The creation of the e-declaration system had been plagued with technical issues in the course of its formation. The deadline for the declarations was this past Sunday, and the system almost crashed several times during the crunch of last-minute filings as Ukrainian politicians unhappily scrambled to fulfill their legal obligations. In some Ukrainian journalistic circles it became a jocular topic of debate to wonder whether or not the very wealthiest and most high profile MPs would file, and how much of their actual holdings would be exposed to the world's scrutiny. Ukrainian politicians are also known for declaring themselves impoverished while living in mansions owned by their wives or brothers and driving luxury automobiles owned by their cousins.

Ukraine's Prime Minister Volodymyr Groysman revealed cash holdings of more than a total of $1.2 million in cash as well as a stockpile of luxury watches. Dozens of MPs likewise declared millions in cash, luxury cars, jewelry, land and industrial holdings, and rare bottles of wine. Unsurprisingly, the most fervently populist members of parliament, such as Radical party head Oleh Lyashko, who once showed up in parliament with a pitchfork, held some of the most impressive hoards of cash.

The revelations have sent Ukrainian politics into paroxysms of mutual recriminations. When American writer Sophie Pinkham, author of an excellent recently published memoir of post-Maidan Ukraine, saw the Reuters headline "Ukrainians shocked as politicians declare vast wealth," she commented that she "thought [it] was an Onion article." The tenor of Ukrainian social media was indeed one of outrage. In a Facebook post, journalist Kristina Berdynskykh publicly asked colleagues who run into Poroshenko bloc MP Andrei Pavleno to ask him where he lives because he had left that part of his e-declaration blank. "Does he live in the Rada itself?" she retorted, wondering about a man known to own multiple expensive watches.

Ukraine's political class is infamous for its venality. Many members of parliament are representatives of big business who entered the Verkhovna Rada for the express purpose of siphoning resources from the state budget or to acquire parliamentary immunity against possible prosecution. Ironically, the reverse side of Ukraine's widespread kleptocracy is its puritanical public relationship to wealth that is a leftover legacy of Soviet communism. Ukrainians' income has been slashed by a war-driven recession, and their buying power has been further reduced by the twin scourges of a depreciation of the currency against the dollar and sharply rising inflation.

In a defensive Facebook post published Tuesday morning, Prime Minister Groysman's press secretary accused Fatherland party leader Yulia Tymoshenko of making a salary five times higher when she had served as prime minister about a decade ago. In an unrelated but particularly bad case of timing, Ukraine's parliament is now in the midst of voting in a retroactive pay raise that would more than double their salaries. Many skeptical local political observers as well as international experts of the declaration process pointedly wondered why any member of the ordinary Ukrainian population should be expected to entrust the banking system with his life savings when large swathes of the political elite choose to keep their wealth tucked under their mattress or in the form of expensive wine bottles. That is a reasonable question to ask as Ukraine struggles to create strong public institutions and cleanse its public sphere of corruption.

Tablet Magazine 2016

.

Kompromat vs. Maskirovka

Yesterday, after having gone six months without a proper press conference, Donald Trump was forced into one in the midst of a breaking espionage scandal. A secret dossier had appeared, compiled by a British intelligence operative who was now on the run after the BBC had blown his anonymity and shown his picture on television. The unverified dossier included revelations that Trump associates or campaign figures had secretly met with Russian officials and concluded a deal which would include the conclusion of sanctions against Russia and allow Putin to have his way with Ukraine. Russia's part of the deal would be to obtain and deliver compromising material on the Democratic National Committee. The most salacious revelation, however, was about Trump's 2013 stay at the Moscow Ritz, during which he had allegedly hired a pair of prostitutes to defile the hotel bed in which the Obamas had once slept. A week before he would become leader of the free world, Trump was reduced to reminding people that he was a germaphobe.

The Russian concept of "kompromat" describes the spycraft practice of gathering compromising personal information, which is then filed away for later use in blackmailing operations. The technique was a beloved tactic of Soviet security agencies and was deployed against both domestic and foreign opponents of the Soviet Union. The Kremlin's powerful Spokesman Dmitry Peskov dismissed the dossier however as "complete fabrication and utter nonsense," and swore to the heavens that Putin's government "does not engage in the collection of compromising material." Likewise, Nikolai Kovalyov, Putin's predecessors as head of Russia's Federal Security Service, the successor to the KGB, also denied Moscow ever gathering any compromising secrets about Trump's activities on his many business visits to Moscow over the years. That none of these revelations have surprised (or convinced) anyone in Russia is revealing, but what is far more concerning is the fact of their exportation to American soil.

Though the lessons of postmodern theory are becoming more germane by the day for understanding our political situation, one need not invoke "the absent mediating subject" to see that President Obama's foreign policy has in fact been in full alignment with Putin in the Middle East for quite some time. This later also became true of Eastern Europe despite all the necessary protestations to the contrary. Obama single-handedly ignored a bipartisan Washington consensus to arm the Ukrainians with lethal defensive weapons. In Syria, his administration stood by as the slow-motion sacking of Aleppo by Assad regime forces changed the calculus of the war. The recapture of the rebel city was accomplished by an alliance of what was left of the Syrian army, and local militias backed by Iranian Shiite expeditionary brigades and Russian special forces wearing the military patches of their new friends in Hezbollah.

A hollow man with no agenda besides winning, grifting, becoming more famous, and accumulating more money, Donald Trump never imagined that once he had grasped power he would be humiliated in this fashion. Buttressed by his immense wealth and a lifetime of power, which abetted his fleeing responsibility for his serially brackish actions, Trump is the opposite of a reflective man.

A week before he is due to become president, Trump has seen his position cardinally weakened. The damage control will continue for the duration of his presidency. Even before Trump has been sworn in, he has been radically undermined by Putin, who is winning in exactly the brutal kind of way that Trump promised his voters he would.

Just as he has in Russia and Ukraine, Putin has successfully sown epistemic doubts about what is true and what is false, and about our capacity to comprehend the concept of truth, while gaining the upper hand to continue the exact same policies he successfully urged on the last President. Even better, the claustrophobic political culture of Russian "managed democracy" is quickly being exported to America. The devious populist Stephen K. Bannon, for example, is being elevated to a consigliere position in the White House to fulfill a role that is not dissimilar from the incantatory dark magic that the "political technologist" Vladislav Surkov carries out for the Kremlin.

"Optics," as the Obama administration understands, are well served by claims that Trump is a Kremlin agent. The broader interest of securing cover for the Obama administration's legacy by disguising its actual alignment with the Kremlin is part of this play. Trump is left holding the bag and bearing responsibility for whatever happens. If Trump now aligns with Putin (unilaterally drops sanctions, de facto dissolves NATO, recognizes the annexation of Crimea, publicly abandons Ukraine), he will be open to attack from the Democrats led in semi-retirement by Obama—while in fact continuing with Obama's actual core policies in the Middle East and Eastern Europe, which simply could not have been more favorable to the Kremlin, especially over the past three years. If, on the other hand, Trump splits with Putin and confronts Russia, the Kremlin will have the kompromat hanging over him, real or fake—which the American media will all too eagerly disseminate. It seems obvious under that calculation that the winners in this scenario are Putin and Obama and the loser is Trump. "Sad," as the new commander-in-chief might pronounce.

It is important to recall how unlikely this whole situation may have seemed just a few months ago. Moscow, not unlike many other ostensibly rational actors, placed its wager on a Clinton victory while also hedging its bets and methodically feeding the Trump campaign scraps of toxic intel.

Kyiv, on the other hand, bet heavily on Clinton and crossed the rubicon into exactly the sort of manipulation with which American liberals had accused the Russians—minus the skill, grace, results and deniably. It has long been known to us journalists and analysts of Ukrainian politics that the Ukrainians played their hand in abominable fashion. The investigative report on their haphazard efforts to sabotage Trump published yesterday in Politico has very neatly tied together everything that we know about Kyiv's calculations.

It was apparent to all of us in Ukraine this summer that Kyiv was funneling information on Trump campaign manager Paul Manafort's backroom dealings with President Yanukovich and Putin through revelations of the "black ledger" of secret cash payments of the Russia-backed (and since dissolved) Party of Regions. Kyiv doubled down on warring with the Trump transition team even after the election shocker showed them that they had lost the wager. It got so bad that various British and American commentators living in Ukraine began writing op-eds pleading with Kyiv to hire a well-connected Republican lobbying firm.

Yet, the cruel cosmic joke on the Russians (as well as the rest of us now) is the widespread casting of blame for the election's outcome on Moscow—which from Putin's standpoint has both positive and negative connotations. On the one hand, the American press is making Putin out to be an evil genius who "hacked" the American election, which is fantastic for Russian domestic consumption and Putin's approval ratings as it confirms Russian television talking points about the inherent fakeness of American democracy: American elections are now apparently no less falsified than Russian elections. On the other hand, Trump, before this scandal broke, was on track to offer positive overtures to Putin. Now, there is a huge spotlight on everything Russia-related that Trump does, which may well tie his hands in many instances and leave the decision-making to the Russia hawks whom he has appointed to crucial defense and diplomacy portfolios in his cabinet. The Russian public has been primed by Russian television to view Trump as a great friend of Russia, which there is no reason to believe he is, or will necessarily continue to be.

So what in the final analysis is Moscow's endgame? Despite the sardonic grins on the faces of Russian Kremlin spokesmen and spooks turned statesmen as they deny ever having engaged in active measures, Moscow surely files away kompromat on myriad American elected officials. It is likely they had such material on Obama. They axiomatically have it on the Clintons. So, do they have it on Trump? It would be hard for them not to.

Yet the telling clue in this story is our knowledge that Russian intelligence agencies certainly have access to all the emails that Clinton sent from her private server as Secretary of State. All the "sordid" revelations, but actually quite bland scandals of the late campaign season involved the timed releases of John Podesta's campaign emails through Wikileaks. The fact that none of the important emails featuring actual state secrets had been handed over to Assange—not a single email or phone call from Hillary Clinton's personal account—intimates that the Kremlin was relatively sure that Hillary Clinton would win the election. They were always saving the truly incriminating and salacious materials to blackmail her once she became President—and they were too scared to release it during the campaign, knowing that American intelligence has its own kompromat on the billions of dollars worth of assets that Putin has pilfered from the Russian people over his decade and a half in power. This in turn suggests that they were similarly saving the best material on Trump.

The most likely meaning of the Trump dossier is therefore that it is maskirovka—a form of disinformation conveying the threat of a real compromise by publicizing implausible, fake kompromat. The message to Trump might be read as "remember every perverted thing you ever did in a hotel room." The message to Clinton, who is also named in the dossier, would be "think about every email that you have ever sent out over your server."

Being both maximalist and magical realist, Russian political culture had long ago catapulted far ahead of America into the realms of postmodern simulacrum. Now, American politics has been reduced—or according to one's politics—elevated to the level of a lurid potboiler thriller. Before this election, conspiracy theories and le Carre-like machinations did not explain most things in American politics in the way that they typically do in Russia. The American body politic, it turned out, has yet to develop antibodies against a potent new infection.

Tablet 2017

A Damning Report

The inquiry into systematic Russian interference prevalent in British life and politics that we have all been waiting for has finally been published. Along with every other Russian analyst, journalist and observer of Post-Soviet politics, I have been waiting for the release of the report with great anticipation. It did not disappoint. Compiled by Parliament's Intelligence and Security Committee amid storied political infighting, the subject of intense political jockeying, the report has already caused as much chaos and damage as we had expected. It commences by judging the aims of the Russian state to be "fundamentally nihilistic". The report does seem to give credence to accusations that British intelligence services truly did not want to get involved in its preparation – they prefer to avoid getting involved in such politicized matters at all cost – but the issue of whether they had been told to stand down for political reasons remains unanswered.

Did successive British leaders prefer to play tennis with agents of the Kremlin's influence while British citizens were being murdered on British soil by (sometimes hapless) hitmen sent by the Russian security apparatus? Was the report kept under lock and key in order to protect a series of Tory governments which had systematically denied the realities of Russian interference in British life as British financial institutions became ever more dependent on Russian money?

Was the report's release really delayed for more than a year in anticipation of the parliamentary elections? Is Prime Minister Johnson personally too close to people who are Russian plants? Did Russian money or disinformation sway the voting in either direction during the Brexit 2016 referendum?

My friends in the British press who have been waiting for the report to become public have told me that it contains exactly more or less what they had expected for 18 months, and my British colleagues can provide better answers to those questions. As a Russian-American who has spent the last decade reporting from Eastern Europe I am more interested in what lessons Americans might imbibe from London's experience.

The influence of Russian money and influence in London has been a topic of discussion in Washington and New York for the better part of a decade. If we avoid the puerile pastime of scoring points against successive Tory governments (amusing as that can be, it is in any case a British problem) the publication of the report proffers up a perfect opportunity for starting a vigorous public debate by American policy makers and the general public on this issue. That is before our own situation becomes as seemingly hopeless as that of London. My American colleagues, including everyone who works in the burgeoning think tank field of "Kleptocracy studies" inside of newly founded "Kleptocracy Institutes," have been waiting for the British to get their house in order for years. Perhaps it is already too late, and the British economy is too tightly interwoven with Russian money and influence. Incidentally, the aforementioned "Kleptocracy Institutes" do themselves routinely get into trouble with minor scandals for accepting contributions from disreputable Post-Soviet characters. The problems of Kyiv and Moscow all too quickly arrive in London before touching down in New York City and Washington D.C.

For Americans, London is indeed the proverbial canary in the coal mine. The US Congress is nowhere as deeply compromised – or not yet anyway – as the House of Lords has become. But the British experience of the penetration of its elites has been – or at least should be – instructive to Americans. Former United States Senators routinely lobby on behalf of Russian oligarchs and causes, while former Attorney Generals and high level Justice department officials retire into private practice and represent those same oligarchs in court. Part of the problem is that there remains no post-Cold War consensus on what constitutes the moral and legal red lines for Anglo-American elites. Both the fine print of the law and the social norms and etiquette are entirely opaque. What constitutes acceptable behavior remains a subjective question, to which different people will have different, and often self serving, answers. This, of course, projects a debilitating lack of cohesion back to Moscow (and also Beijing) and further strengthens the feedback loop of ever more flamboyant probing and coercive influence operations against our democratic institutions.

Even after an entire term of President Trump's administration, we had expected the improbable events of 2015-16 to spearhead massive reform, but FARA violations remain so selectively prosecuted as to render the process to be almost arbitrary. Which in effect undermines the intended deterrence effect. Indeed whenever I am asked if I follow any sport, I typically respond that the bloodsport competition that I most enjoy is keeping track of which Ukrainian and Russian oligarchs hire which D.C. lobbying firms against one another.

Likewise, the New York City and Miami property markets are nowhere near as distorted by Post-Soviet cash flows as the London market is, but it is a real issue and a metastasising one. It is also a genuinely confusing one for the general public. President Donald Trump's real estate business engaged in the same sort of squalid business practices of selling apartments to Post-Soviet kleptocrats for cash as everyone else had. It was very much an industry-wide phenomenon that everyone at the upper echelons of New York real estate had engaged in. Numerous conspiracy theories centering on Trump's relationship to Moscow have spread over the years and many of these are based in large measure on his disreputable business activities over the course of decades. These have been spread like infectious diseases by the American media, and many were at least on the karmic level, an outcome of the way that he had behaved for decades. "Russiagate" was a tremendous farce and squandered a great deal of public trust in our media as an institution, but it underlined Washington's bracing need for a similar sort of commission. The Mueller report de facto played the role of such an investigation, but the scope and remit of the report were far too politicized and narrow to really do justice to the problem. The rest of the world is starting to understand what those of us who follow Russian politics have known for a long time. London has numerous problems, but admirably enough, a lack of capacity for lucid analysis and self criticism are not among of them.

The Critic 2020

We Need More Lord Lebedevs

What does it mean for British liberal democracy when the son of a senior Russian KGB agent, a 90s era oligarch with complex relations with the Kremlin, is elevated to the House of Lords? The appointment takes place in the context of an inquiry into systematic Russian interference prevalent in British life. The announcement seems almost farcical. The timing of the government's release of the list of 36 peers, which includes Prime Minister Boris Johnson's own brother but did not include John Bercow, the former Speaker of the Commons, could not have been more surreal. Or perhaps merely gauche.

I do not know if the rumors of Theresa May having kept Russia related intel from Johnson while he was her Foreign Secretary are true. Those rumors are indicative however. It is more than a run of the mill kleptocracy when the Prime Minister, who is doing his best to downplay the report, genuinely likes the fellow and routinely parties with him. The optics of the appointment actually tell us more about Boris Johnson than they do about Lebedev or his record, abilities and capacity to bring value to the House. The fury against the appointment emanating from every corner of British society is eminently understandable, I would like to take the heterodox view and defend it.

Many reasonable commentators have pointed out that ennobling socialite press barons is a fine and harmless British tradition. Lebedev is very well dressed and he has dash. He will surely bring fresh blood to Parliament. I am told that he throws fantastic parties. This is all to the good. We can only hope that he will turn Westminster Parliament into the set of the next "Party Like a Russian" music video.

Much of the criticism of the appointment has understandably focused on the symbolic absurdity of it rather than on any substantive criticisms of Lebedev personally. After all, there are far more malicious, outrageous, dilettantish and ignoble characters to be found in the ageing and ever expanding House of Lords. My British contacts inform me that around a dozen members of the chamber are already viscerally disdained by the British intelligence community as de facto traitors to the nation. These are, to repeat, peers – without naming names – who are actively distrusted by British intelligence agencies for their clubby connections to wealthy and influential Russians. So why not?

We might be forgiven for flippantly asking: what difference does one more make? Is Lebedev a bigger threat to the maintenance of British state secrets than British peers whose ancestors had lived in the UK for centuries, and yet who make money directly from dealings with Moscow? Almost surely not. In fact, we should attempt to be fair to Lebedev: he is not himself a Russian oligarch. I empathize with the position of a son who does not want to be associated with the sins – or business practices – of his prominent father.

Lebedev is a British educated gentleman who has lived in England since he was eight and who has almost no political influence to speak of back in Kremlin court politics. His newspaper holdings actually took the opposite line of Moscow's intel operations on central questions such as Brexit and he more or less saved that failing paper (a phrase that will now for all time be associated with America's own playboy Commander in Chief).

Colleagues and acquaintances who had worked for *The Independent* have informed me that he had never complained about Russia-related stories. He cannot be accused of spiking such pieces, nor of any improper meddling in the reporting. He was doubtless very silly in his youth. Sure, he tried to save the elephant. Who amongst us would not want to save elephants? The worst judgment that can be made of Lebedev is that he is an extravagant, hedonistic, peacock aesthete of a Russian dandy enjoying himself ceaselessly and with panache. Most of which has also been said about me.

Let him who has never tried to hug an elephant cast the first stone!

As my colleague, British national treasure, Mark Galeotti wrote in the *Moscow Times*:

"It is hard to believe that Johnson was unaware of the media storm it would provoke. He probably feels that he is currently at his strongest politically, with the news cycle still dominated by Covid-19, parliament on recess, and his majority overwhelming, such that this is the best time to reward his friends and ride out any ensuing turbulence. He may have been less aware, though, of the potential damage to the U.K.'s international credibility."

The greatest risk of the appointment is in fact as Galeotti sagely notes, of the UK seeming to be more compromised than it actually is. Symbolically, the appointment very much resembles a season conclusion cliffhanger in the "McMafia" series. It is a Balzacian act of grace that redeems the underlying crime that besmirches a family name and raises it to triumphal heights of respectability – with the added benefit of throwing contempt in the faces of one's critics. In terms of chutzpah, Boris Johnson has outdone himself on this occasion. Bravo to him. Thirty years after the collapse of the Soviet Union, we are beginning to approach the dynastic transition phase of imperial breakup, where we get to see the ways in which the inheritance of numerous newly minted fortunes plays out. The first generation of the international Post-Soviet de facto aristocracy are being transmuted into actual aristocrats. Will they prove worthy of the opportunities handed to them?

A parting anecdote: a Russian speaking journalist friend of mine who was then working for the BBC had accompanied Lebedev on his journalistic junket by private plane to Belarus, where he quizzed "the last dictator in Europe," Alexander Lukashenko on his opinions on group sex. Which is exactly the sort of transgressive dadaist thrill that anyone might entertain if they were a billionaire playboy who got to interview the arch conservative, repressive and repressed Lukashenko. I would have given him a peerage for that alone.

Lord Lebedev, you and I would get on just fine and I await my invitation to the next bacchanal!

The Critic 2020

How Ukraine Became Chinatown

This essay was published a week after President Donald Trump left the white house and before his second impeachment trial.

The "Ukrainegate" scandal triggered Donald Trump's first impeachment trial, and it's winding down just in time for the former president's second impeachment. The scandal's denouement is a shockingly tidy end to what started as a convoluted and confusing set of overlapping scandals. It came when Treasury Secretary Steve Mnuchin, one of the few Trump officials to serve out his entire four-year term, announced the sanctioning of seven former and current Ukrainian officials who he claimed were tied to "a Russia-linked foreign influence network."

The announcement of the new sanctions ended a sordid and surreal chapter of American political history. It also served as a de facto rebuke of former New York City Mayor Rudy Giuliani, Trump's confidant and lawyer who faithfully carried out Trump's frenzied quest for oppo, or so-called "Kompromat," regarding the Ukrainian activities of Joe Biden's troubled son Hunter. Giuliani had gathered a piratical assemblage of shadowy middlemen — exactly the sort of characters that he had made his name prosecuting back in New York City — to deliver the goods to the American press, which mostly declined to report on the scandal. Those few who did found their accounts locked and tweets blocked by social media giants, America's new arbiters of what news is fit to print.

Individuals sanctioned by Treasury included serving parliamentarian Oleksandr Dubinsky; the fugitive former lawmaker and international playboy Oleksandr Onyshchenko (he had been leaking the tapes); former midtier prosecutor Konstatin Kulyk; and the former diplomat-turned-lobbyist Andrii Telizhenko, who had served as Giuliani's personal political fixer in Kyiv. All five men had taken part in the campaign to prove that former Vice President Joe Biden had behaved inappropriately to defend his son: Biden was overseeing the Ukraine anti-corruption portfolio as President Obama's point man in Kyiv at the time that Hunter was receiving $50,000 a month from a Ukrainian gas company. Several media companies connected to Andrii Derkach, a member of the Ukrainian parliament known in Ukrainian political circles for his pro-Moscow posture, were used to publicize the various accusations against the Bidens. (Those companies were also sanctioned.)

The fact that Giuliani was searching for compromising material against the Bidens created an energetic market for that commodity. Supply arose to meet the demand, and a host of political operatives, Russian connected spymasters, disgraced former prosecutors, and corrupt members of parliament soon responded to the call with relish—each with their own agenda, and each to be paid in their own currency (including access, television interviews and arranged meetings). The professional fixer Telizhenko connected the others with Giuliani. Since the going price for the goods was high, these unscrupulous individuals happily fed the obsessive, bitter, and cunning former mayor with information — some of what they provided was totally true, some doctored or speculative, and much of it simply unverifiable.

I myself wound up as a United States law enforcement witness regarding various parts of the conspiracy involving Giuliani and his fixer Telizhenko—after the latter tried to bribe me to illegally lobby the United States Senate on behalf of Russian political interests in Ukraine.

The latest round of sanctions began in early September, when the Treasury Department first sanctioned Derkach, as the pivotal figure behind a plot involving Ukrainians, Russians, and their various proxies to use "a wide range of influence methods and actors to target our electoral process, including targeting U.S. presidential candidates." The sanctioning underlined that he had "directly or indirectly engaged in, sponsored, concealed, or otherwise been complicit in foreign interference in an attempt to undermine the upcoming 2020 U.S. presidential election."

Derkach is a truly nefarious figure whose father was the head of the Ukrainian intelligence services in the 1990s and who himself was educated in the Moscow KGB academy. He is known in intelligence circles to have made large sums of money in the nuclear fuel trade between

Russia and Ukraine when he headed the Ukrainian parliamentary commission on nuclear energy issues. While the term "agent of influence" has admittedly lost much of its pungency due to its frequent misuse by the American media as well as amateur social media investigators, Derkach surely fits the bill.

He and his Ukrainian confreres were feeding a combination of toxic rumors, carefully engineered disinformation and torqued-up facts directly into the ear of President Trump. And I don't mean that figuratively.

Though it was grounded in actual facts, Ukrainegate, like it's big sister Russiagate, highlighted America's descent into banana republic territory under the dual influence of Trump's dime-store Juan Peron act (and very nasty nativism), and the unhinged conspiracy-theorizing of his self-righteous "resistance" foes. It also showcased the endemic credulousness, unprofessionalism, and partisanship of whole swathes of the legacy American media. Reporters competed with each other to distort basic facts and confuse motives and timelines without the slightest apology. They displayed little understanding of the vexed relationships between what in fact were often mutually loathing and competing local factions. The lack of local context and language skills of the international press, their pervasive amateurishness shading into conspiracy theorizing, made the local media in Kyiv look good by comparison.

Ukrainegate is not just a tremendous political scandal, it was a political scandal and a media scandal rolled into one. Various American journalists had relied too heavily on the deeply unreliable narrative and self-serving agenda of Telizhenko himself, soon after he'd been sacked from his low-level position with the Ukrainian Embassy in Washington, D.C. for an array of questionable behaviors.

To categorize the purpose of Ukrainegate as "misinformation" is itself a form of conceptual word-bending, because contrary to the versions of reality that today's American political operatives would like to enforce, more than one truth can be true at the same time—a worldview that Ukrainians and Russians are forced to imbibe with their mother's milk. While Derkach and his fellows were indeed part of a Russian-linked influence network that actively sought to interfere in the 2020 election, it can also be true that the substance of the accusations against Hunter Biden were not entirely false. None of it was fake news, or rather, none of it was *only* fake news.

In accepting a position on the board of directors of Burisma, an energy company owned by the former Yanukovich government minister Mykola Zlochevsky, Hunter Biden undoubtedly created a tremendous political liability for his father. That the younger Biden—a sad and self-destructive figure with a messy personal life—was engaged in influence-peddling and profiteering off his family name seems undeniably true. It is also absolutely true, as Republican counsel proposed during the first impeachment trial, that Hunter Biden had never worked in that sector or in Eastern Europe or had any relevant experience that would seem to necessitate such a large monthly retainer for his services—aside from the hope of influencing his father or providing the intimation of political cover for the company. That Joe Biden should never have tolerated his son's compromising positions, and that the former vice president deserved criticism for doing so is also true, even if his personal behavior may not have risen to the level of the unhinged-seeming accusations of corruption leveled by Giuliani in the final days of the presidential campaign.

Hunter Biden is hardly the exception. He is part of a spreading class of decadent, hereditary princelings who exist throughout both political parties. He is the louche and coddled progeny of an oligarchic elite that is currently ruling a country that was explicitly founded in opposition to the idea of oligarchic elites.

With a demonic gift for sharp political judgments and capacity to instantaneously grasp the vulnerabilities of his opponents, Trump seemed to instinctively identify the Hunter Biden story as the narrative that would be the most damaging to Joe Biden's campaign. Ordinary Americans understandably resent living in a modern iteration of late imperial Rome, complete with a class of sybaritic ne'er-do-wells who fly around the world using their family name to extract wealth from places like Ukraine, or who profited by exporting American manufacturing capabilities and jobs to China. Hunter Biden's checkered past and willingness to take cash from anyone seemed tailor-made for the populist tirades of the Trump campaign.

The accusation that Joe Biden had intervened to protect his troubled and brash son by compromising an anti-corruption campaign in a country where he was supposed to be the main outside arbiter of good governance was a powerful and ugly narrative, if the Trump team could prove it. The only problem was that it didn't make any sense to locals or to Western journalists who had devoted their professional lives to the country. It was difficult for those of us who were active in Kyiv during the whole affair to explain to outsiders, politically motivated or not, that the Obama-Biden policy of calling for President Petro Poroshenko to sack his loyal Prosecutor General Viktor Shokin was not that far-fetched; it was in fact the same view held by America's allies.

Shokin was *not* a great reformer. Indeed, he typically signaled far more interest in sitting in the *banya* with a cool drink after a long day of protecting the remnants of the old political elite from prosecution than in actually reforming the Ukrainian judiciary. The one time that I was briefly introduced to him by an oligarch source whom I was dining with in a Kyiv hotel, he struck me as being inordinately — perhaps even obscenely — relaxed. Hunter Biden was surely under less judicial threat with Shokin in place. Yet the claim that the Obama administration was trying to oust Shokin in order to protect the vice president's son was the basic premise underlying the accusations against Biden.

Clearly, the younger Biden's business dealings were the correct card to play if you were looking to undermine Joe Biden's reputation as an honest "straight shooter," but the Trump team played it completely wrong. They were as unlucky in 2020 as they had been lucky four years earlier.

The Russian intervention in the 2016 elections, which has produced libraries of analytical commentary and was later adumbrated in full detail by the Mueller report, was a relatively simple mischief-making affair, whose aim was more or less to cause maximum chaos on a small budget. It seems fair to call that operation a categorical success. But the 2020 American influence operation that attempted to use Hunter Biden's actions to destroy his father was a "massively overengineered and overly complicated disinformation operation that was always destined to fail," as one Western intelligence agent who worked on the matter informed me after the election.

The coordination of too many moving parts — including the complexity of explaining Eastern European political culture and Ukrainian factional infighting to an American audience — guaranteed the scheme's failure. Sen. Ron Johnson's Senate committee hearings on the matter planned for mid-March 2020, fell apart for a variety of reasons. There was the political pressure from different sides, and the tremendously bad timing regarding COVID-19. Trump tried to raise the scandal during one of his presidential debates with Biden in September, but the set up for the narrative wasn't in place, and the story fizzled.

Despite the failure of the 2020 gambit, foreign influence operations against American elections, whether instigated by foreign intelligence services or in concert with domestic campaign operatives, are here to stay. The new social media technology, coupled with the dissipation of the protective filtering function of the media, ensures it. The possibility of tremendous political outcomes stemming from very low-cost and deniable influence operations ensures that such operations will be far too tempting to pass up in the future.

While this was surely not the first time that foreign actors attempted to intervene in internal American elections, what was notable this time was that they were legitimized by media operations on both sides of the American partisan divide (and very few, if any, *nonpartisan* forms of media exist anymore in the United States). American party politics have become globalized. Foreign governments hire K Street lobbyists and former attorneys general to influence and even corrupt the American legislative and sanctioning process, just as the American government takes for granted its right to engage in nation-building projects abroad. Thanks to increased political polarization and the breakdown of a bipartisan foreign policy consensus, foreign actors are forced to choose sides within American political feuds at the expense of institutional arrangements based on values, norms, interests, or commonsensical alliances. Picking a partisan side to play on is of course not a useful way to maintain civil relations with both sides. In this, as in much else, Trump's presidency exacerbated preexisting trends and dragged a long simmering issue out into the daylight. It also demonstrates that there remains literally nothing left from the crumbling edifice of the post-Cold War consensus.

Fairly or not, the Ukrainian state will for some time be seen as having entangled itself in American politics. Worse still: Kyiv appears to have backed the wrong horse two elections in a row. (Even if it was various factional elements within the government who made the unwise decision, but try explaining that to skeptical outsiders.)

A deeper issue is that for a generation of American politicians, political operatives, and consultants, Ukraine was always a source of easy cash. John McCain, to his credit, figured out that various people close to him who had been orbiting the Paul Manafort circle were radioactive, and he never gave Manafort the top job as his 2008 presidential campaign chairman. The Ukrainegate scandal is the harbinger of much greater political skirmishing to come. In a dramatic first, the tech monopolies dropped their facade of political neutrality during the Hunter Biden affair when they intervened to keep a poorly sourced and partisan *New York Post* piece on Hunter Biden's errant laptops from being shared on their platform, regardless of whether the story was true or not. As it turned out, an uncomfortable portion of the story *did* turn out to be true.

Ukrainegate is the future. The jokes that those of us who have spent years reporting in Eastern Europe make about the systematic Ukrainization of American politics are as apt as they are glib.

My beloved Ukraine is the new Chinatown.

Tablet Magazine 2021

Difficult Neighbors: How the Belarus Crisis has Strained Ties Between Minsk and Kyiv

The unprecedented pro-democracy protest movement that erupted in Belarus last summer has unleashed a geopolitical shock wave throughout the wider region. Since the crisis first began in August 2020, international attention has tended to focus on the challenges created for Russia and the European Union. However, the Belarusian relationship with neighboring Ukraine has also come under significant strain. In many ways, the democratic awakening in Belarus has fractured and realigned the economic, military, diplomatic, and security relationship between Minsk and Kyiv.

For years, bilateral ties between Ukraine and Belarus were shaped by the often radically different approaches adopted by the two nations towards managing their respective relationships with Moscow. Given the Kremlin's ambitions to maintain its dominant position within the post-Soviet region, the Russian factor has weighed heavily in both Minsk and Kyiv. The need to manage ties with Russia has in many ways defined Ukrainian-Belarusian engagement, creating an often antagonistic but mutually dependent relationship that continues to oscillate wildly.

Belarusian strongman Alyaksandr Lukashenka has recently returned home from his latest summit meeting in Sochi, during which he pleaded for additional assistance from Russian President Vladimir Putin. The visit in turn sparked the latest round of speculation over Lukashenka's readiness to accept Russian demands for deeper integration. As the Western world grows ever more distant with every act of repression from his security services, the Belarus dictator appears to have little option but to accept greater Russian dominance in return for desperately needed support.

Meanwhile, diplomatic relations between Belarus and Ukraine remain significantly strained. This deterioration began in the early days of the crisis last summer. In line with broader international opinion, Ukraine declined to recognize the official results of the flawed August 2020 Belarusian presidential election. This sparked an indignant response from Lukashenka, who accused Kyiv of having sided with the West against him.

As the crisis escalated, Lukashenka repeatedly claimed Ukraine was part of an insidious plot against him masterminded by NATO, the Poles, the Lithuanians, and the Western world in general. Bilateral relations deteriorated rapidly as a consequence, with the Ukrainian Ambassador to Belarus subjected to the seemingly calculated diplomatic indignity of a border crossing search in early September.

Tensions with Ukraine continued to simmer throughout the final months of 2020. The Lukashenka regime was furious over Kyiv's moral support for the Belarusian pro-democracy movement and the Ukrainian government's apparent readiness to help Belarusian dissidents. Many suspected that Lukashenka's vocal criticism of Ukraine was also designed to win favor in Moscow.

There was considerable additional anger within the Lukashenka regime at Ukraine's decision to extend a red carpet welcome to Belarusian tech companies and IT professionals looking to relocate from Minsk. Ukrainian efforts to benefit from Belarus's growing IT industry exodus drew sharp criticism from Belarusian officials as an unfriendly act. However, the breakdown in bilateral ties remained far from complete, with Ukraine continuing to discreetly purchase electricity from Belarus.

There were indications that the war of words between the Ukrainian and Belarusian foreign ministries was beginning to cool off by the end of year. Some Belarusian analysts have since hinted that Minsk may not have been taking the confrontation very seriously, despite the strong language employed.

"Relations still exist but it would perhaps be better if both foreign ministries took a very deep breath and a long pause," says Denis Bukonkin, Director of the Foreign Policy and Security Research Center. "From the Belarus perspective, it looks as if the Ukrainian Ministry of Foreign Affairs is leaning toward EU policy and is obliged to take the same positions as the EU. The Belarusian Foreign Ministry sees any Ukrainian statements as being primarily geared toward their EU allies and therefore does not take these statements personally." According to Bukonkin, the current diplomatic chill between Kyiv and Minsk is unlikely to give way to a thaw any time soon unless EU-Belarus ties also improve. While Kyiv has more or less openly backed the Belarusian pro-democracy protest movement, the leadership of the Belarusian opposition has not entirely returned the favor. With a view to keeping a window open for future conversations with Moscow, Belarusian opposition leader Sviatlana Tsikhanouskaya has been cautious about adopting pro-Ukrainian positions on key geopolitical issues such as the 2014 Russian seizure of Ukraine's Crimean peninsula.

"The Belarusian opposition has maintained its distance from Kyiv. There are officially no issues between Ukraine and Belarus but in reality, relations are frozen," explains Andrei Kazakevich, Director of Political Studies at the Political Sphere think tank. "Tsikhanouskaya's refusal to make a clear statement on the question of Crimea has kept the Ukrainians from further developing relations with the Belarusian opposition leadership in exile. Other opposition leaders such as Pavel Latushka are also in no rush to make such pronouncements [on Crimea] in order not to foreclose the possibility of further contacts with Moscow."

The rise in bilateral tensions between Kyiv and Minsk over the past seven months follows on from a period of intensified engagement dating back to the onset of Russian aggression against Ukraine in early 2014. The outbreak of hostilities between Russia and Ukraine placed Belarus in an extremely delicate position and tested Lukashenka's diplomatic skills to the maximum.

Since 2014, the Belarus strongman had sought to play both sides off against one another, while at the same time resolutely taking the Russian side during important votes in international bodies. Belarus was one of only 11 nations to vote against Ukrainian territorial integrity at the United Nations on March 27, 2014, following the Russian invasion and occupation of Crimea. Minsk would also go on to take Moscow's side during subsequent United Nations votes pertaining to territorial integrity issues as well as human rights abuses committed against the Crimean Tatars.

Despite this support for Moscow on the global stage, the Belarusian strongman has sought to occupy the middle ground whenever possible. Lukashenka's geopolitical balancing act has involved making himself useful to everyone in the region. Crucially, he has offered Ukraine ironclad guarantees of neutrality and pledged to prevent Russian troops or proxies from posing a threat to Ukraine's northern borders from Belarusian territory.

These security assurances are hugely significant for the military balance in the region. Ukraine and Belarus share a border of over 1,000km. Any Russian military pressure from the north would totally redefine the current conflict and would force Ukraine to radically rethink the country's entire defense posture. In this context, Lukashenka's repeated jokes about arriving at the Ukrainian border on a tractor rather than a tank have been part of his efforts to calm nerves in Kyiv.

Faced by the overwhelming might of Russia, Belarus and Ukraine have had good reason to develop security cooperation in recent years. Prior to the current crisis in Belarus, Kyiv and Minsk regularly exchanged intelligence reports and other sensitive information. It was by all accounts a relationship that Kyiv valued. I have been informed that much of the intelligence shared by the Belarusian intelligence services with their Ukrainian colleagues was deemed to be exceedingly useful.

Beginning in September 2014, a key aspect of Belarus-Ukraine ties has been the role of Minsk as the location for peace negotiations between Moscow and Kyiv. This status had allowed Lukashenka to considerably bolster his international reputation as a reliable partner and gracious host for the leaders of the Normandy Format countries (France, Germany, Russia, and Ukraine).

Until the outbreak of pro-democracy protests in Belarus last summer, this role as host of the Russo-Ukrainian peace negotiations had been seen as important enough to regional defense arrangements for European and American leaders to increasingly put aside their qualms about dealing with Lukashenka.

However, the new geopolitical realities created by Lukashenka's brutal crackdown on pro-democracy demonstrations have served to undo any advantages accrued as a result of the Minsk peace process. With

Lukashenka isolated from the West and reliant on Russia, the entire future of the Minsk negotiation format has been thrown into question. It is now obvious that the Ukrainian delegation no longer regards Minsk as a neutral venue, while human rights concerns also make Lukashenka an entirely unsuitable host from a European point of view.

These issues have arisen at a time when the situation in Russian-occupied eastern Ukraine is once again entering into a period of escalation. There has been an uptick in Ukrainian military casualties during the first months of 2021 as Moscow has responded aggressively to President Zelenskyy's moves against Russian proxy political forces and television stations inside Ukraine.

In the current circumstances, it is difficult to imagine the Ukrainian side agreeing to continue with the Minsk negotiation format. Meanwhile, it is equally hard to envisage Russia agreeing to any fundamental changes.

"The situation with Minsk remaining the negotiating platform for further contacts between Kyiv and Moscow has not been fully resolved, even though it is obvious that the Belarusian capital can no longer serve as the location for neutral talks under these circumstances," says Yauheni Priherman, Director at the Minsk Dialogue on International Relations. "I am not entirely sure that this is a settled matter as Ukraine is insisting on changing the location of future negotiations, but the Europeans have no idea what to do about the issue. It does not look like any decision will be made anytime soon."

With Lukashenka more and more dependent on Russia, Moscow continues to explore opportunities to increase military pressure on Ukraine and the European Union via Belarus. Lukashenka has long resisted Russian efforts to establish permanent military bases on Belarusian territory, but the Kremlin already manages two strategic facilities in Belarus. One is a long range submarine communications hub, while the other is an anti-rocket radar facility.

Talks are currently underway to extend the treaties governing these Russian facilities, with most observers expecting Moscow to retain its current presence in Belarus. The real issue is whether the Kremlin will prove able to acquire a further military foothold. Putin has long set his sights on a Russian air base in Belarus, which Lukashenka has always seen as unacceptable. However, this may be part of the terms and conditions for continued Russian backing. For obvious reasons, any increase in the Russian military presence in Belarus would be viewed with extreme alarm by Ukraine.

The military component is just one aspect of the complex relationship between Kyiv and Minsk. Ukraine's desire to pursue Euro-Atlantic integration and Belarus's focus on closer ties with Moscow have placed the two countries on sharply diverging geopolitical trajectories, but a shared desire to manage Russian imperial ambitions has also created considerable common ground.

The unexpected and unprecedented pro-democracy uprising of the past seven months in Belarus has served to further complicate bilateral ties and fueled increasingly public tensions in what has traditionally been a diplomatically courteous and outwardly friendly relationship. This has caused significant damage, but ties between the two countries are surely not beyond repair.

With hopes fading for a rapid conclusion to the pro-democracy uprising in Belarus, both Kyiv and Minsk now appear to be looking to dial down the diplomatic belligerence of late 2020 and settle into a new period of comparative calm.

Tellingly, Lukashenka has recently ceased including Ukrainians in the paranoid pantheon of his imagined enemies. The Belarusian dictator is nothing if not politically cunning. During his 26-year reign, he has learned to avoid turning opponents into mortal enemies. He may now be seeking to adopt a similarly pragmatic approach towards future relations with Ukraine.

The Atlantic Council 2021

VI. On Statues

Monument to Isaac Babel Erected in Odessa

Eighty-five years after bestowing "The Odessa Tales" and "Red Cavalry" to both the Russian and the Jewish modernist literary canons; 71 years after a 20-minute show trial resulted in execution by firing squad; 54 years after his posthumous rehabilitation by Soviet authorities, and several decades after plans were first laid, a monument to Isaac Babel has been erected in his home town of Odessa, across the street from his former apartment building on the corner of Rishelyevskaya and Zhukovskaya streets.

Located in a plaza in front of the lumpy neo-Soviet columns of high school number 117, the monument depicts a frocked Babel sitting next to a massive "wheel of fate," scribbling in a notebook while gazing dreamily into the distance.

The tribute was dedicated September 4 by The World Odessite Club, a loose confederation of associations that produces nostalgic get-togethers. Expatriates of the cosmopolitan port town collected money for the sculpture over the better part of the last five years, one donation at a time.

Until now, the discerning Babel fan in search of a public tribute to the scribe of the Jewish tough guy had to content himself with a nicely etched marble plaque hanging over the entrance to Babel's former apartment building. This is the house in which Babel spent his productive adult years, occupying it (as the plaque tells us in Ukrainian) from 1909 to 1924. The ornate door and doorknob are the only visible architectural motifs that hint at the building's former sumptuousness. A mere 15-minute walk from the city's opera house and port, it was probably a nice place to work.

But for several years the structure has been enclosed by construction scaffolding, which in turn has been plastered over with advertising and graffiti. A massive billboard for a Paul & Shark clothing shop located next door obscures the plaque, and one has to step around a set of aluminum sided walls and lift up a heavy plastic construction tarp to get a peek at it.

Everyone involved in the new tribute proudly points out that the funds for the monument to Russia's national poet, Alexander Pushkin, which stands with its back to city hall due to the city's refusal to help finance it, took twice as long to collect. The Russian celebrity sculptor Georgy Frangulyan, best known for his statues of singer-songwriter Bulat Okudzhava in Moscow, Pushkin in Brussels, Peter the Great in Antwerp and, entertainingly enough (and to this Russian, grotesquely also), Boris Yeltsin in Yekaterinburg, reportedly took a hefty pay cut to work on the statue, out of his love for Babel's stories.

Fittingly, this being Odessa, the story is not without hints of lurid machinations. The New York and Odessa branches of the club broke off relations after allegations that the former was keeping a portion of the donations for their own club's coffers. The Odessan Diaspora in Los Angeles, however, was heartily thanked for its generosity.

The Forward 2011

Ukraine's Post-Soviet Identity Through the Murky Lens of Its Statues

On Wednesday, the Ukrainian cabinet of ministers announced it would be erecting a statue in the coming years dedicated to Symon Petliura, a Ukrainian soldier and statesman who fought for the country's independence from Russia, Poland, and Germany. The politics of the construction—and destruction—of Soviet-era monuments in Ukraine continues to rage unabated as the nation carries on with the process of decommunization and the building of a truly post-Soviet identity. The construction of Ukrainian statehood outside of the parameters of the Soviet legacy requires a historical foundation in a country whose historical legacy of freedom fighting is firmly bound up with unsavory political identities.

The nationalist Petliura was assassinated in Paris in 1926 by Jewish anarchist Sholom Schwartzbard. Petliura is an infamously complex character in terms of Jewish-Ukrainian relations and his historical legacy remains contested. That legacy is marked by his having been unable to control elements of his army from committing anti-Jewish pogroms as well as numerous instances of his personal kindness to Jews in the midst of a truly horrific, multi-sided conflict.

The Ukrainian Minister of Culture Yevhen Nyshchuk drew parallels between the forthcoming anniversary events marking the celebration of the existence of the short-lived Ukrainian National Republic "with activities related to the events of the Ukrainian revolution of 1917-1921." The passing of decommunization legislation in May of 2015 by the Ukrainian parliament adopted a package of laws which condemned equally both the Communist and Nazi regimes, and stipulated that the statues of Russian revolutionary leader Vladimir Lenin be brought down.

Earlier this week, multiple Ukrainian media reported that the dismantling of the statue of Lenin in the Ukrainian city of Novgorod-

Seversky constituted the fall of the last statue to the revolution within unoccupied Ukrainian territory.

An estimated 1000 statues of Lenin have been pulled down across Ukraine over the last two years. Meanwhile, Russian-backed separatists and Russian occupation forces in the so-called "breakaway republics" of Donetsk and Lugansk have gone in the other direction and revived a cult of Soviet nostalgia.

Ukraine is not alone in its newfound appetite for the erection of politicized historical monuments however. Signaling it's renewed revanchist conservative stance towards the West, Russia has also recently erected its first statue to Ivan The Terrible in the city of Oryol, some 200 hundred miles south of Moscow.

A month after the nation's impressive show of seriousness in organizing extensive commemorations of the 75th anniversary of Babyn Yar massacres, renewed bouts of criticism of Ukraine's handling of it's exceedingly complex wartime past have emerged. Recently, the Kyiv city council had renamed the Moscow highway in Kyiv after the OUN wartime leader Stepan Bandera, a move which was met with glee on Russian television and concerted outrage in the Polish parliament. That move was taken by Kyiv city authorities several days before an important NATO summit in Warsaw and created prolonged diplomatic fiasco with the Poles, who are Ukraine's closest ally in Europe.

Yesterday, Andreas Umland, a preeminent German expert on Ukrainian politics and identity issues published the latest in a wave of articles signaling that the patience of Ukraine'e Western partners would not be unlimited. Writing in *Foreign Policy* he pointed out that the embrace of nationalist historical figures runs exactly counter to the founding principles of the European Union and thus served as a countermeasure to future integration. Of this "dilemma," he writes:

[W]hile many of the OUN-B's leaders and ordinary members gave their lives in Ukraine's fight for independence, most were also virulent nationalists, to the point of outright xenophobia. Some were even complicit in the Holocaust and other mass crimes against civilians. As a result, though the group enjoys considerable sympathy among Ukraine's governing class and large parts of the intellectual elite, it is highly controversial among the country's Russian-leaning population, its Jews, its liberal intelligentsia, and its foreign partners. The question of how Ukrainians should interpret this wartime history requires nuance and restraint.

Tablet Magazine 2016

Sculptor Ernst Neizvestny, Who Challenged the Soviet Regime, Dies at 91

It is symbolic that the Russian-American sculptor Ernst Neizvestny's passing in New York City at the age of 91 has taken place amid renewed tensions between Russia and the U.S. The sculptures of Neizvestny (his last name means "unknown" in Russian), who died on August 9 in Stony Brook, New York, brought modernist techniques perfected in Western Europe to the Soviet Union, but his tremendous brutalist-heroic sculptures varied widely in quality and were certainly not to everyone's tastes. From *The Economist*:

[Neizvestny's] paintings, and especially his sculptures, were about: struggle, contradiction, multiplicity, flesh against spirit, all within one unity, the human body. His works turned humans into robots, centaurs, giants or machines, with hard and soft, metallic and organic flowing into and transforming each other.

Nikita Khrushchev, the former premier of the Soviet Union, once called Neizvestny's 1962 show near the Kremlin "filth" and "dog shit." An obit in *The Art Newspaper* recalls that "Khrushchev's comments signaled an end to the cultural thaw he started after the death of Joseph Stalin."

"Why do you disfigure the faces of Soviet people?" the Soviet leader asked Neizvestny. The two became embroiled in an infamous yelling match during which Neizvestny impressed upon the premier of the Soviet Union his force of personality. The incident encapsulated and rehashed 50 years of debates on the meaning and place of art under socialism, which inspired art critic John Berger's classic book *Art and Revolution*.

However, when Khrushchev died in 1971 (following his ouster in 1964), his family asked Neizvestny to design a tombstone for his grave at Moscow's Novodevichy Cemetery. The sculptor created a bust of

Khrushchev starkly surrounded with black marble slabs on one side, and white on the other, symbolizing the premier's good and bad sides. "We chose Ernst because my father had great respect for him," Khushchev's son, Sergei, told Western reporters when the monument was installed in 1974, according to *The New York Times*.

Neizvestny was born in 1925 in Sverdlovsk, which is now called Yekaterinburg, and was highly decorated for his World War II service before commencing his art studies in Moscow and Riga. When he arrived in New York City in 1976, he became a grand figure in the Russian artist émigré community. He remained so until the end of his life. Though Neizvestny often spoke openly in interviews of his experience of anti-Semitic persecution at the hands of Soviet authorities, Neizvestny's family experience was certainly irregular in comparison to that of other Russian Jews. Neizvevestny's father, a prominent and respected pediatrician, had changed the family name after the Russian Civil War to conceal the fact that he had fought for the White Army. No English language appraisal, and few in Russian, ever speak of Neizvestny's remarkable mother, the aristocratic Sephardi poetess Bella DeJour, who was in her own right an important figure, and lived until the age of 102 in New York City.

My beloved aesthete grandmother, Galina Seryabrikova, knew and socialized with DeJour in Brooklyn in the early 1990s. They would take tea together and I do believe that DeJour unsuccessfully tried to convert my grandmother into becoming a member of "Jews for Jesus".

Neizvestny was close to the editorial committee of the legendary émigré dissident journal *Kontinent*, which focused on the politics of the Soviet Union. His gigantic sculpture "The Mask Of Sorrow," erected in 1996 in Magadan, commemorated the victims of the gulag system. Yet, like many other Russian artists and writers of his generation, including his friend, Russian novelist Alexander Solzhenitsyn, who had spent decades in the political wilderness of exile, he had already made his peace with the post-Soviet Russian government.

In a public telegram addressed to Neizvestny's family and friends, Russian President Vladimir Putin described the artist as "one of the greatest sculptors of our times." It also included the president's plaintive declaration that his death represented a "grievous loss for world culture," which is much more than mere political boilerplate. As a young man Neizvestny had challenged the Soviet state and Khrushchev; as an old man he socialized with Putin and accepted numerous state accolades. The Russia state became an enthusiastic sponsor of Neizvestny's late career works. The high-brow channels of Russian television have spent the last week screening documentaries about his life continuously.

Still, as a young man he had challenged the aesthetic and political character of the Soviet regime at its ideological peak. We should strive to remember him at his best: a great independent and irreverent spirit and a moralizing political dissident in the great Russian tradition.

Tablet Magazine 2016

Invitation to a Beheading:
What can American Statue-Topplers
Learn from Europe?

Are we living through a truly revolutionary moment or merely the jejune simulacrum of one? Either way, this is undeniably a moment of tempestuous iconoclasm. Monuments and statues to the "problematic" heroes of the grand narratives of an older order are being defaced and toppled across multiple continents. As the American-inspired protests sweep across Western Europe from Marseille to Bristol, and from Amsterdam to London, we should be satisfied that America in the midst of the epoch of Trump has not experienced the oft-predicted decline of its cultural hegemony.

Needless to say, judging historical figures according to the ideological standards of the present constitutes both a mental and spiritual category error. On the other hand, that basic axiom must be balanced against the almost universally held moral intuition that the most terrifying and egregious monsters of history should not and can not be memorialized by a just and healthy society. Yet Americans and Western Europe are only now catching up to the statue wars that took place in Eastern Europe five years ago. In the process they are mostly reenacting the same exact arguments that we Eastern Europeans engaged in and observed half a decade ago.

But before returning to the East and what my experiences there suggest about the course of events playing out in the current protests, let me describe the scene that I recently observed in Western Europe.

The weekend before last, a statue of the Prussian ruler Otto von Bismarck in Altona, a borough of Hamburg, Germany, was splattered with cherry red paint. At that very same moment during which activists were providing the "Iron Chancellor" with his new red coat, the Place de la

République square in Paris was being transformed into a warzone. A minority of the protesters who had been brandishing Black Lives Matter signs stenciled with English slogans engaged in brutal raiding sorties against the phalanxes of French gendarmes. I watched one protester with a particularly fierce visage run up to a fallen riot policeman who had gotten separated from his unit, and crumple him with a precisely delivered kick to the back of the kneecap. The French riot police drove the rioters off the square with truncheons and tear gas. On Sunday night, French President Emmanuel Macron was forced to confront the obvious while delivering the speech that unwound the last of the quarantine prohibitions: "the Republic will erase no trace or name from our history, it will tear down no statue," he promised. In the United Kingdom, the process began with mob attacks on various British slavers. Statues were toppled from their plinths or thrown headfirst into the harbor by frenzied crowds who did not seem to be guided by a careful study of history and may have only recently learned of these men's deeds.

Troublingly for many, the frenzy soon leapt from the unambiguously controversial cases of minor historical figures to attacks on those whose lives constitute the core of Western history books. Such processes, as any student or observer of revolutionary times will know, have a way of quickly escalating to the point where the most emotionally and politically maximal position is the one that carries the moment. Gandhi, progenitor of the doctrine of peaceful resistance (but who indeed held chauvinist ideas about Africans that were endemic to his time and milieu) was quickly branded and spray-painted a racist. Winston Churchill's statue in front of the British parliament has been ensconced in a protective steel cocoon in the middle of London. Churchill's granddaughter acknowledged that the statue of this "complex man, with infinitely more good than bad in the ledger of his life" would likely have to be transferred to a museum for its own good.

So what can Americans and Western Europeans learn from recent, similar historical events in Eastern Europe?

Soon upon ascending to political power, the post-revolutionary Ukrainian government of Petro Poroshenko passed a wide-ranging package of "decommunization" laws, whose measures included the renaming of streets, the opening up of former KGB archives to historians, and the mandated removal of Communist heroes from public spaces. The cumulative taking down of literally thousands of Lenin statues across Ukrainian territory that took place between 2014 and 2016 came to be known as the "Leninopad" or the "Leninfall."

Moscow, as I have previously written for Tablet, selected the opposite approach and, even after the fall of Communism, chose to construct statues to Communist Soviet heroes as the Putin regime tied its legitimacy to nostalgia for WWII Soviet memory. Those statues continue to be erected. Between 2015 and 2018, I lived in and reported from Ukraine while editing my literary journal, *The Odessa Review*, and so had the chance to observe at first hand the process of the toppling and removing of thousands of Communist-era monuments. Watching the statues of Lenin taken down across Southern and Eastern Ukraine was deeply instructive. The ones in Odessa city proper were taken down by Odessa's popular Jewish Mayor Eduard Gurvits in the 1990s, with the Communist-era street names all reverting back to their pre-revolutionary equivalents. Yet, there were many people who refused the new order of things. Twenty-five years after the first wave of Ukrainian decommunization some old timers would still tell their friends to meet them on the corner of "Karl Marx" Street rather than on the corner of "Ekaterininskaya" (named after Catherine the Great).

In Kyiv the atmosphere of the toppling of Lenin at the conclusion of the Euromaidan revolution was raucous, revolutionary, liberatory, and carnivalesque. In other parts of Ukraine (the solidly anti-Soviet Western Ukrainians had done it decades ago in the early '90s of their own accord) the process was carried out in a controlled manner by the police or Interior Ministry troops as the locals gazed on with satisfaction, curiosity, wonder or simmering resentment. In many of the small towns across Odessa region (and others farther east), I observed the process taking place in a haphazard and uncontrolled manner. Large groups of men, many dressed in fatigues, would assemble to yell at each other, with the police often reduced to observing them and being barely able to keep large-scale brawls from breaking out. At some point, amid scuffling and pushing, some of the younger men gripped by feelings of Ukrainian patriotism would either push the statue down by force or connect it to a truck with cables. This divisive spectacle of hours of yelling between neighbors split on the question was very grim.

As Tom de Waal, a most keen observer of Eastern European and Caucasian politics, wrote at the time:

There are two extreme positions. One is that everything must be kept, regardless of whose name it bears. That is surely untenable. No one wants to see a street called Adolf-Hitler-Straße. Cities in the former Soviet Union should not have to keep statues of Lenin and Stalin in their central squares. The other position is to take down all reminders of the past that do not fit with current-day orthodoxies. That approach too is problematic. In Eastern Europe, it has made history a kaleidoscope of vanishing images, in which the past is instantly forgotten and its lessons unheeded.

Many more seminal and central figures of European history and intellectual life were all complicit to one degree or another in the unreflective racism or anti-Semitism of the epochs in which they lived. Changing social mores fairly applied could bring down at least half of the statues to the monarchs of Europe. No one in post-religious Europe is — at least not yet — going to come knocking for the statues of Martin Luther. (Was his rabid theological anti-Semitism a crime? The question is ridiculous on its face.) Yet what would the reaction of European Protestants be in the case that an energized and ideologically committed minority did?

Monuments are the products of the mores and ideological fixations of their time. They glorify and immortalize the figures who shaped the world in which they lived through either their brute force of will, their creativity, or their capacity to wage war. If the very idea of putting up statues to kings and war leaders and renowned writers now seems antiquarian to some, well, logically so should the carnal pagan act of tearing them down to dispel their aura. The arguments of those who believe that statues are merely hunks of steel that we erect in the midst of our cities, and which lack any meaning outside of those impulses with which we wish to imbue them, do not account for the strong passions that accompany the act of erecting and toppling them. These are acts that continue to bind the average stroller in the street to the great men or women who lived alongside them in societies that are descended both intellectually and aesthetically from Greek and Roman traditions. Conversely, the desecration and destruction of the statues of the ancestors of one's enemies is the first order of business upon seizing their territory. Vigilante attacks on the statues one despises can and surely will bring retaliatory strikes on the statues and monuments that one venerates.

The Belgian King Leopold, for example (a statue was removed in a suburb of Antwerp—he constitutes an understandably major target for the movement), it should be noted finally and unequivocally, was responsible for some of the most unspeakable crimes and atrocities against humanity. He was a villain under any fair-minded contemporary reading of history. He was also an ancestor of the reigning King of Belgium in a monarchy where the crown represents the only institution that binds together French-speaking and Dutch-speaking Belgians. Which is not to say, lest there be any misunderstandings, that I personally care in the least about the fate of the Belgium monarchy. I myself am personally romantic about the deposed Romanian monarchy of my Chernowitz-born great-grandparents (God save Queen Margaret of Romania, Custodian of the Crown) and if my own ancestors had not been Soviet revolutionaries and Communist Party apparatchiks, I would have much preferred on the aesthetic level that they had fought with the Russian White cavalry like the young men of the Gunzburg family had. (In more civilized times, the cavalry officers, even the odd Jewish ones, were issued horses whose coloration matched the color of their handlebar mustaches.) Which is to simply admit that one does not get to choose one's history or the side on which one's ancestors may have toiled or fought.

It seems that we are living through a moment in which we are all being forced to relearn the basic tenets of political theory in real time. Attempts to impose minority-held beliefs — based on either authentic or a pretense of radical tolerance — on pluralities without first engaging in the liberal democratic process of honest debate and argumentation will lead to those questions being solved by the deployment force.

It is undeniable that there were those among Eastern Ukrainians who had sided with the Kremlin's war against Ukraine in the wake of imbibing deftly produced and propagandistic Russian television reports of Lenin being thrown off his pedestal in other parts of the country.

If the Leninopad has taught us anything, it is that once the statues are breathed to life and placed on pedestals, they are our co-citizens. Like any other man or woman who has behaved badly, they are entitled to procedural democratic rights and a fair hearing before they can be bundled off to a lonely place and banished from the public square.

Tablet Magazine 2018

The Viking Who Defeated the Odessa Mafia and Erected a Runestone

One of the first major laws that the Ukrainian wartime president President Petro Poroshenko first passed upon election was a wide ranging "decommunization" bill. Signed into law in April of 2015, the new law represented a serious attempt to deal with the trauma of the Communist past. The KGB archives would be opened to historians, researchers and descendants of repressed individuals. Streets glorifying the memory of Communist-era heroes would be renamed. Tens of thousands of Communist-era monuments and statues, including every single statue of Vladimir Lenin, would be removed. A moment of great iconoclasm was upon us. Ideologically inappropriate statues were being torn down, from Izmail to Chernihiv. To the collective joy of political reformers and publishers of deluxe coffee table books the world over, the phenomenon known as 'Leninfall' had commenced.

Perched atop pedestals across the country, the statues of the Bolshevik leader met varied fates. The majority were simply knocked over. Others wound up in private museums or collections. Fragments of Lenin's broken visage and limbs were arranged, often with a touch of languid great poetry, in barns, attics and storerooms. The southern port town of Odessa commissioned a local sculptor to convert a Lenin statue standing in a city park into one of Darth Vader and install a Wifi router inside the Sith Lord's helmet. The international media flocked to this easy story, and hipster photographers from the four corners of the globe made pilgrimages to pay homage to the statue.

Around the same time, a local political broker, a libertarian hacker who happened to be wanted by the American authorities for tens of millions of dollars-worth of credit-card fraud, set up a *Star Wars*-themed political party and flooded the streets of Odessa with stormtroopers riding on top of military-grade Hummers. Through a fantastical and uniquely Odessan turn of events, the statue of the Dark Sith Lord had been trumped.

My friend Thomas Sillesen is a proud Viking. He is very tall, totally bald and built like a roving berserker. He is a Danish businessman with a taste for off-color jokes and high-stakes risk. He and I once drove across the border from Moldova into Transnistria, the Russian-dominated separatist enclave: a territory struck outside of time, an embalmed slice of Seventies-vintage Soviet Union. On the drive back, we passed a checkpoint manned by the Russian peacekeepers who had been placed there at the end of the Transnistrian war in the summer of 1992. The Moldovans do not really control their own border, so it was easy for us to have neglected getting the Moldovan stamp on our passports. A Moldovan border guard lectured me for having violated his country's sovereignty. The argument degenerated, and I instructed him to fight the Russians better in the next war if he wanted the right to harangue people at the border. Afterward, Sillesen remarked that usually it was him who was the belligerent one. This would prove to be accurate.

After serving out his term in the Queens Life Regiment of the Danish army, and while working on a master's in economics at Aarhus University, Sillesen had supported himself by working as a bouncer at a local music club. He does not think highly of the masculinity of the Swedes. If asked politely, he will proudly relate the exact patrimony of a fierce Viking heritage which he can trace back to AD 950. His illustrious ancestor, the Danish chieftain Thorgil Sprakling, sired multiple grandsons who wore the crowns of Denmark and England.

The Dane was in the wind-turbine business. When the Ukraine war broke out in 2014, members of the Russian-led separatist forces broke into his office in Luhansk and threw a pair of Molotov cocktails into the company's boardroom. He decided to pull his company out of Luhansk, and took them to Odessa for the summer. This was supposed to be a temporary move, but then the Ukrainian army, which had been swiftly retaking territory from the dispersing, hybrid force of separatists and Russian special forces, retook control of the city. Like many provisional solutions, the move would end up being all too permanent. The Regular

Russian army would invade in August of 2014 and would quickly route the Ukrainian forces.

The Dane decided to establish his company headquarters in the burned-out ruin of an old hotel which stood on the decrepit old road that runs along the eastern/western side of the port. The space was not much to look at, yet it was easy enough to imagine the seafront developing quickly after the war. In November 2017, Sillesen bought the building directly from the bank which had taken possession of it after foreclosing on the delinquent previous owner. The court documents and deed would be checked over thrice and the lawyers pronounced the paperwork to be in order.

The same evening that the deal was finalized and the ownership of the building was formally amended, the director of the company received a curious call from the former owner. The man claimed that he had in fact been the victim of bank fraud and that the building had been illegally expropriated from him. That, he said, annulled Sillesen's paperwork and title deed . 'I am a Danish guy, and property disputes based on obscure legal loopholes is simply a non-existent problem back in my country, so my lawyer and I were shocked,' Sillesen tells me. 'We thought it was a joke.'

It was not a joke. It was a shakedown. The former owner had defaulted on his bank loan and lost control of the property years ago, but had continued to use it. Now he was attempting to regain control of the building. Meanwhile the bank wanted to keep the money that the Dane had paid for it. A series of absurd court decisions followed. It it soon became evident that the former owner was a close friend of an influential city lawyer. The court would neither grant Sillesen control of the property nor direct the bank to return the money, as would happen in any ordinary country. A minute error in the legal documents was used as a pretext for declaring them void, but no one wanted to refund Sillesen's investment. He made repeated appeals, but the politicized courts continued to award the building and the mortgage to the former owner. This was port side robbery, abetted by a brazenly corrupt judicial system.

Sillesen had no intention of standing down or letting himself be swindled. He hired political consultants and experts in government relations who would assist him in a campaign which would quickly morph into a quest. One of them was the canny American consultant Brian Mefford, an experienced hand in Kyiv's raucous politics who knew who to call in Odessa. Sillesen also began attending high-profile investment meetings with the government and publicly haranguing ministers and functionaries to take an interest in the case. At one meeting, Sillesen raised the issue directly with President Poroshenko. Hearing him out, Poroshenko swore to the heavens to do all that was possible to ameliorate the situation. The president graciously gestured toward an aide and instructed him to be in touch. He also intimated that he would himself be making a personal visit to the Danish company's headquarters during his next visit to Odessa.

It soon became obvious that these grandiose flourishes meant nothing. There was no presidential visit. As a serious businessman from northern Europe, Sillesen was totally unprepared for a culture of such florid and empty promising. He decided to step up the political pressure. Once again he confronted President Poroshenko during a closed meeting of the Ukrainian-European Business Association. On this occasion, the chastened Poroshenko was forced to admit that he 'could help with a property dispute anywhere in Ukraine with the exception of Odessa' which he declared to be a veritable "state within the state." When Sillesen inquired about that with the senior brass of the SBU intelligence agency in Kyiv, they admitted that they had virtually no control over their colleagues in Odessa.

The Dane learned that, much like a medieval Italian city state, Odessa was run by an intersecting set of political families and mafia elites. No state assistance was forthcoming. He would have to reclaim his property through less conventional tactics. 'We realized that these were not good guys, and that the police, prosecutors and judges in Odessa were all crooked. Unless the dynamic was changed, they would always stick together against a foreign investor such as myself,' he explains.

At Sillesen's behest, Mefford deployed his connections in Odessa and set up a back channel to a rival clan of business interests. He familiarized anyone who would listen with the details of the case and looked for a possible opening. Using open-source information, Sillesen procured the home addresses of the city judges, then bought Facebook ads decrying theft from foreign investors, calibrated to be seen by individuals with a legal education living in particular streets.

Soon, Mefford found his man: a muscular Bessarabian gentleman of questionable vocation whose day job was being a member of the Ukrainian parliament. The political clan that the Bessarabian gentleman headed was, Medford reported, "battling the former owner's clan over several pieces of prime real estate around the city." Like the influential lawyer of the building's former owner, this clan also controlled and influenced its own share of city judges. From the very start of the process, multiple individuals materialized to offer to mediate the dispute. Typically they would offer to make the problem disappear in exchange for a sizable cash payment. The stubborn and valiant Dane refused the offers out of hand. There would be no bribe or any other activity which would compromise his acutely sharp sense of ethics.

Instead, he invited all the men who had influence on the Odessa judiciary to a reception in his headquarters. Like the Vikings of old, he plied his enemies with a mighty feast of meat and mead before declaring total war on them (it should be admitted that your humble servant himself attended the feast and got massively smashed on the excellent cognac on offer). Sillesen figured that he should look his opponents in the eyes before continuing his campaign. The munificent show of traditional Viking hospitality was surely a wise investment.

Shortly thereafter the Bessarabian gentleman invited Mefford to his office for a drink. Familiar with the fabled code of Odessa business customs, Mefford brought along his reliable Georgian partner Irakli. "I figured that in such matters, it was always good to have a fiesty Georgian watching your back". The meeting took place in the private office of the Bessarabian gangster. Food was served by a blonde secretary and a bottle of Chivas Regal was opened over manly banter. It was only after the second bottle was mostly finished, that the host brought up the issue at hand. "When you get invited to such a meeting, you always let your host initiate the discussion" the courtly southerner Mefford later explained. Finally the obvious question would be put on the table: "Who is this guy to you and is he willing to pay?" Mefford casually but intently seized the moment. "He's just a legit guy, you know, a real man's man like you. Your city gets a bad rap because of the crap that this other clan does and it brings down heat on you guys. It's your chance to screw your enemies and do a boy scout deed for the day that will help the city's image". A third bottle of Chivas Regal was opened and the glasses were clinked to a toast for friendship and 'bratani". Mefford remarked that "an elucidation had been planted that would last beyond the next morning's hangover".

Five days later the appeals court would finally issue a decision in favor of the Danish engineering company. If one did not count Odessa's former mayor Hurevitz (who holds Israeli citizenship), this was the first time that any foreign investor had won a case in an Odessa court in decades. "We fought the court order out of principle but the victory burnished the company image," explained the victorious Sillesen. Less than an hour after the court decision was proffered, Mefford received a congratulatory call from the chuckling Bessarabian politician.

To mark his victory over the Odessa gangsters in the traditional Viking style, Sillesen decided to erect a traditional Viking rune stone at the base of his newly secured property. Several decades ago, when he had been very young, he had met a Danish rune stone carver. The craftsman was a black metal musician and an old-time follower of Odin named Eric the Red. Sillesen had long fantasized about commissioning his own rune stone and realized that this victory would likely be the great signal battle of his life. This was the moment to summon forth his Viking ancestors.

The Obelisk would be carved in Denmark. Weighing more than six and a half tons, it had to be delivered to Odessa by truck. Eric the Red was flown out to Odessa and spent a week finishing the painting of it on site. An emblem of Odin's mask was carved into its side in order to protect those living with it from the machinations of evil spirits. It also featured a raven - the warbird of the Vikings - in the act of mutilating a snake. The old Norse inscription carved into the stone explained that the raven had slaughtered the dragon - which in the case of this modern scenario likely represented the specter of corruption. "It also commemorates the friends who helped in the fight," explained the triumphant Viking.

Having placed the rock in its new home along the shoreline of the Odessa port, Sillesen took the time to re-read the Viking chronicles. Upon which point he realized that his predicament was in fact as old as the Varangian war songs. The old Viking chronicles foretold that after a Viking ship would pass through the end of the Dnipro river and would turn right at the entrance to the Black Sea, a man had to prepare himself for combat. "One arrives at Odessa and one has to be prepared to fight, this is just the standard operating procedure in the chronicles of old" Sillesen marveled. "And my ancestors were right about that!"

VII. Views and Reviews

Culture Under Threat: The Odessa Philharmonic Orchestra As Case Study

In the last two years, it has become routine to acknowledge that the EuroMaidan Revolution unleashed torrents of creative energy in Ukraine. Myriad articles have been written about the ferment of cultural activity taking place across every discipline in every major city in the country. Yet while this is doubtless true of many aspects of contemporary and youth culture, classic cultural institutions and performing arts groups continue to face many of the same problems they have faced over the past twenty-five years. The overwhelming political and economic constraints aside, Ukraine has not systematically prioritized the promotion of its culture outside the borders of the nation as other advanced countries do.

It is critical to remember that the Ukrainian state is constrained by budget shortfalls and an austerity plan mandated by the IMF. Eliminating corruption, reforming the judicial system, securing the border, and raising living standards for millions of people are certainly the highest priorities in the short term. But the human spirit cannot survive on security alone. In the long term, the transmission and reproduction of elite and high culture is of utter importance and should be counted among the nation's existential priorities.

The Odessa Philharmonic Orchestra is a fine institution as well as being a representative microcosm of the universally shared problems plaguing all of Ukraine's elite performing arts institutions. While the Ukrainian cinema and art sectors have their own unique problems, all Ukrainian cultural institutions are constrained by similar problems with lack of capital as well as by systematic management issues and corruption.

Led by Venezuelan-born American conductor Hobart Earle for the entirety of its twenty-five years of post-Soviet existence, the orchestra routinely functions at the highest levels on exceedingly limited resources. The first Ukrainian orchestra to cross the Atlantic and the Equator, it continues to tour the world and perform upwards of sixty-five concerts a year at home, continually producing original programming. Though the dictum of "De gustibus non est disputandum" remains in unimpeachable effect in Ukraine as elsewhere, discerning observers of the Ukrainian cultural scene have often judged the OPO to be among the premiere, if not the most singular performing arts institution in the whole country. No other orchestra in Ukraine routinely fields ten double basses on stage, as they did in the beginning of September for a wonderful rendition of Alexander Scriabin's third symphony.

To Ukraine's great credit, despite systematic financing issues, no national-level government-backed performing arts institution has ever folded since Ukraine's independence day. However, Earle's stewardship of a perennially underfunded orchestra is largely a testament to his administrative powers: it has survived this long without having been forced to make personnel cuts or having hemorrhaged staff. Ukraine's federal budget does not provide for anything other than payroll, and, like other cultural institutions, it is expected to make do and fend for itself. There are the occasional scares about budget cuts emanating from Kyiv; these are usually couched in the language of patriotism, calling for sacrifices in the name of defense.

Like many other concert halls and museums in the country, Odessa's Philharmonic Hall is in dire need of restoration and repair. In the '90s, Earle invited the renowned American acoustician Russell Johnson to appraise its quality. Johnson reported that "with full scale restoration, this hall can rival the major concert halls of Europe." A remarkable building in a prime location, it has been the target of repeated instances of rent-seeking by those who have access to the authorities. A historical monument under the jurisdiction of the Odessa Region, half of the building has been appropriated and has served as a casino since 1993, with the revenues passing to unknown parties shielded by officials at the highest levels of the Odessa Regional State Administration.

The collapse of the Soviet Union wrought catastrophic effects on cultural and performing arts institutions, whose work requires the mobilization of significant resources. A command economy was fairly apt at distributing costs and mobilizing economies of scale; during Soviet times, provincial orchestras could call on their colleagues in Moscow and receive precious sheet music free of charge. Needless to say, there is no one in Moscow who will do that today. Other Ukrainian orchestras will only waive the customarily hefty photocopy fees in exchange for sheet music they need themselves.

Another loss from Soviet times is the sharing of solo performers. Talented soloists would be routinely circulated around the Soviet Union, thus making sure that even far flung orchestras in the periphery of the Soviet bloc had relatively equal access to the world-famous stars of the Soviet musical scene.

Like all of its Ukrainian contemporaries, the OPO's touring of Europe and North America has always been funded by private money: cultural sponsors, private sponsorships, scattershot philanthropy, and concert presenters in the various countries. The Ukrainian government has no dedicated funding in its cultural budget for touring, and sending an entire orchestra abroad is a significant expenditure.

"We probably have more guest artists on an annual basis than any of the other national performing arts organizations," Earle explained "but there is no funding for that from the federal budget. I use my reserve of goodwill and friendship in order to persuade people to come here and perform as guests. Pianists like Yefim Bronfman and Piotr Anderszewski, violinists like Sergey Krylov and Valeriy Sokolov have come here. There is a natural limit to how far that goes, however."

At the same time, an organic tradition of connoisseurship by the aristocracy and educated elites was quashed by the Russian Revolution, and the generation that was born since the dissolution of the Soviet Union has not had enough time to replicate centuries of lost cultural capital. A much debated "Law on Philanthropy," which would allow for Western-style contributions to cultural institutions, remains to be tabled for a vote in parliament. Nor does the tax code yet permit for the sorts of deductions that American cultural institutions depend on.

The OPO, like every other performing institution in the country, also has no endowment fund and no reserves for a rainy day, a concept that Earle describes as a "revolutionary idea" for a Ukrainian cultural institution. However, if these were established, they would need to be created separately for individual organizations, as creating a single multi-purpose endowment fund for multiple cultural institutions would be an inefficient bureaucratic mess. It would also create many opportunities for gross misappropriation of funds.

Despite the nation's constraints and penurious situation, a great deal remains to be done in order to ensure the continuation of Ukraine's high culture. A society is represented by its cultural institutions and a great country unabashedly deserves at least one great philharmonic orchestra.

The Atlantic Council 2016

Trouble on the Dnieper

A review of "Independence Square," by A.D. Miller.
Pegasus Books

Ukrainian politics are undoubtedly some of the most complex, fractious, and fascinating in Europe. This fact became universally known in January, when Kyiv's quotidian political maneuverings took center stage during President Trump's impeachment trial. American audiences were exposed to the country's campaign against endemic corruption, its oligarchic capture, and its weak governance (all of which is exaggerated by Kyiv's ruthless adversary in the Kremlin). Certainly, Ukraine's political elites are second to none in their flamboyance. The country is currently governed by Volodymyr Zelensky, an actor and comedian who became the real president of Ukraine after convincingly playing the president of Ukraine on TV.

Yet unlike the Russians, who spent the chaotic 1990s generating novels and satirical literary movements at a remarkable pace, post-independence Ukrainians never quite forged their own political literary tradition. Canonical contemporary Ukrainian writers Yurii Andrukhovych, Serhiy Zhadan, and Andrey Kurkov often deal with social matters, but in an oblique, roundabout fashion. (Oksana Zabuzhko's multigenerational The Museum of Abandoned Secrets, published in 2009, constitutes the rare exception.) This is not for want of material: The nation's politics constitute a surreal and never-ending drama. Curiously, however, the role of novelizing recent Ukrainian political history, of processing and interpreting it for a global literary audience, has fallen to outsiders.

The journalist A.D. Miller is a veteran hand in covering the post-Soviet world, experience from which he has liberally drawn in his novels. He reworked his journalistic experiences in Russia, where he served as the Moscow bureau chief for the Economist, into his previous political thriller, Snowdrops, which was nominated for the Booker Prize. Later, Miller covered the 2004 Orange Revolution in Kyiv, which he used as the basis for his latest novel, Independence Square. The square of the book's title is Kyiv's Maidan Nezalezhnosti, where Ukrainians routinely gather to protest and occasionally to bring down their government.

The plot of Independence Square centers on the brief and ultimately destructive romance between Simon Davey, the deputy head of mission at the British Embassy in Kyiv, and Olesya, a young and glamorously idealistic Ukrainian activist. Their relationship blooms against the backdrop of the 2004 revolution, when Ukrainians turned out en masse to protest the illegitimate election of Viktor Yanukovych. (Though the novel mostly leaves oligarchs and politicians unnamed, those familiar with Ukrainian politics will be able to deduce their identities.) Olesya is quickly swept up into the events that follow.

The novel transcribes in minute detail the course of the 2004 revolution: the rigged vote, the mass protests, the mandated recount, the standoff in the streets of Kyiv between massed representatives of two divergent visions of Ukraine's future, and the poisoning of the main opposition candidate. The city is overtaken by chaos and the wartime rumor mill. "Rumor," Miller writes, "was its queen. She had grown grander in her prophecies and scope. No longer predicting drunken miners, busloads of Titushky (thugs for hire), or released convicts, rumor was anticipating war. War with Russia, civil wars, coups, sabotage, states of emergency. Already, rumor maintained Russian spetsnaz (special forces) had been secreted in position, ready to open fire if the order came from Moscow."

The romance and revolutionary carnage take place amid an evocatively (if sparely) described Kyiv, borne along in a lapidary tone. Chapters alternate vantage points between the events of the 2004 revolution and London 12 years later. The plot pivots around the moment when Kyiv's Moscow-aligned government is on the cusp of ordering troops to open fire on the protesters.

Simon becomes romantically ensnared with Olesya and is compromised by the calculating oligarch Korvin. A loquacious TV baron, Korvin is a ruthless and amoral political operator who takes pleasure in delivering devilish monologues. "You know this old ... not joke ...

proverb: my friends are near, but my belly is nearer. No? So my businesses are nearer than these big dramas. From my point of view, when this election story is finished, there must be rules of the game for business — who gets, who keeps." Korvin is a convincing composite of the oligarchs who control Ukraine's politics and whom any journalist covering the country will have encountered.

In the square and later again in his home, Korvin lectures Simon in dialectical fashion on the laws of history and the way that business is done in post-Soviet Ukraine. ("We are not angels, okay? Not absolutely clean. I am not a Hollywood hero, this is a fact.") Angling for his ambassadorship and also wanting to do what he thinks is right, Simon disregards diplomatic protocol and personally intervenes in order to avert the imminent showdown between the revolutionaries and representatives of the pro-Russian portion of the political class.

His brave and sentimental actions are intended to secure a peaceful political transition, but he walks into a trap laid for him by the clever Korvin. Coupled with his affair with Olesya, this leads to the unraveling of Simon's personal life and his ouster from the diplomatic service. Back in the present, we meet the disgraced Simon as he is driving an Uber to make ends meet while ruminating on the past. One day, he catches sight of Olesya on London's Tube and takes after her in obsessive pursuit. The book shifts from a political fable to a slowly simmering detective story as Simon desperately tries to figure out why his life and history turned out the way that they did.

Though written by an Englishman, Independence Square is a worthy addition to the genre of Ukrainian political novels. One hopes it is only the first of many to come.

The Washington Examiner 2020

Fake News From Cannes

The opening of the 71st iteration of the Cannes Film Festival is upon us, along with all the pomp and splendor that it entails. As usual, the festival is a temple to both cinema and extreme sensuous hedonism, with tremendous parties thrown by film companies and oligarchs on private yachts (some of which dwarf many small islands, and some this Tablet correspondent will do his best to attend for the sake of our readers).

Another annual tradition also lovingly kept up is the surfeit of political and legal drama accompanying the world's most glamorous film festival. Terry Gilliam's *The Man Who Killed Don Quixote*, a near mythical production awaited by fans of cinema for decades, will be screened after all as the Festival's closing film in the wake of a last-minute Paris court decision to throw out a lawsuit from an irate producer and his lawyer son. (The Festival sent out a gloating triumphalist press release earlier Thursday claiming to be "a unique forum for freedom of expression.") Elsewhere, the renowned French filmmaker Jean-Luc Godard, long accused of anti-Semitism, announced at the start of the competition that he would be joining a boycott of Israeli cinema by several dozen French film-industry professionals. Numerous campaigns for increased representation of women in competition ended with institutional disappointment as only a handful were selected, despite the ghost of Harvey Weinstein hovering over festivities. A pair of celebrated Russian and Iranian dissident film makers in the competition program were not allowed to travel to their openings because of house arrests by their respective nations.

The commencement of the Cannes Film Festival also coincided with an even more auspicious historical moment: Yesterday marked the 73rd anniversary of Nazi Germany's unconditional surrender to the Soviet Union. As is now commonly understood, the memory of World War II has become an ideological flashpoint across the post-Soviet world. Some commentators have even gone so far as to make the case that manipulated memories of the Soviet victory over the Nazis now constitute the primary ideological pillar of Russian President Vladimir Putin's rule of the Russian Federation. Across Ukraine, the tense annual tradition of dueling historical commemorations of the conclusion of the war took place on May 8 and 9. In the south of Ukraine, in my beloved Odessa, a large pro-Russian crowd of demonstrators marched along the "Alley of Glory" carrying pictures of their veteran ancestors while chanting "Donbas, we are with you!" It is a tremendous pity that none of those marching in support of the benighted region will likely have a chance to watch the acerbic *Donbas* by Ukraine's storied auteur Sergei Loznitsa.

While the blooming of the Ukrainian film industry since the start of the conflict with Russia has been the great story of the coalescing of Ukrainian civic nationalism, Loznitsa's formally rigorous vision has constituted the crown jewel of Ukrainian cinema for more than a decade. Loznitsa's films are astringent, humanistic, urbane, and dark works of formalist art cinema. The Ukrainians sent a vice-prime minister to lead the delegation to the opening. (Full disclosure: Loznitsa and I know each other a bit from the Ukrainian film festival circuit and being good Russians we have shared a few glasses on several occasions.) A Cannes festival veteran, Loznitsa's sardonic war film opened the *Un Certain Regard* parallel program. For those who might have wondered why a star of world cinema and a special favorite of Cannes power director Thierry Frémaux was being passed over for the main competition, Loznitsa explained in his English language comments that the film had only been completed six weeks earlier. Fremaux would himself admit on stage the fact that the festival's strict filing deadline had been waived in this case.

During the opening ceremony, Fremaux also recalled having once inquired of Loznitsa whether the auteur considered himself to be a Russian or a Ukrainian. Loznitsa replied that he had a Ukrainian passport and a Russian soul, but that it was all very much more complicated. Indeed, having been born in Belarus, coming of age in Kyiv, learning his film craft in Moscow, and having spent exactly half his life in the Soviet Union, Loznitsa's culture is in fact totally and unambiguously Russian. Though he makes films about the Russian world, with last year's *A Gentle*

Creature explicitly ruminating on Dostoevsky and the phantasmagoric tinge of bureaucratic proceduralism, the realm of Russian culture that Loznitsa's cinema inhabits is decidedly liberal. (I previously wrote about his *Maidan* protest documentary in my 2014 Cannes dispatch for Tablet Magazine). Loznitsa's geographically unmoored post-Soviet culture is categorically not the revanchist *"Russkiy Mir"* (the so-called "Russian world" of Kremlin propaganda) of authoritarian Putinism. It has nothing to do with the neo-imperialist fantasia of the sort upheld by the malevolent cast of mercenaries, brigands, fanatics, and soldiers of fortune who run rampant in Ukraine's occupied eastern regions (though the spelling of the film's name in the Russian manner has not gone unnoticed by certain Ukrainian nationalists).

Donbas is the work of a Russophone patriot of sovereign Ukraine and it is composed of 13 interwoven vignettes, all based on grotesque or comic real life events, that will be familiar to anyone who has followed the course of the war over the last four years. *Donbas* is set in Ukraine's eastern regions, torn asunder by a chaotic occupation by Russian-led separatist militias . Almost surrealist levels of satire portray the opportunists, bandits, and lowlifes who menace a society in the wake of a collapse of civilized social structures. Corruption reigns supreme as property is expropriated by greedy warlords and gangsters under the guise of fighting fascism. A separatist mercenary who stops a bus full of civilians takes a cut of meat from an old woman for his soup. At the next roadblock a Russian servicewoman lines the men in the bus up and harangues them with patriotic speeches before stripping them naked. The film is unabashedly patriotic, yet one of the scenes suggests a Ukrainian army officer takes bribes to let a separatist commander through a checkpoint.

A sequence set in an underground bunker, where refugees of the conflict live in misery and squalor, points to the human costs of the war for the ordinary residents of the Donbas. A woman disrupts a meeting of the city council, dumping a bucket of feces over the head of the chairman, and gets embroiled in a screaming match with a Ukrainian journalist. A harrowing scene (once again based on real events) concerns a Ukrainian POW tied to a pole and debased by a crowd in the middle of Donetsk, with enraged babushkas in headscarves leading the crowd in beating the humiliated Ukrainian soldier with their fists and canes. Accompanied by a bemused local translator, a German journalist asks Russian military servicemen with the Asian facial features of residents of Russia's Siberian Buryat Republic if they are locals. Much of the film deals with the literal production of "fake news," with the opening set piece showing actors preparing for the role of sobbing on television—and Loznitsa takes a cruel satisfaction in having the separatists exact a fitting cost from these opportunistic characters at the film's conclusion. (In real life there were indeed amateur actors who travelled from Ukrainian city to Ukrainian city to partake in weepy television interviews for the sake of Russian nightly news shows.)

The staging and framing of the film is scabrous; the film's director of photography is the Romanian new-wave stalwart Oleg Mutu, who returns to collaborate with Loznitsa. Several early reviews of *Donbas* have uniformly empathized with the complexity and opaque quality of the material with which Loznitsa worked. Several of my critic colleagues admitted to me after the screening that certain parts of the film were difficult to follow for anyone who was not thoroughly steeped in the minutiae of the conflict. While acknowledging the film to be Loznitsa's "arguably most dramatically coherent and accessible," one critic nonetheless inveighed that the director "risks creating a dry formalist exercise that's hard to understand and engage with for non-Slavs or anyone averse to High Art-House cinema." Telling apart the different groups of soldiers and separatists in their almost identical camo outfits is indeed difficult, even if one can tell Novorossiya patches from Ukrainian army ones, and this is likely part of the point.

Loznitsa is not likely to be concerned by critiques of incomprehensibility, even if *Donbas* offers us the best fictionalized account of the Ukrainian-Russian conflict to have appeared to date. One of the last segments of the film, an extended portrait of a raucous wedding taking place under the auspices of the newly codified laws of Novorossiya — complete with flowery and grotesque extended toasts read out by drunken commanders of mercenary forces — drives home the point. The elegant, urbane, and ironic Loznitsa is an unabashed cultural elitist and

Donbas makes clear a personal view that the new regime constructed in Ukraine's occupied territories constitutes an assault on Russian culture (not to mention taste) as well as universal human rights.

Tablet Magazine 2018

VIII. Obituaries and Appreciations

All That Is Solid Melts Into Berman: The Unkempt Emperor of New York Intellectuals

Many fine appraisals and recollections of the life and works of Marshall Berman, the great political theorist, urbanist, Marxist philosopher, and supreme lyricist of the enchantments of metropolitan life, have been penned following his recent passing at the age of 72 — felled by a heart attack while eating breakfast with a friend at his beloved Metro Diner on 100th Street in Manhattan. These have included the many elaborate sketches of his early grappling with the Faustian figure of Robert Moses, who leveled Marshall's Bronx neighborhood of Tremont to make room for the Cross Bronx Expressway. From deep within the bowels of academia came accounts of his place in the neo-formalist and structuralist debates of the 1980s. Marshall's colleagues and friends at *Dissent*, which published some of his greatest essays and whose board he sat on for many years, fondly recalled his contributions to the life of the storied social democratic magazine. His great friend Michael Walzer remembered his idiosyncratic personality and his boundless kindness. In Tablet, Todd Gitlin, like Marshall an important participant/chronicler of the tumult of the 1960s, wrote the very first obituary to appear after Marshall's passing: He spoke of a "Marxist Mensch," a phrase that provoked the editor of *Commentary*, John Podhoretz, to assert on Twitter that no one would ever speak of a "Nazi Humanist Mensch." Podhoretz apologized for the comment the following day, clarifying that he meant to highlight the difference with which Marxism and Nazism are treated in contemporary public discourse. In death as in life, Marshall had the honor of being involved in internecine ideological warfare between small, New York-based literary journals of ideas.

Having cataloged the encomiums of his public achievements, I want to add one to his private ones. Marshall was my teacher as well as the coordinator of my undergraduate studies at the City University of New York, where I finished my university studies with a double degree in Intellectual History and Russian Literature. Marshall took me under his protective wing, and I adored him.

Marshall's second- and third-generation Jewish immigrant milieu in the South Bronx resembled my own upbringing in Brighton Beach, the major difference between that "world of our fathers" and my own being the absence of any discernibly radical or self-aware politics: Everyday life in the worker's paradise had the near-universal effect of turning most people exceedingly right-wing. Not only did the Soviet Union strip people of their cultural patrimony and knowledge, but it also unwittingly stripped away any possibility of a belief in positivist progress. Having emigrated from the Soviet Union with my family at a young age, I had not been old enough to imbibe the crushing noxiousness of life under state Communism. Growing up in Brighton Beach, my (then) stridently left-wing politics were a fluke—though, statistically speaking, it had to have happened to someone.

After reneging on art school and moving around from college to college as a transitive and feckless misfit, I wound up, by a stroke of luck, in the inspired and relaxed environs of the CUNY B.A. program, which allows self-directed students to compile their own program of study. One could, for example, take a class at the downtown business college Baruch on Monday morning, travel to uptown Hunter in the evening for a chemistry class, and then up to John Jay for criminal law on Tuesdays and Thursdays. I wanted to be at CCNY's uptown campus merely for the pleasure of taking the train up to the campus and fantasizing about the fratricidal conflicts that had taken place between Trotskyists and Communists in the first and second annexes of the CCNY cafeteria. What I craved more than anything else was to have been there in the 1930s and '40s, in that romantic New York where conflicts over ideas mattered. Lost in my dreamy fantasies, I was intoxicated by the myth of the august intensity of the New York Intellectuals. I scoured used bookstores for old copies of *Partisan Review* and Dwight McDonald's *Politics*, contemplated what Morris Raphael Cohen had taught William Phillips, and read Lionel Trilling, F.W. Dupee, Richard Hofstadter, Daniel Bell, Meyer Schapiro, Clement Greenberg, Saul Bellow, and C. Wright Mills. I rode the subway and read their memoirs, Norman Podhoretz's *Making It*, William Phillips *Partisan View*, and Alfred Kazin's *Walker in the City*. Their struggle to align the Thanatos of a roiling inner world and the demands of immigrant integration while speculating about the fashion in which one might live a politically engaged life mirrored my own.

I was precocious enough to have read Marshall's essays and book reviews in *Dissent* and the *Times Book Review* and to direct myself to his doorstep without quite knowing what it was that I needed or expected from him. The syllabus for "Marxism," the class I stumbled into, was like nothing I had ever seen before: It was scribbled out in a thick, rickety scrawl of block letters across a purposefully crude photocopy. Dispensing with all academic conventions, it had nothing on it other than Prof. Berman's name, contact information, and a reading list of five or six books.

The professor himself was even more strikingly contemptuous of any trace of conformism. With his thick, unruly mane of hair and unkempt beard, he was a stout and gentle giant, perennially shambling, with his bad back and ruined knees. He was the consummate anti-dandy, but with his orange jackets and tie-dyed T-shirts, he was still very much a peacock. I thought he was aesthetically marvelous, the very portrait of the scabrous, irascible, and cantankerous old Jewish intellectual I imagined I myself would one day become. The class was a remarkable and electrifying riff over 20th-century left-wing history ranging from Lassalle's influence on Lenin to Bakunin's reading of Burke, ending in Nietzsche's idea of the nature of sensibility. Marshall would talk about various theories of repression and veer off on a tangent about Thorstein Veblen before delving into the fate of his Dickens-reading Iranian students who were being consumed by the ayatollah's revolution.

In hindsight, I am impressed by how neatly he synthesized the brackish world of 19th-century Russian revolutionary politics for American undergraduates, light-years removed from it. I see, on opening my notes from that autumn, that the first line I wrote down in my notebook in that class might be taken for Marshall's credo. "Must we wait for after the revolution for joy?" This was followed by a resounding "No!"

The centerpiece of Berman's reading list was his magnum opus *All That Is Solid Melts Into Air*. Reading that book was a revelation, and I experienced a variant of his well-known reaction to his first (what came to be known as a "humanist") reading of Marx's 1844 manuscript: "Suddenly I was in a sweat, melting, shedding clothes and tears, flashing hot and cold."

The immediate context for the book, the conditions under which it had been written and to which it responded viscerally was a vigil over the charred remains of the burned-out New Left and the cultural backlash that coalesced against the '60s counter-culture. Before books like Zygmunt Bauman's *Liquid Modernity* and Christopher Lasch's *The Culture of Narcissism* diagnosed the disintegration of the incorporated, coherent psychological self, Marshall pinpointed the unraveling of the identity structures of contemporary man. The book's core insight was that the seams of received identity had become unglued, and inherited formulas no longer held, so it was the duty of modern man to construct and reconstruct himself and fill his own vessel.

Marshall's magpie response was a call for a feverishly grasping appropriation of all that is best in literature, philosophy, and the social sciences. In a 1982 review of the book, John Leonard deduced quite lucidly that "according to Mr. Berman, all that is modern, in literature and the arts, in architecture and in politics, is sexy." Whenever I met someone who was carrying a copy of *All That Is Solid Melts Into Air*, I knew immediately that this person was a kindred spirit, worth striking up a conversation with. Most often it would be an earnest Argentine or Turkish intellectual who would tell me ecstatically that Berman's book changed their life. I knew what they meant. And how could one not love a man who slotted yiddishisms like mamzer and narishkeit into erudite essays like his rebuke of Irving's rebuke of the New Left?

For a man of his stature and accomplishment, Marshall was an exceedingly generous mentor, though never a coddling one. He would forward me recommendations for fellowships to apply for and books to read, and he responded to every single one of the fledgling publications that I sent his way with equal parts praise and ribaldry, as well as humiliatingly incisive criticism. "Why have you made yourself into a Le Carré character, addressing us from some anonymous East European City?" he once asked me about a piece I had written about Rosa Luxembourg. After reading my appraisal of a Slovenian poet, he wrote back to rebuke me: "I don't like the way you disparage Max Jacob. He isn't my fave poet either, but people who die in Nazi concentration camps shouldn't be dug up & dissed." His correspondence was as inimitable as his conversation. Terse, cagey, and luxurious, it channeled his idiosyncratic character through shorthand and orthographic syntax. His letters and emails always ended with an exhorting *"shalom."*

Here is one email he sent me last year urging me to get in contact with an up-and-coming Polish left-wing group of Revisionist Marxists whom he had visited in Poland:

Dear V—

There was an * I forgot to fill in. They translated my ADVENTURES IN MARXISM– & a bk of Mike W & one by Mike K– remarkably fast, w a delightful cover of M on a motorcycle. It contains an essay on Lukacs, 1st written in 1985, where I tell story of him & Irma Seidler, & I Say "What a great Hungarian movie this might have made!" But now [written in 90s] it's too late…. All this was before I knew of H's post-Waidja work as a director. But I mentioned the essay, & I said she was one of few authors I knew who cd put "love" & "communism" in same sentence & make it mean something–& I mentioned L in 1968, who said Russian Rev had exhausted its creative power, & "cinema is now the world's avant-garde". She was fascinated by this—others in aud yelled what were probably Polish curses at L….Who knows if anything will come of this?

Though it is written in a coded cipher, this letter makes perfect sense to me—as it probably does to others who spoke this hermetic language.

The last time we spoke was at the end of June, when I called him from Paris at his home on the Upper West Side. The day afterward, I was slated to catch the Eurostar to London and a train to Oxford for the 50th anniversary conference of the *New York Review of Books*, which was devoted to the memory of Isaiah Berlin, under whom Marshall had written his fateful dissertation on Marx during his graduate studies at Oxford. Berlin was the towering Russian Jewish émigré intellectual par excellence, and Marshall's presence in Berlin's circle in Oxford thrilled me, as it confirmed my own patrimony in the history of ideas I was obsessed with. Over the phone Marshall told me of his own disappointment that though "Berlin had been a great teacher and wonderful person in my life, for years people had been compiling a 'kosher list' of Berlin's students that I and many others never made."

During that call I related to Marshall what seemed to me to be a bittersweet tale of rejection: I had recently been invited by a common friend over to the palatial *hôtel particulier* of Isaiah Berlin's adopted grandson, an important man in the administration of Sotheby's auction house in Paris. Inside the mansion's exquisite library stood Berlin's desk, and over it hung the original of the David Levine portrait of the philosopher that had graced his pieces in the *New York Review of Books*. The gentleman's art collection, full of Monets, Bretons, and Picassos, as well as his library, were suitably grand. The evening had gone well enough, I had thought at the time. The guy even got the Pasternak manuscripts out to show me and had me translate Pasternak's faded wartime inscriptions to Berlin from the Russian ("Only you understand everything Isaiah"). He even pulled out the condolence telegram the queen had sent the family before the funeral ("I so enjoyed my afternoon teas and talks with Isaiah. My deepest condolences. Yours truly, Elizabeth").

Afterward, my friend informed me that Sir Isaiah Berlin's honorable descendant requested that he no longer bring the "weirdo intellectual" around. I was shocked and aghast at the world's perfidy. Could this man truly not care about my encyclopedic knowledge of his grandfather's obscure positions in the Oxford language debates of the 1930s! I complained about the incident to Marshall, who was typically livid at my lack of self-awareness: "C'mon man! What's wrong with you!?" he bellowed at me through the phone, brusque and loving as always. "Not everybody can go everywhere and do everything! You're from Brighton Beach! You should know better!"

Anyway, he went on, he loved my last article about the movies in Cannes and hoped that I could get to write more stories like that. It was a great way to spend one's youth. He was waiting with bated breath to see the new Coen Brothers movie, and wasn't it great that Jerry Lewis was still causing trouble at his age? I invited him to my wedding in the fall, knowing of course that he had teaching obligations and would decline graciously, secretly hoping of course that he would be in Europe for some talk and so might drop in.

After 40 minutes the conversation began to wind down, and I began to blurt out my gratitude to him. I thanked him for always having been so kind to me and for having taken an interest in me for all those years. "I was always glad to do it," he told me. I did not know then why I had said it.

Tablet Magazine 2013

Boris Nemtsov, Murdered in the Shadow of the Kremlin

This obituary was published immediately after the murder of Russian opposition leader Boris Nemtsov.

Russian opposition leader and former Vice Premier of the Russian Federation Boris Nemtsov was publicly executed in Moscow shortly before midnight on Friday while crossing the Moskvoretsky bridge several hundred feet away from the Kremlin. He was shot while strolling home from dinner with his Ukrainian girlfriend after having spoken on the independent radio station Echo of Moscow in support of a planned opposition march and protest against the economic crisis and the war in Ukraine. The gunmen fired seven or eight shots at Nemtsov's back, with four bullets meeting their mark, destroying his inner organs on impact and killing him instantly. The killers then evaporated effortlessly into the eternal Moscow traffic jam in a white vehicle bearing North Caucasian license plates.

The killing was cinematic in a rancid way: Nemtsov died beneath the glimmering domes of St. Basil's Cathedral and was covered in a black body bag after having his buff torso exposed to the pitiless gaze of the television cameras by the responding officers at the scene. Sunday's rally drew between 50,000 and 100,000 Russians to a march in his memory despite the climate of acute ultra-nationalism now prevalent in the country. It is the most significant political assassination to take place in a decade and perhaps in the 25-year history of the Russian Federation.

The former first deputy prime minister was youthful, brave, nimble, and possessed of curly haired good-looks. He also had a quality rarely found in Russian politics: dash. The lurid finish of his story was a calculated rebuke to a glamorous life lived in the public eye, which despite its myriad failings symbolized a transitory epoch of Russian political life.

Boris Yeltsin's protégé, Nemtsov was a gifted politician and former scientist, tasked with the reformation of the energy sector. He had once been groomed as a possible successor to the presidency. He had been a kinetically hyperactive governor of Nizhny Novgorod and a deputy speaker of the Duma before being ousted from parliament in 2004. By necessity he had originally taken a stance of tepid accommodation toward Vladimir Putin when he had first come to power at the turn of the millennium. (At the time, Nemtsov co-authored a *New York Times* op-ed that now makes for heartrending reading for its complete lack of judgment.) Putin's increasing authoritarianism led Nemtsov to join up as a standard bearer and leader of the liberal opposition.

The audacious killing of a famed and charismatic figure has left Russia's embattled liberals struggling to interpret the meaning of the symbolic public execution. Bernard-Henri Lévy told Tablet that, with Nemtsov's death, we have lost "the anti-Putin. The bright side of Russia — Putin being its dark side, as well as the honor of the Russian people and the true heir of Sakharov and of the spirit of dissidence." Nemtsov's friend Garry Kasparov wrote that "Boris Nemtsov was a tireless fighter and one of the most skilled critics of the Putin government, a role that was by no means his only possible destiny." The Anglophone world's most learned Kremlinologists, Russia hands, and Slavic scholars are currently engaged in an arcane debate comparing the killing to the 1934 murder of Leningrad Communist Party leader Sergei Kirov. That December assassination of the Bolshevik leader was the pretext for setting off the Great Purges of the late 1930s that precipitated Joseph Stalin's consolidation of ultimate power over the Soviets. A historically minded minority instead compared the killing to Mussolini's expunging of Italian Socialist politician Giacomo Matteotti in 1924. Whether the murder does indeed augur a repetition of history by presaging a wider culling of the Kremlin's opponents remains to be seen.

Nemtsov was a vivacious character and an unrepentant playboy in comparison to whom the only other politicians of his generation who might be described as noble — the economist Grigory Yavlinsky and the army Gen. Alexander Lebed — were plodding characters. Of the smooth and sleek young reformist politicians of his generation he was probably the smoothest and sleekest, the closest to being a Russian variant of a Clinton-Blair-style third way. Nemtsov is certainly a martyr of the Russian liberal opposition whose death will "change everything," just as a thousand op-eds have already prophesied. Yet the actual policy prescriptions of his neoliberal reformism and its effects on '90s-era Russia have been understandably elided by the communal response to his killing. The neoliberal doctrine of shock reforms was carried out with brazen disregard for Russia's most vulnerable citizens and did incalculable damage to the social fabric of the country. Mark Ames' typically acerbic and raucous appraisal of Nemtsov's tenure as the handsome liberal face of Yeltsin's government is a rare dissenting view that bears careful study. It is a necessary corrective to the never-ending multitude of slavish panegyrics to the man penned by confused liberals who in their own countries would be defenders of Nordic-style welfare state-ism.

The habitually cavalier and occasionally squalid privatization schemes that Nemtsov and his ideological cohort of liberal anti-corruption activists had administered were dubious affairs of invidious power politics that likely would have been carried out in similar fashion by whoever had come to power in the '90s. In a country without large or indeed any reserves of capital, the concepts of value and prices were largely meaningless. The arbitrary distribution of colossal amounts of Russia's communally held assets to a few private individuals for what amounted to a pittance could not have been anything but radically unjust. Nemtsov's complex and belligerent political relations at the time with Boris Berezovsky bubbled over into personal friction over the privatization of a massive telecommunications firm.

This led to a personality clash in which he was handily outgunned by the more transparently brutish Berezovsky. In turn, Berezovsky's infamously impudent putdown of Nemtsov's presidential ambitions was proffered via pithy wordplay over their shared liability of bearing Jewish patronymics in Russian politics: "It seems to me that Mr. Nemtsov has a purely genetic problem," Berezovsky said at a 1997 press conference. "He is a Boris Yefimovich, at times he is a Boris Abramovich, but he wants to be Boris Nikolayevich (Yeltsin). You don't become a president, presidents are born."

Though the impious Nemtsov had been baptized by his Russian grandmother at an early age, Berezovsky's observation was as correct as it was cruel. Nemtsov and his cabinet were sacked, and his presidential aspirations were finally derailed by the August 1998 Russian financial crisis and debt default.

In hindsight, the mundane-seeming Putin's ascent to power over such opponents as Foreign Intelligence Service Director Yevgeny Primakov and the rough-hewn Moscow Mayor Yuri Luzhkov seems to be both over-determined and bizarre at once. But Stalin too seemed to have been the lesser of all his opponents until he finished them all off.

It was not until he was firmly ousted from power as the face of establishmentarian Russian reformism that Nemtsov began transforming himself into the quixotically noble figure that he is remembered as today. Ardently opposed to the Sochi Olympics, which he viewed as a debacle for his hometown, he ran a doomed campaign and was trounced in the city's 2009 mayoral elections. In 2013, he returned to electoral politics having won a regional election on the Yaroslavl regional city council— which is a significant step down for a former vice prime minister.

The Kremlin's response to the assassination was self-exculpatory to the point of self pity. Putin's powerful Press Secretary Dmitry Peskov gave a testy and dismissive interview during which he characterized Nemtsov's assassination as "a contract job that bears an exclusively provocational character." *Provocational* here being a paranoiac euphemism for a "set up." That widely reported proclamation of victim-blaming was followed up with the much less reported but infinitely more brazen comparison of Nemtsov's and Putin's "ratings," which proved that "all in all Boris Nemtsov was only slightly more important than the average statistical citizen." This carried the jarring reverberations of Putin's analogous debasement of crusading journalist Anna Politkovskaya as "politically insignificant" in the wake of her own 2006 murder.

Myriad defenders of the Kremlin quickly stepped forward to assert that there had actually existed no rational reason whatsoever for Putin to eliminate Nemtsov. The crime could only have been committed by crazed Caucasian Islamists, lone operators, or by the martyr-hungry liberals cannibalizing one of their own. A firm defender of Ukraine and embattled

President Poroshenko, Nemtsov had begun meeting with families of Russian soldiers killed in Ukraine. The Kremlin's proxies wasted no time fomenting rumors that his killing was somehow related to dalliances with aggrieved shadowy Ukrainian forces. Another version claimed that he was killed by a jealous lover of his 23-year-old Ukrainian girlfriend Anna Duritska, whom he had allegedly recently flown to Switzerland for an abortion.

The day after the killing, Poroshenko made public claims that Nemtsov had planned to reveal official Russian links to the East Ukrainian separatists. Many liberals, such as Nemtsov's friend and close collaborator Ilya Yashin, insist that he was eliminated at the moment that he was preparing a damning report with extensive documentation of the presence of Russian troops in Eastern Ukraine. Only the most crude or transparently cynical commentators placed the blame on a perfidious Ukrainian complot carried out by the CIA. Putin personally took the reins of the investigation and appointed the head of the Investigative Committee domestic law enforcement agency Alexander Bastrykin to lead the investigation: Bastrykin is widely beloved by liberals and journalists alike for threatening to have a journalist killed in the woods.

Nemtsov had confided his private dread to his friends and had recently spent several semi-concealed months in Israel and complained to police of having received social media threats. Eventually he had become lucid — and perhaps desperate — enough to admit fearing for his life in an interview earlier this month with the *Sobesednik* newspaper. He continued to rely, perhaps blithely, on the unwritten compact of reciprocal imperviousness enjoyed by former high-ranking Russian government officials. There are many who compare his murder to that of crusading journalist Politkovskaya, but the comparison unduly minimizes the fact that Nemtsov was a former deputy prime minister, and as such ostensibly untouchable. That Politkovskaya, too, was murdered on Putin's birthday — a "gift from the intelligence services" — is something that Russian liberals whisper to each other. The day before the killing, Putin had signed a decree declaring that Feb. 28 be celebrated in Russia as Special Operations Forces Day.

On Monday *Vedemosti* published the final posthumous interview in which Nemtsov speaks of Putin as "a completely amoral person. He is Leviathan."

Tablet Magazine 2015

Ukraine's Capital Names a 'Nemtsov Square' After Slain Leader of Russian Opposition

The Kyiv city council passed the measure to rename the street after a long campaign to honor Boris Nemtsov, who was a staunch supporter of Ukraine's Euromaidan revolution.

The assassination of Boris Nemtsov, a renowned physicist and leader of Russia's political opposition, on a bridge outside of the Kremlin in February 2015, was widely seen as a watershed moment in Russian politics. Yesterday, the Kyiv city council passed a resolution to rename the street housing the Russian Embassy in Ukraine's capital after Nemtsov.

Nemtsov had come to power in the '90s as an energetic young governor before becoming a favorite of Boris Yeltsin and was once seen as a possible heir to the Russian presidency. In the end, though, he was passed over by Yeltsin as a successor for the leadership of the Russian state in favor of Vladimir Putin. He would rebound from that loss to become the unlikely de facto leader of the organized opposition and to emerge as an indefatigable critic of the Putin regime. Observers of Russian politics view Nemtsov's killing as the event that symbolically broke an unspoken compact that had previously kept high-ranking members of the Russian government immune from political violence. With Nemtsov out of the picture, there was no other obvious candidate who could unite Russia's opposition. His killing stands as a testament to the Russian state's brutality towards perceived internal threats.

With the newly named Nemtsov street, Kyiv will become the third city after Washington, D.C. and the Lithuanian capital, Vilnius, where Russian diplomats will have to come to work on a street named after the slain politician. The vote was the culmination of a 13-month-long campaign, which passed through numerous bureaucratic obstacles. Sixty-nine Kyiv city councilmen voted in favor, 18 abstained and none voted against the resolution to rename the square after Nemtsov.

Nemtsov was a passionate supporter of Ukraine's EuroMaidan revolution and so it is appropriate that his memory be honored in Kyiv. At the same time, Moscow city authorities have continually prohibited any sort of public memorial to him in the Russian capital. Members of the Russian opposition bring flowers to the spot where Nemtsov was killed, only to have them bulldozed away on a weekly basis.

The campaign to honor Nemtsov's name was led by a coalition of Russian dissidents living in Kyiv, along with numerous Ukrainian civil society activists. Free Russia House Kyiv, an organization devoted to a Putin-free Russia, which serves as an "alternative" consul for Russian liberals, was one of the organizations that initiated the resolution.

"Nemtsov was a unique figure, not just in Russian politics, but for Ukraine as well," explained Greg Frolov, head of Free Russia House Kyiv. "He spent a large portion of his life not only fighting for Russian liberal democracy but also for Ukrainian independence, and he was killed at a moment while he was severely criticizing Putin's intervention in Ukraine, and while he was also crucially preparing a 'Putin's War Report' detailing the evidence of Russian troops fighting in Ukraine."

Tablet Magazine 2018

In Memory of Isaiah Berlin

Today marks the 109th birthday of Isaiah Berlin, the great Riga-born Russian-British political philosopher and historian of ideas. It is difficult to overstate the influence that Berlin held over British cultural institutions and the effect that his work continues to have on political thought.

The 20th anniversary of Berlin's death last November saw numerous conferences, exhibitions, television programs, lectures, and memorial events commemorating his life and legacy, many of which will be published this fall or gave rise to projects that are still ongoing. The Yale historian Timothy Snyder, now one of America's foremost public intellectuals, delivered last year's Isaiah Berlin Lecture in Riga. Titled "The Politics of Inevitability," the lecture's two-part conceptual structure was patterned on Berlin's famous theory of "two concepts of freedom," and constituted a kind of prelude to Snyder's new book *The Road to Unfreedom*, in which Snyder's debt to Berlin's thought is proudly displayed. Yale University hosted a major conference, with the scholarly papers being presented forming the core of what is to become the *Cambridge Companion to Isaiah Berlin*, which is slated for publication this fall. The art historian and filmmaker Judith Wechsler, known for her film about Walter Benjamin, is in the midst of completing a documentary film exploring the philosopher's life.

Yet the Berlin revival seems to owe as much to nostalgia for a fast-vanishing academic world of educated insights and sharp argument mediated by good manners as it does to the philosopher's ideas themselves. The Yale conference saw the world's preeminent experts on Berlin gather in his natural habitat, a wood-paneled hall, to give papers on his core concepts and concerns: the tension between cosmopolitanism and populism, his Cold War liberalism, the dangers of monism, the interplay between irrationality and the capacity of reason to know the world. Yet, what was so remarkable about it was the sense of genial camaraderie and something resembling almost low-key mirth. It felt very much like the family reunion in honor of a beloved uncle. Perhaps no more than a dozen of those who spoke or attended the conference, at most, had actually met Berlin or had studied with him.

The most memorable moment of the conference came when Berlin's loyal editor Henry Hardy stood at the podium to deliver the keynote speech. It was a beautiful speech, with Hardy speaking about the way that his commitment to Berlin's work and legacy had given his life meaning, and how otherwise he would have been an unremarkable but competent editor at a trade house. When Hardy stopped speaking, the entire crowd of 50 academics got up and gave him a standing ovation. Afterward, all present gathered in the private chamber of a Yale dining club for dinner and fond reminiscences. As Snyder correctly noted to me that week, "This is not the sort of relationship that people have to most political theorists." I myself was a student of Berlin's student, the Marxist philosopher Marshall Berman, who always told me of his great love for Berlin. It is an intellectual lineage that I am proud of.

The conventional wisdom is that the recent completion of the publication of Berlin's selected letters, lovingly edited by Mark Pottle and Hardy, have drastically changed our view of the Oxford philosopher by adding warts to what had hereto been an unblemished and highly idealized portrait. It is true that alongside some remarkable literary ruminations in chatty, conversational epistles written to anyone worth corresponding with over six decades at the center of public life, the volumes reveal Berlin to have been a canny academic infighter — but he never denied being anything other than a British establishmentarian. Berlin's posthumous reputation is widely assumed to have been secured by Hardy's meticulous editing and rummaging through Berlin's papers for lost treasures.

Berlin lived through remarkable times in a period when being an academic still meant that one was firmly ensconced in intellectual life, which at that point was still deeply integrated to the wider society. Berlin and his Oxbridge friends took advantage of working arrangements present before academia had been ruined by overspecialization and corrupted by the worst aspects of corporate governance. At another recent conference dedicated to Berlin's legacy, the British philosopher John Gray opined that Berlin's leisurely career would have been totally impossible in the contemporary academic environment, with its onerous administrative drudgery, teaching loads, and ceaseless demands for publication.

The manner in which Berlin lived his life remains eminently, even achingly, attractive and a stirring example of how to compose one's being in the world. Perhaps more than any other thinker of the 20th century, Berlin personified the contemplative life with an engagement with the world—an engaged connoisseurship with the arts coupled with a tireless pursuit of pleasure and friendship. Berlin took part in likely every interesting cultural phenomenon of his time, and personally engaged in the cultural politics that involved the occasional bout of espionage — like his assistance in getting the manuscript of Boris Pasternak's banned novel *Doctor Zhivago* out of the Soviet Union.

Berlin's pluralism was most keenly connected to his thinking about the multiple selves of an individual with multiple contradictory allegiances — a truly British-Russian Jew.

Haunted by childhood experiences of having to flee the Russian Empire in the midst of the carnal violence wrought by the Bolshevik revolution, Berlin was also throughout the course of his long career a keen student of the character, internal processes, aesthetics, ideological structures, and cultural apparatus of totalitarian systems.

We are now bombarded by a nearly continuous stream of articles and think pieces urging us to rediscover the philosophical tracts of Hannah Arendt and the novels and essays of George Orwell as practical guides to survival in the age of Trump. It is Berlin however who provides a more refined schemata for understanding the developmental vectors of totalitarianism — and his lesser-read essays on Soviet culture constitute a useful and timely adumbration of the deformation that is wrought upon the arts by their coerced politicization. There should by all rights be a run on his books.

In a manner that was taxonomically similar to that of Susan Sontag's literary project, Berlin rummaged through the canon of obscure and elided 18th-century political thinkers to construct an alternative canon. In the process he created an entire sub-discipline of intellectual history, the "counter enlightenment" pantheon — a convocation of anti-rationalist figures of European philosophy against whose anti-rationalist and reactionary arguments he measured a skeptical and anti-utopian understanding of human nature.

Personally amenable and moderate of character, Berlin was intellectually drawn to wild histrionic extremists such as the aristocratic revolutionary Joseph de Maistre whom he identified as "certainly the most brilliant and the most polemical of the critics of the philosophy that underlay the French Revolution." Having penned numerous scholarly studies of figures such as Giambattista Vico, J.G. Hamann, and Johann Gottfried Herder, Berlin would certainly have known what to make of the luminaries of the so-called alt-right movement. He also likely would have been fascinated with and would have studied carefully the lineages and intellectual taxonomies of the anti-democratic thinkers and neo-reactionaries who have become more widely known over the last few years, and which have lately been popularized and weaponized by noxious characters of the sort that Russians refer to as "political technologists," like Steve Bannon. The impulses animating the "neo- traditionalism" of the Italian philosopher Julius Evola, or the "Eurasianism" of the Russian Alexandr Dugin as well as the various tendencies associated with the so-called dark enlightenment would have been all too familiar to the man who wrote *Three Critics of the Enlightenment*.

Berlin's fascinating study of illiberal thought was carried out at least partly with the intention of injecting salutary antibodies to opposition to democratic norms into the bloodstream of Cold War liberalism. If he were here to observe our contemporary American or European politics, Berlin would have made an excellent guide to diagnosing and diagramming the ideological intonations and historical antecedents of the "illiberal democratic" wave that is cresting on both the right and the left, in a surreal moment when the *New York Times* publishes quirky pieces about Evola. Whether Berlin would categorize a figure like Jordan Peterson as being a representative of the enlightenment or the counter-enlightenment is a fascinating and important question.

Reading Berlin provides an excellent preparation for thinking about contemporary identity politics as well. Contemporary accusations of globalism (as distinct from internationalism) aimed at what some "rooted" peoples view as a deracinated, postnational, self-dealing, and globe-trotting elite would have surprised Berlin only at the generally primitive and derivative level at which the discourse is being waged. He thought of the individual as being intimately embedded in a tribe, a folk, a nation, and a civilization, and he would have dismissed out of hand both the rejection of sophisticated cosmopolitanism as well as its corollary impulse to denounce even the liberal defense of the nation-state or national borders as being illegitimate.

Berlin was always an immigrant, who came from a fragile minority in a small nation, and who maintained an exquisite sympathy for the plight of small peoples and never took the idea of home for granted. He maintained an equal sensitivity to the warmth and comfort of national feeling and the damage that it could do. "In our modern age, nationalism is not resurgent; it never died," he told an interviewer immediately after the collapse of the Soviet Union, and "neither did racism. They are the most powerful movements in the world today, cutting across many social systems."

Tablet Magazine 2018

Your Guide to the Next, Never-Ending War

At the start of January of this year, General Sir Nicholas Carter, now the newly appointed head of the British armed forces, delivered a widely noticed, doctrine-setting speech on the nature of contemporary armed conflict in the age of social media at the Royal United Services Institute. Over the last half decade, he posited, radical innovations in social media had revolutionized the capacities of state and nonstate actors to wage war, with connected individuals and groups now possessing weapons of mass propaganda that had hereto been the purview of powerful states with a well-funded military. The brightest lights of the British armed forces (as well as their counterparts the world over) had taken notice, and were preparing to adapt to fight back. In the midst of his speech, General Carter observed that "social media is throwing up digital supermen, hyperconnected and hyperempowered online individuals," and added that "I'd like a few of those in 77 Brigade, please."

The quote, and several other references in the speech, were taken from David Patrikarakos' *War in 140 Characters: How Social Media Is Reshaping Conflict in the Twenty-First Century*, whose lessons are based on ground reportage conducted during the last Israeli-Gaza and Russian-Ukrainian conflicts. Both of those conflicts were fought in cyberspace as much as they were on the field of battle, and the book posits the birth of "homo digitalis," a tech-savvy postmodern creature, who inhabits the online world and whose fighting prowess is equal to that of a battalion of infantry. Writing on the asymmetry between Hamas and Israeli narratives for Tablet last month, Patrikarakos stipulated that

"As ever in modern conflict—from Syria to Iraq to even Occupy Wall Street—two battles are taking place between Israel and Hamas in Gaza: one on the ground and the other in cyberspace. This latter battle centers on questions of outrage, perceived culpability, blaming (on both sides), and is played out in cycles that are determined by the mechanics and rhythms of social media. In terms of substance, this clash is between two opposing narratives."

The book has received a great deal of attention because it captured the innovative ways in which the act of shaping political narratives over social media—also known as "disinformation warfare," as well as other new names for the ancient art of propaganda—are now ascendant. In fact, the radical timeliness and importance of the book's message was underlined when Twitter instituted long debated changes by doubling the platform's character limit a week before the publication date.

Patrikarakos describes the Russian-Ukrainian conflict as the first truly modern war, and his is the first concentrated study of the ways in which media have been weaponized on the ground. His innate gift for explaining the wide-ranging social implications of complex technological innovations to popular audiences quickly catapulted him to the forefront of a newly forged class of social media explainers of politics in the age of "post truth." Unlike the majority of these commentators, however, his analysis and prescriptions are based on rigorous on-the-ground reportage. The book marked a transition from his being an old-school war correspondent to being a public intellectual.

Yet, taking up the pen, the Middle East, and the study of military conflict seems to have been almost predetermined for Patrikarakos. He descends, on his Greek side, from the statesman and soldier Georgios Sisinis, a great revolutionary who fought against the Turks and whose portrait hangs in the Greek national museum. On his mother's side, Patrikarakos is descended from the master kabbalist and de facto chief Rabbi of Babylon, Yosef Hayyim. Another great-grandfather was Rabbi Abdallah Somekh, who was instrumental in the process of the codification of Iraqi kosher laws. Sylvia Kedourie, the wife of the great Middle East scholar Elie Kedourie was also a cousin.

Patrikarakos was born in London, and grew up in the British capital living mostly with his mother after his parents divorced when he was 11 years old. His father ran a software company, and his mother was an art collector who lived off of money inherited from Naim Javid, her grandfather. An Iraqi businessman who had made a tremendous fortune in Baghdad, Javid was typical of his generation of Baghdadi Jews, a generation whose fortunes were wiped out when they were forced to flee Baghdad in the wake of the founding of the state of Israel. Javid decamped for Tehran in the early 1950s, and somewhat improbably recreated his fortune in Iran before being forced to flee again by the next geopolitical earthquake, the 1979 revolution in Iran. After attending the private University College school in Hampstead, Patrikarakos studied English literature at university. He spent his time there mostly reading the novels of Martin Amis, Evelyn Waugh, Dickens, Wodehouse, George Eliot, and Phillip Roth, and drinking through his studies instead of doing his coursework. An impressionable early reading of Fitzroy Maclean's *Eastern Approaches* would later prove to influence his choice of vocation. How could it not?

Being a self described "nice North London Jewish boy," Patrikarakos followed family expectations after university and made a halfhearted effort at starting a career as a commercial lawyer after attending law school. A depressing stint at a law firm specializing in international arbitration ended in spectacular failure. Patrikarakos informed me that he was sacked from the job after six months, being "escorted from the building by security guards in a gentle and civilized manner".

In his late 20s, he returned to Oxford to pursue his postgraduate studies at Wadham College. He admits that his time at Oxford was noteworthy chiefly for his "somewhat lax attitude toward traditional college rules," an attitude that on occasion landed him in the dean's office. Which, of course, is a timeless tradition for literary men. The degree work concluded in a stint studying Persian at the University of Tehran. He left Oxford, and took the plunge into journalism. writing first for the *Financial Times*, which was followed by a stint writing for *The New Statesman*. Early globe trotting war exploits included a stretch of time embedded with the U.N. peacekeeping force in the Congolese jungle as it faced off against the maniacal Joseph Kony and his Lord's Resistance Army, and Patrikarakos admits that he encountered some deeply visceral stuff in the jungle. He covered the Kurdish referendum and traveled the breadth of the Middle East.

Yet it was Patrikarakos' Oxford thesis on the history of the Iranian atomic program that would constitute the germ of his first book, *Nuclear Iran: The Birth of an Atomic State*. Minutely researched, deeply immersive, and written with flair, *Nuclear Iran* was the first full-length historical study of the Iranian nuclear program to have appeared in the English language. The narrative arc begins with Iranian humiliation in the 1950s and goes all the way to the present day, buttressed by impressive and wide-ranging interviews with the principal architects of the Iranian nuclear program. The timing of its publication, as the world debated the Obama administration policy of rapprochement with Tehran, was impeccable and the book was unusually well received for a freshman effort in foreign policy analysis, being a *New York Times* editors' choice, and landing on the shortlist for the international affairs book of the year and being nominated for the political book award in Great Britain.

Patrikarakos arrived in Ukraine in March of 2014, right after the Maidan revolution concluded with the kleptocratic former President Viktor Yanukovych fleeing the country. He stayed in Ukraine for just under a year, covering the conflict, with his experiences there and in Israel constituting the core ideas for *War in 140 Characters*. During his time there, he traveled throughout the occupied cities Luhansk, Donetsk, and Slovyansk, and was embedded with the Ukrainian army. During the course of his reporting on the conflict, he befriended the Ukraine volunteer activist Anna Sandalova, who was a pioneer of social media assisted crowd-sourced support for the Ukrainian army at a moment when the Ukrainian state was unable to offer basic service or arm its own troops.

Not that it much mattered: Modern warfare, Patrikarakos soon learned, was very different from the traditional model we've come to know and expect. Nowadays, he learned, propaganda no longer served war on the ground, with maneuvering on the ground instead serving to advance and buttress particular propaganda narratives. President Putin's Russian forces, the book notes, could've easily defeated their neighbor militaristically, but instead focused on using social media to convince many that the Ukrainian government was a junta-dominated fascist regime hell-bent on persecuting Russians. This form of social media based battle not only deepened the fissures, but turned war into a never-ending affair, a state of mind perpetuated by troll farms churning out countless posts designed to sow discord and animosity.

The book that Patrikarakos wrote is not only an excellent guide to living in such times of never-ending conflict, but also a damning account of what happens to us when we descend from the barbarism of violence to the arguably even more depraved depths of vile tweets, malicious posts, and fake news.

Tablet Magazine 2018

Stephen Cohen: Historian, Polemicist and Friend of Gorbachev

Cohen was an anti-American prophet of the decline of legacy American media during the partisanship and conspiracy theorizing of Russiagate.

The passing of Stephen Cohen — historian, polemicist and friend of Soviet Premier Mikhail Gorbachev — at the age of eighty-one brought to a close an important chapter of American intellectual life.

Along with being a lifelong supporter of détente between Moscow and Washington D.C., he emerged as the most prominent American leftist critic of the so-called "Russiagate" narrative — a conspiratorial confusion which contributed to the thorough collapse of the American public's trust in whole swathes of the prestige American media. While an investigation into the possible collusion of the Trump campaign was surely warranted, for more than two years supposedly unbiased print and television journalists hyperbolically reported on a story that would mostly fizzle out.

In unapologetic and apocalyptic tones, incessant political proclamations — rather than reporting — took place amid unfulfilled promises of imminent grandiose revelations from the Mueller report. This helped propel along our partisan polarization as Americans quickly retreated into their own private epistemic spheres of knowledge. It was truly bittersweet that Cohen did not live another ten days. The acerbic political bruiser would have been thrilled by the revelations of the *New York Times* investigation into President Trump's tax returns.

Along with piquant revelations of the ways in which Trump spent his life gaming the US tax code, the *New York Times* confirmed that the documents it had received contained no previously unknown information regarding business dealings with Russia. Thus, through internal logic particular to each side, skepticism of the "Russiagate" narrative united American conservatives and old school left-wingers in an unholy alliance.

Professor Cohen proceeded to gamble a lifetime of credibility commenting on Soviet and Russian politics on his unyielding denunciations of "Russiagate". Despite Cohen's undeniable intelligence and scholarly contribution, he turned out to have been invariably wrong in most every major debate of his life. Yet in the final argument of an archly quarrelsome career, he was proven to be perfectly correct, if for all the wrong reasons.

The course of the historian's life and later influence was set in motion with the publication of his Magnum Opus: *Bukharin and the Bolshevik Revolution: A Political Biography, 1888-1938*. Published when he was thirty-five years old, the book was met with universal acclamation for its revolutionary scholarship and revelations on the life and times of the lovable rascal. Bukharin possessed by far the most appealing personality among the dour, ascetic, doctrinaire and mostly pitiless old Bolshevik leaders. The book posited Bukharin as the emblematic figurehead of an untaken and humane Soviet Socialist future. The great Russia scholar Leonard Shapiro pronounced it to be magnificent in a somewhat sly 1974 essay review in the *New York Review of Books*: it was a "full, fair, balanced, enormously well-documented, sympathetic yet not uncritical study of Bukharin's life and thought". Shapiro asked, "what is the significance of Bukharin for posterity?" The book's implicit answer was that "for those socialists to whom Stalinism has proved a disillusionment, and for those who see little to hope for from the various forms of violent revolution in which followers of Trotsky or Mao see the vision of a happy future, Bukharin offers the only alternative—a form of post-revolutionary revisionism." Everything would have worked out perfectly fine if only Stalin had not killed Bukharin and the other old Bolsheviks.

The book heralded Cohen's concerns over the next half century at the exact same moment that its great feat of scholarship was becoming outdated. "The opening of the Soviet archives in the late 1980s and early 1990s has rendered all research on Bukharin which had been conducted without access to those relevant archives pretty much obsolete," the Harvard historian Serhii Plohii informed me. Instead, Cohen abandoned the field, never returning to the research or big question that had launched his career. Instead he embarked upon a transformation from being an acclaimed and promising historian into a giddy bomb-throwing polemicist. It was a role for which he possessed undeniable gifts, including a properly acerbic temperament and the gait of a born dueller.

The Russian translation arrived at an optimal moment to create waves just as Gorbachev launched Perestroika. It appeared at the exact moment when the crumbling system began grappling for alternative interpretations of early Soviet events and different ways forward. Gorbachev became a fan and befriended Cohen, bringing him into his inner circle.

The political access that Professor Cohen enjoyed offered him ringside access to historic events that his colleagues in academia could only have dreamed of. He opined on reforming Soviet communism along gradualist transition lines into a mixed economy, which was not radically dissimilar an impulse from the "New Economic Plan" that Stalin had rendered moot when he had Bukharin and the other old Bolshevik leaders executed. This was faintly ludicrous as a solution to Soviet problems, even as the economic transition that actually transpired likely could not have been any worse. Scholars of Russia who had known Cohen in the late 80's judged him very harshly for having failed to predict the oncoming dissolution of the Soviet Union. He missed the Communist Party apparatus losing its grip over the union despite standing with them up on the tribunal while observing victory day parades with Gorbachev.

Professor Cohen's atavistic leftism was characterized by a deeply reflexive, uncompromising and austere anti-Americanism. For decades he had advocated a return to Kissingerian Realism in relations with Russia, which he thought needed to be allowed to retain its traditional sphere of influence. That impulse made him sympathetic to the 2016 Trump presidential campaign for its openly promising the latest in a series of doomed resets of relations with Moscow. That ideal was always held at the expense of the democratic and national aspirations of former imperial subjects who yearned for liberty, for their own nations. His remarkable lack of curiosity regarding the Soviet Union's so-called "nationalities question" led to him having a reputation for never having taken very much interest in the thoughts and desires of anyone other than the most elite Russians living in the major cities.

Likewise, Cohen lacked all understanding of the dynamics taking place within the Baltics, which he never seemed to have visited (and which one needed to have done in order to understand that the Soviet system was definitively on its way out). Despite all of the many years of producing polemics on the Ukrainian relationship with Russia, several Ukrainian-Americans who knew him have related to me Cohen's admission that he never visited Kyiv. After the 2014 Russian invasion of Ukraine and the annexation of the Crimean Peninsula, he emerged as perhaps the fiercest defender of the Kremlin position within American intellectual and public life: he habitually blamed Crimean annexation on NATO expansion.

Cohen's marriage to Katrina vanden Heuvel, the editor and publisher of *The Nation*, ensured that his views on Soviet history, Russian politics and the war in Ukraine were firmly stamped on *The Nation*'s editorial line. Vanden Heuvel's moving and ethereally naive account of their romance ("In fact, it was samizdat manuscripts that first brought us together") is very much worthy of a mid-period Woody Allen film. A fellowship that they had planned to offer in Cohen's honor to the Association for Slavic, East European and Eurasian Studies foundered in scandal after many association members objected to being associated with Cohen's divisive politics. At the time, *The New York Times* noted that "his largesse and his divisive reputation have collided, opening a rift in the main scholarly association covering the post-Soviet world and spurring charges that the polarizing politics of the Ukraine crisis are stifling free speech and compromising the group's scholarly mission".

In every instance Cohen would blame America "first, second, third and last," a member of the Council on Foreign Relations once told me. Cohen's tempestuous 2000 book *Failed Crusade: America and the Tragedy of Post-Communist Russia* blamed the stilted Russian democratic transition process almost entirely on the malign advice of the American advisors, journalists and diplomats whom he judged to have led Russia astray. No one familiar with what transpired in Russia during the 1990s would argue that the advice was always good. Yet the over-determined judgment and intense castigation of American policymakers characteristically denied all agency to the Russians, who, let us face it, did not need American assistance to make a total mess of an already catastrophic situation.

The Russian transition to liberal democracy likely would not have taken place in any different manner even if not a single third-rate American expatriate had arrived to find his fortune in Moscow. The chaotic and criminality-inflected transition process that followed the total collapse of societal values was no more likely to have produced Swedish-style governance than the Bolshevik revolution was to have produced Communism and universal brotherly love, if only Bukharin could have outwitted Stalin. The pitch of Cohen's rage was not entirely fair or well directed, but it was very much born of honest disappointment.

Habitually visiting the Soviet Union during its twilight years, Cohen cultivated strategically close ties amongst the nomenklatura and the intelligentsia. Spending time with the dissidents, he quite understandably came to love them. This was understandable. No one – especially no feisty Jewish-American lefty – who had spent his life emotionally immersed in Russian history while drinking with Russian intellectuals in their grubby perestroika kitchens could have avoided absorbing some of our more glorious and nasty character traits. Still, many of the Russian dissidents whom he had cultivated and came to love in the '80s (such as Solzhenitsyn), went on to disappoint him with their embrace of embarrassingly conservative nationalist politics.

The children of the Russian emigrés whom he had helped emigrate to America have universally spoken to me in warm tones of his personal decency to them. "Young Russians were about the only people that he was nice to," an academic who knew him quipped. The only time that I personally interacted with Cohen fifteen years ago was at the New York City retirement party of *The Nation*'s legendary editor Victor Navasky. Cohen was affable enough and remained deeply enthused in defending Bukharin's legacy to a young Russian. Re-reading the volumes that Cohen later published of his deeply sympathetic conversations with dissidents and Gulag survivors, I almost forgave him his endless depredations against my beloved Ukraine.

By the end of his life, Cohen was reduced to publishing collections of his increasingly crankish pro-Kremlin apologias and incidental polemics with ever more obscure publishers. He also continually claimed that "no Russian attack had occurred on America during the 2016 election". That was not strictly true but it did have the salutary effect of coinciding with his emotional commitments as well as his deep need to see America as the responsible actor in every conflict.

Despite being totally outside of the mainstream on most political questions in his worldview, he clearly understood what large swathes of ostensibly professional American journalists did not. The short-sighted, histrionic and often desperate attempts to tie Moscow to a Trump conspiracy that largely did not exist did far more damage to American institutions than they did to either Trump or Moscow. They also constituted an existential threat to the credibility of American media. Cohen was a prophet of its decline, and he stamped the anti-imperialist left with his views. Somewhere in either heaven or hell Cohen, Trotsky and Bukharin are spending the rest of eternity arguing in a musty kitchen over the meaning of socialism and the Russian way.

The Critic 2020

A Clown's Funeral

When I first heard that the deeply beloved, Odessa-born Soviet satirist Mikhail Zhvanetsky had died at the age of 86, I inadvertently thought back to his earnest explanation for the reason that he chose to write. "What did I need to write for?" the diminutive everyman comedian pantomimed, "well, I was short, fat, bald, and ugly, but as a composer I knew once told me, 'I just have to get her to walk over to the piano.'"

It is true that Zhvanetsky was short, bald, and fat, but he was far from badly formed. With his rounded shoulders, gregarious smile, and aquiline nose, Zhvanetsky looked like a Soviet Wallace Shawn with a touch of late perestroika-period Seinfeld.

During the 1980s and into Gorbachev's reign, the jowly Jewish mechanical engineer from Odessa was arguably the most famous comic in the Soviet Union. Almost 300 million Soviet citizens could recite his routines. His well-turned aphoristic phrases entered the lexicon of everyday Russian speech throughout the Union from Arkhangelsk to Ashgabat and from Tbilisi to Tomsk.

The persona of the cheerful Jewish everyman from Odessa who dealt with the unceasing privations and ritual humiliations of quotidian life in the worker's paradise with a laugh and a shrug and a good anecdote did a great deal to disenchant swaths of the population with the regime, though he was not a hero or any sort of dissident and his humor was surely tolerated by the party. He was a man who had to get by, but who hummed along with the party's tune in a passive, resisting manner.

Born in the early '30s, and first having studied to be an engineer, Zhvanetsky did not achieve renown in his vocation as humorist until his 40s. It was while working fixing cranes in the Odessa port that he met his future collaborators Viktor Ilchenko and Roman Kartsev, with whom he founded a comic trio. For a long time before he started a solo career, he toiled in writer's rooms giving his best material to more famous comedians. Eventually, the comic trio moved to Leningrad under the patronage of the Soviet comedian Arkady Raikin, to write his jokes and monologues for him.

It took Zhvanetsky many years of channeling dogged self-effacement before he emerged as a comic frontman. He excelled as an exacting phrase-maker and a witty aphorist and he composed books of his collected stand-up material.

Zhvanetsky's wry Odessan humor was totally, categorically, and thoroughly Jewish in cast and tone, and he played up being a Jewish funnyman to Soviet audiences with a self-referential wink. The American writer and translator Boris Dralyuk, himself a native of Odessa, is incontrovertibly correct in describing Zhvanetsky as a "kitchen-table existentialist" as well as "Odessa incarnate, and no one since Babel was a purer product of the city, a purer expression of its sardonic yet sentimental, warm yet pugnacious character." The one time that I met him at the glammed-up after-party of a film festival, he kept teasing me about my obviously Jewish surname.

Basing one's legacy on scabrous routines about ordinary Soviet stoicism in the face of privation and ritual humiliation was always a losing bet — a fact that Zhvanetsky understood well. The jokes for which he was famous were very much contingent upon a specific time and place, and after the dissolution of the Soviet Union those concerns became of merely historical interest.

Yet Zhvanetsky yearned during his later years to be taken seriously as a contributor to the great Russian literary canon. He went on to befriend and socialize with some of the most renowned Russian literary authors of his time, and he not so secretly measured his jovial and popular work against their highbrow productions. Obviously, such a comparison could only end with disappointment, and his late-period work turned more and more to philosophical ruminations, a great deal of which were quite charming and poignant and showcased his distinctive timing and wit. Whether the comedian's thoughts on the meaning of life, women and men, and aging will in fact be read by Russian readers in half a century's time is an open question, though.

I myself was born during perestroika in the mid-1980s, so I am far too young to have experienced Zhvanetsky in his prime. My own affection for his work is rooted in a sentimental affection for the cultural references of my parents' generation. Those in my own generation who got the humor and the references did so ironically, and because he had entered city history and lore. When I lived in Odessa he was mostly treated by the city as a living statue.

When I attended a packed hall performance of his greatest hits in Odessa four years ago, Zhvanetsky was already in his early 80s. There were many young families there as well as numerous young people, but the audience was very much living out the later stages of its life. In fact, one member of the audience had a heart attack in the middle of the second act. Several dozen doctors present in the audience sprung out of their seats to attend to him.

As any professional stand-up man would in that situation, Zhvanetsky looked up from his sheath of joke material and quizzically inquired of the audience, "what, are my jokes so bad, are they bombing tonight? I promise that this usually does not happen."

It should be said that Zhvanetsky was conspicuous among his late Soviet peers in not having fallen into the trap of what Russians refer to as "ruining his obituary"—a reference to an oblique adage about an honorable individual who behaved badly and compromised himself in an unseemly matter with the authorities in old age after having lived an otherwise blameless and even heroic life. Zhvanetsky was indeed embraced by the regime in his old age, as were many others who had been even more rebellious against Soviet authorities. He even amiably accepted a prize directly from Putin's hands in the wake of the commencement of Russia's war with Ukraine. In his 80s and buffered by a lifetime of acclaim, there really would have been no political penalty for not having accepted the accolade. Yet he did so, going along with the show in Putin's Russia just as he did in Brezhnev's Soviet Union.

But it should also be noted that the comedian demurred from signing on to any of the truly noxious jingoistic public letters that some of his peers signed on to in the overheated atmospherics of 2015. As a result, he was to the very end beloved in Ukraine no less than he was in Russia.

Ukrainian President and former comic actor Volodymyr Zelensky doffed his cap to him as a master fellow performer: "His satire became wisdom for many of us."

Zhvanestsky remained committed to the craft of the professional funnyman to the very end. He even went beyond the call of duty by working the room into the afterlife. A suitably comical situation ensued after the state funeral, which took place in Moscow's grand Novodevichy Cemetery, where the comic joined his fellow Russian ironists Gogol and Chekov in a ceremony attended by the Russian minister of culture as well as the preternaturally scandalous Russian pop star Alla Pugacheva.

As soon as the ceremony concluded, Russian social media networks erupted with scandalized shock at the picture of the grave broadcast from inside the cemetery, which seemed to depict an Orthodox cross having been erected over Zhvanetsky's grave. However, upon closer observation it emerged that this was in fact the product of an optical illusion: The cross was protruding from the grave located directly behind that of Zhvanetsky's neighbor, the Russian Jewish actress Galina Volchek. This was *finita la commedia* for the Russian Jewish entertainer's dream of appearing to go along with a crowd while retaining his own irreducible essence by cracking wise.

Tablet Magazine 2020

Swaggering Gangster Mayor Hennadiy Kernes, Reluctant Savior of Kharkiv, Is Felled by COVID-19

The mayor of Ukraine's second-largest city of Kharkiv, the charismatic politician and gangster Hennadiy Kernes, has succumbed to COVID-19 at the age of 61. Known for his weightlifting and trash-talking, the gangster mayor was an intense and canny political survivor who had found himself starting out on the wrong side of two Ukrainian political revolutions, both of which he somehow managed to survive politically. A diminutive, physically brave wise-guy hoodlum, he enjoyed posting pictures of his jacked up pecs on Instagram (*The New York Times* referred to it as "eccentric," which is an estimable accomplishment) and possessed a wondrously handsome schnoz straight out of a late 19th-century anti-Semitic newspaper caricature.

A masterful regional politician, Kernes excelled at the arts of political skulduggery while also being renowned across the Russian-speaking world for his hilarious and untranslatable expletive-fueled tirades. Kernes will also be remembered for having been strong-armed into keeping the region of Kharkiv from falling to Russian-led separatist forces in the spring of 2014.

The government of Petro Poroshenko had leveraged its control over Kernes by having him put on simmering trial, over the course of several years, on charges related to his alleged kidnapping, torture, and death threats against local activists of the Euromaidan Revolution. The case would be unceremoniously and unexpectedly closed by the government last summer, without a verdict being delivered, in advance of last fall's local elections.

As the transactional mayor of a city 20 miles from the Russian border, Kernes had openly flirted with separatism when Ukraine was first invaded in 2014. He supported President Victor Yanukovych's Party of Regions, and was deeply tied to Russia through his personal business relations. The city he led, Kharkiv, was central to the Russian project of carving up Ukraine and establishing an economically and politically viable "Novorossiya" Russian proxy state.

Yet, the Russians had in fact badly miscalculated the level of resistance that would arise against the sort of deniable tactics that had succeeded flawlessly in the takeover of Crimea. As a result, the geography of Europe and the very course of 21st-century European history would be decided partly in Kharkiv between late February and mid-April 2014.

On Feb. 22, 2014, the day after President Yanukovych fled Kyiv, a conference of separatist and Russian delegates gathered in Kharkiv from all across Eastern and Southern Ukraine. Kernes was at that time a central figure in the Russophone Party of Regions, and was known to have sympathies with the pro-Russian separatists after already having switched sides twice during the previous Orange Revolution. Wearing the ribbon of St. George on his lapel (the World War II symbol has since been adapted by pro-Russian and separatist forces), Kernes delivered a speech in which he surprised the gathered attendees by hedging his bets and calling for Ukrainian national sovereignty to be respected.

It is likely that almost no one in the audience or back in Kyiv believed him. More ardent men stood up and gave revolutionary speeches, and the city soon degenerated into weeks of demonstrations and counterdemonstrations between loyalists of Kyiv and Moscow. The Russian flag was soon hoisted over the regional state administration building after it was stormed by locals and Russian men who had arrived by bus from Russia.

By the first week of April, the Ukrainian government prudently sent in units of patriotically minded commandos from Kyiv to retake the regional state administration building from the men huddled inside of it with guns. The Russian flag was swiftly pulled down, and by the middle of April the Ukrainian state had more or less regained control of the city center. The Russian takeover plan had taken too long to unfurl and had effectively been neutralized. Kernes was now once again in favor of national territorial sovereignty.

The mayor's transparently transactional decision—eventually taken under duress from Kyiv—to throw his lot in with the post-revolutionary Maidan government cemented the fact that Kharkiv (which is, after all, the most Russified city in Ukraine) would remain Ukrainian territory. Kernes quickly reached an accommodation with the new authorities, and somehow reinvented himself as a critical but loyal pillar of Ukrainian statehood. This may very well be the reason that one of his numerous enemies first ordered a hit on him.

On April 28, just as the war in the East began escalating, Kernes was out for his morning jog when an assassin caught up with him and put a pair of well-placed sniper rifle shots into his back. To this day the identity of the attempted assassin and his paymaster remain unknown—though many speculate that the hit was ordered by Russia and its allies as retribution for his having changed sides.

Israeli doctors saved Kernes life, but his health was ruined and his slow decline after the shooting was inexorable. He had by that time occupied the main hotel in the city, which resembled an armed bunker, and lived there mostly alone, with the exception of his 27 dogs and numerous birds. My colleagues who had interviewed him over the last several years described a formerly vigorous man who was now wheelchair-bound, his once-powerful body atrophied and bloated from the secondary effects of the attempted killing.

The flamboyant mayor was so beloved by the residents of Kharkiv that he cruised to reelection in October with more than 60% of the vote despite having disappeared from view for treatment for what turned out to be a terminal case of COVID, which he appears to have caught at a massive public rally back in August. In fact, he had been gone from public view for so long after having been reelected to City Hall that his political opponents had triggered a police search for him. It had been reported that his kidneys had ceased functioning a week before his death and that he had been placed on dialysis. Rumors of his death may have been greatly exaggerated for months, but in the end they turned out to be true.

Kernes' "simple straightforward man of the people" populist act occluded the animal political cunning that had been finely honed in the waning days of the Soviet Union. These talents naturally come in handy during the period of extreme violence that descended over Eastern Ukraine in the early '90s. Kernes sprang from a very modest family and was naturally canny rather than educated, and he was often seen in the leather jackets favored by authentic tough guys.

Kharkiv was a hub of late Soviet criminality under the slow motion dilapidation of the Brezhnev era. While Kernes had worked as a watch repairman and milk delivery man for a time, rumors of his youthful start indicate that he had once been a street criminal who specialized in three-card monte. As Perestroika commenced in the mid-'80s Kernes was sentenced to several years of imprisonment for petty larceny and fraud. It is a time in his life that he preferred not to speak about later.

Before the seat of power was moved to Kyiv, Kharkiv had been the original capital of the Soviet Socialist Republic of Ukraine. The city retains its independent cultural identity and deep sense of self. Citizens of the city are proud of its highly intellectual character and cultural achievements from Soviet modernism onward. No less than rambunctious Odessa, it is also very much a city characterized by trade as well as inventive and flamboyant criminality.

Shimon Briman, an Israeli journalist and historian as well as a native of Kharkiv, explained to Tablet that "Kernes personified the spirit and style of Kharkiv — which is why he was so incredibly popular in the city. Kharkiv has a very specific mentality — it is deeply mercantile as well as being stolidly artistic and remains proud of being the 'first' capital of the Ukrainian Soviet Republic. Kernes bridged that divide between the mores of the city intelligentsia elite and its extensive semi-criminal business underground." The organizing living principle of the city being "live and let live."

Indeed, Kernes possessed an undeniable and authentic emotional connection to his city even as he robbed it blind. He was an adequate steward of city interests, but possessed no particular grand vision for its long-term development. Briman recalled having numerous conversations with Kharkovites of all different social classes who would tell him that, "Yes, of course we know that he is a criminal and that he steals, but he also does good for the city which he surely loves." Such was the ethos of the town, and in some quarters Kernes was downright worshipped: A visiting American professor of Ukrainian studies wrote that, in early 2014, he observed an old Kharkovite woman of Russian sympathies haranguing a pro-Maidan Ukrainian supporter with the induction to "pray for the soul of Hennadiy Adolfovich. It is because of him that you have warm water and electricity!"

Along with his friend, Kharkiv-born Russian-Ukrainian billionaire developer Pavel Fuks, who became a prime character in "UkraineGate," Kernes soon became embroiled in the scandals surrounding a certain Italian-American politician who had first made his name prosecuting New York gangsters. A business partner of former New York City Mayor Rudolph Giuliani, Fuks brought Giuliani along to a comical 2017 junket in Kharkiv, and the city soon began funneling what were likely outrageous fees to provide farcical "Cyber Security consulting" to Giuliani's own consulting firm.

When Kernes eventually rose to the mayor's office after having first chaired the city council, he became known for his florid put-downs of his political enemies. One French journalist who interviewed him reported that in the midst of intense questioning Kernes retorted that, "If monsieur journalist is so smart, why is monsieur journalist so poor?"

The citizenry of the city loved his ritual theatrical emasculation of members of the city council, which were broadcast live and insured his continual reelection. "You son of a bitch, I will multiply you by zero!" he once memorably yelled at an inept bureaucrat. On another occasion, a city councilwoman stood up to him in a public argument regarding a permit issue. Kernes stared at her with patient contempt and softly demanded to know if she could bake a carrot cake. Many of those aphorisms entered the argot of the local folk culture, even if admittedly, they consisted mostly of physical threats.

It is thus deeply appropriate that the last great peacocking conflict of a picturesque life spent in both petty and grandiose conflicts literally involved peacocks. Over the past five years, all of Kharkiv had become entranced with Kernes' feud with another of the city's favorite sons, the Jewish businessman, philanthropist, and parliamentarian Alexander Feldman. The businessman had spent years building his own private tropical zoo in a compound that he owned on the outskirts of the city center. Feldman had filled it with exotic animals and named it "Ecopark Feldman." Naturally everyone loved it.

Enraged at the newly won social renown of his competitor, Kernes proceeded to empty out the city budget of numerous departments in order to funnel the resources into a competing project in the guise of a grandiose reconstruction and refurbishment of the old zoo in the city center. It would be bigger than Feldman's zoo, and would have rarer animals and one would not have to take the city tram to see it.

While Feldman spent his own fortune to build his zoo, Kernes characteristically chose for the city's sidewalks to go unrepaired and the buildings to forgo being repainted in order to build his own nature park with the people's money. It would all be worth it to deny Feldman his glory. Sadly, COVID snatched away his great victory. Kernes did not live to see the day that his grand and beautifully embezzled new zoo would be inaugurated to a grateful public.

Kernes will no doubt be remembered as a swaggering city legend. The scholar Briman added that the entire city of Kharkiv was deeply thrilled by the feud between the mayor and the oligarch. The citizens of Kharkiv were so proud of the zoological competition between the two that they began to say that "typically men compete by measuring their dicks, but here in Kharkiv our Jews compete by measuring their ducks!"

Tablet Magazine 2020

Unravelling the Myth of George Soros

This essay is a reaction to Emily Tamkin's "The Influence of Soros" which was a lucid, subtle and fair-minded attempt to grapple with the tremendously contradictory legacy of the international financier. The Soros conspiracy theories that had circulated the world over were injected into the intellectual life of Ukraine around the autumn of 2018. They were injected into the national conversation by pro-Russian television stations owned by pro-Russian politician Victor Medvechuk, and curiously arrived in Ukraine long after they had become common in other parts of Eastern Europe such as Poland, Hungary and Slovakia.

Late one night, after attending one of those innumerable democratization conferences, I found myself in a run-down bar in an Eastern European capital along with a group of local intellectuals.

The drinking game we played that night was to replace a supernatural figure in an epic poem with that of a contemporary individual. My own contribution to the evening's festivities was to recite Allen Ginsberg's "Howl" – that seminal *cri du coeur* of late-night soul searching – while replacing every mention of "Moloch" with "George Soros". The experiment turned out shockingly well:

"Soros! Soros! Nightmare of Soros! Soros the loveless! Mental Soros! Soros the heavy judger of men!

Soros the incomprehensible prison!

Soros the crossbone soulless jailhouse and Congress of sorrows!

Soros whose buildings are judgment! Soros the vast stone of war! Soros the stunned governments!

Soros whose mind is pure machinery!

Soros whose blood is running money! Soros whose fingers are ten armies!

Soros whose breast is a cannibal dynamo! Soros whose ear is a smoking tomb!"

This seemed like a fitting substitution, as the name of the legendary financier has become synonymous in some circles with that of the evil bronze demi-god who demands a steady stream of human sacrifice to appease his infinite lust for power. While some view Soros as a saintly philanthropist who has done a world of good in his efforts to democratize his native Eastern Europe, others see him as the avatar incarnate of a monstrous conspiracy to subvert democratic popular will through financial and political manipulation.

This begs the question: what sort of creature is Soros really? A new biography penned by Emily Tamkin, the talented US editor at *New Statesman*, attempts to sift the facts from the miasma of intrigue.

The book's title, *The Influence of Soros,* announces its intention to avoid a chronologically thorough biography of the financier in favor of a ruminative investigation of his imprint upon our world.

Structured in nine thematic chapters, this is a book about the myriad contradictions inherent in a man widely considered to be one of the greatest and most brazen investors of the post-war order – Soros founded a revolutionary hedge fund in the late 60s – and the ways in which he has invested and distributed his wealth.

However, this is also a book about the transition from communism to democracy undertaken by the nations of Central Europe and the western Balkans; a transition which Soros nudged along with often contradictory results. It is also a contribution to the history of ideas proper – the ideal of the "The Open Society" to which Soros consecrated his foundation was one that Soros imbibed from his teacher at the London School of Economics: the philosopher Karl Popper.

Tamkin has previously reported on the relationship between Soros and the brimming tide of nationalism currently cresting across Eastern Europe. Her narrative is nimble in expositing the complex historical events of a century ago that led to Hungarian Jewry being blamed for the punitive judgements imposed upon the Hungarians by the Treaty of Trianon. That unfair castigation and demonization – not substantively different from the opprobrium heaped upon Soros today in his native Budapest – concluded with Hungarian Jews being denuded of their secure status as loyal Hungarian citizens. These were the events that set the stage for the nationalist Hungarian repression of the Jews and which likely contributed to lifelong psychic trauma for the young George Soros.

In 1944, when Hitler suspected his Hungarian allies of disloyalty, the Nazis invaded the country and thirteen-year-old George was forced to go into hiding under false identity papers scrounged up by his father. This formative experience would lay at the center of his political philosophy and would spurn his attempts to better the world. It would also prepare him to correctly predict the post-communist national turn that would sweep across Eastern Europe.

Soros engaged with specific regions after forging relationships with interesting individuals that he met and established networks based on those individuals' connections. He identified future leaders very well and empowered them. This approach, however, lent his project a certain cliquey quality which froze some people out and created a caste of outsiders who would come to resent his largesse. The effects of the philanthropic efforts have often been radically unpredictable – with the primary case of unintended consequences being that of his great enemy and former grantee Hungarian Prime Minister Viktor Orbán.

Tamkin is alternatively admiring and critical of the manner in which Soros had structured his foundation and revolutionized the practices of the philanthropic world. The book returns continually to the paradoxical gap between the brazen wagering with which Soros acquired his wealth and the unpredictable political and civic consequences of the ways in which he has distributed it.

Though Soros stipulated a policy of never being directly involved in doing business in the countries where his foundation operated, he continued to engage in finance long after branching out into philanthropy. The Hungarian arm of the Soros Foundation purchased photocopier machines for dissidents and institutions, thus gifting them with (a pre-internet) means of communication.

Resistance to his efforts from the Eastern European governments whom he wished to assist began almost immediately upon his arrival in the region. However, the usefulness of his foundations would not be replicated by anyone else, either in government or in the philanthropic world. No second Marshall Plan to help transition Eastern Europe through a generation of pain was ever forthcoming.

The chapter on the relationship between Soros and American President George W. Bush, against whose re-election Soros intervened massively in 2004, demonstrates the fashion in which Soros undercut his own criticism of the prevalence of "big money" in politics when it suited his whims. His private war against Bush, whom he saw as a unique and world historical evil was another example of his failures. In retrospect, that judgment was naive, histrionic and played a role in the American polarization that has brought us the election of Donald Trump in 2016. Other missteps include Soros having to pull his foundation out in frustration from '80s China and apartheid-era South Africa, though few examples rise to the hubris level of his having proffered a study grant to the young Orbán.

Another thing the book makes clear is that Soros conspiracy theories are not unique to the Twitter age. They began to circulate at the very same moment that Soros first commenced his philanthropy in Eastern Europe three and a half decades ago. This account also tells us that conspiracies grew tall at least partly because of the opaque manner in which the Soros Foundation operated in its earliest days. Criticism of the Soros influence in politics should not be out of bounds, but getting it right without lapsing into bigotry has proven all too difficult for many people.

"Every time that Soros starts to sound like a puppeteer, the conversation crosses over into conspiracy theory territory," Tamkin recently explained to an audience during an Atlantic Council event. The litmus test that Tamkin posits for doing so is one of "agency," as in criticism that keeps track of the difference between an individual and a faceless globalist conspiracy.

Soros has also been heavily criticized within the Jewish world for his relationship (or lack thereof) to Jewish causes and the state of Israel, a continuation of the eternal argument between Hellenistic "universalist Jews" and Hebraic "Jewish" Jews. Ironically, one of the world's most cynical expositors of Soros conspiracy theories is Israeli prime minister Netenyahu.

The book does have selective gaps – it would have been a useful contribution to learn more about the efforts of the Open Society in places such as Myanmar. The characteristic fairness of tone also occasionally leads to judgments that feel too light. The failures of Soros are intimately tied up with the broader failures of Western democratization practices, which the book mostly ignores.

Still, *The Influence of Soros* is a lucid, subtle and fair-minded attempt to grapple with a tremendously complex legacy. Ultimately, Soros lives up to his elusive reputation, the introduction relating the lengthy negotiations for an interview, in which Soros finally granted only epistolary responses to select questions. One might legitimately wonder, outside of the myth, does Soros the man even walk the earth in our reality?

One of the pieces that I am most proud of commissioning and publishing as an editor was an updated, modern version of *Flaubert's Dictionary of Received Ideas* from the excellent American tech writer and memoirist David Auerbach. The entry for "George Soros" reads: "The greatest trick that he ever pulled was convincing conservatives he existed."

The Critic 2020

IX. Conversations

A Conversation with Former United States Ambassador To Ukraine Steven Pifer

"The Eagle and the Trident" was the long awaited memoir of Steven Pifer, the third American ambassador to Ukraine. He was appointed to the position by Bill Clinton in 1998 and served until 2000. From 2001 to 2004, he was a Deputy Assistant Secretary of State in the Bureau of European and Eurasian Affairs, with responsibility for Russia and Ukraine. This volume of diplomatic history constitutes an insider's account of the relationship between the United States and post-Soviet Ukraine. It is also the first comprehensive description of diplomatic relations in the period covering the years 1992 -2004. The book was written using notes that Pifer made while in office and which he had to consult in the State Department archive. The conversation with the former ambassador took place in a Starbucks in McLean, Virginia outside of Washington D.C in late 2017.

Vladislav Davidzon: Tell us a little bit about the genesis of the book. Is this a traditional diplomatic history? And what is it that distinguishes this account from other such accounts?
Steven Pifer (SP): From 1993-2004 I worked on Ukraine at the State Department, at the National Security Council (NSC), the Embassy in Kyiv and then again at the State Department. It was about three years after I retired from government service when I began to think back and realized that there is actually kind of an interesting diplomatic history to tell about how the U.S. engaged with Ukraine, and what worked and what didn't work. So I went down to the Clinton Presidential Library in Little Rock, Arkansas, where it turns out 3 stories underground they have the classified NSC files. I was able to get access to my records, make some notes, which were then declassified.

VD: So you took notes on your own notes?

SP: Yeah, they wouldn't just release my notes, so I took notes on my notes. Then the new notes were declassified. Likewise, I had access to my ambassadorial records and some other things. So then I had a pretty good written record covering that period, and I used that as the basis for the book. In those cases where there were gaps, I would interview people, or I would also reach out to people and say, "Can you look at this chapter? I was in Ukraine, you were working the issue in Washington, what things did I miss?" So I think it's a fairly accurate history. One thing I did that was kind of fun in six of the chapters was that I had a section called "Reflections," in which I would think back on what worked and what didn't work. So for example, when I talked about the removal of nuclear weapons from Ukraine, looking back on it, I think the United States put too much attention on the nuclear weapons issue at the beginning, and we failed to give Kyiv confidence that there would be a relationship once the nuclear weapons were gone. Ukraine became more ready to do the deal on nuclear weapons probably in October-November 1993, in part, because Secretary of State Warren Christopher came to Kyiv and talked about other things; he talked about the economics of the relationship, Ukraine's place in Europe. Things like that.

VD: So, the nuclear weapons issue is resolved and you come in as ambassador in January of '98. This is right before the elections. Right when the second democratically elected Ukrainian president shows up.

SP: A year and a half before the presidential elections, yes. So, the issues that were big when I got there in early 1998, we were still working on Ukraine to align policies on non-proliferation. Which we did in early 1998, and that opened up things. For example, when Ukraine pulled out of the Bushehr nuclear power project in Iran, that allowed us to sign a civil nuclear cooperation agreement with Ukraine, and among other things Ukraine now can buy nuclear fuel from Westinghouse. The United States government spent about 70-80 million dollars to qualify Westinghouse to provide the required fuel for Ukrainian reactors. Other issues that came up in that period. Well, we had a difficult question for Ukraine, which was less than 2 years after Kuchma had gone to Madrid and signed the Charter on a Distinctive Partnership with NATO. To his dismay, he found NATO bombing Serbia. We spent a lot of time on that issue, trying to explain why NATO was doing this. And it was particularly awkward for President Kuchma, because a month after that began, he was supposed to go to Washington for a NATO-Ukraine summit, which he did, but he got some political heat at home for doing that. And then we had the presidential election in 1999. The way I would describe the presidential election was, it was not bad by post-Soviet standards, but that's a pretty low bar, and it fell short of the expectations that we had, primarily because Ukraine talked about its European aspirations and adherence to European and democratic norms. So the dilemma for us was that we saw abuse of administrative resources, with the media being all pro-President Kuchma. We also heard stories that if you were a businessman and you contributed to an opponent of Kuchma, within a week you would be audited by the state tax administration.

VD: It was literally a week? It would literally be that graceless? Three business days and the tax police would be at your door?

SP: This is what we were hearing, yeah. We raised this issue with the foreign ministry and the presidential administration, and got nowhere. And then we had a discussion with Washington saying, should we raise our concerns publicly? And there were two reasons not to do so. One, it wasn't going to change anything. And two, the presidential administration was not going to be happy. But at the end of the day, we at the embassy and Washington concluded that we should raise our objections publicly because democracy had been such a big part of the U.S. vision for Ukraine. So we did speak out publicly. I did so in Kyiv and Deputy Secretary Talbott had a big op-ed interview on the issue, and we made the point. It didn't change anything and the election was still flawed in ways. The presidential administration was not happy with the embassy for some time afterward. But I was struck by the number of times people in the embassy — they were traveling and people would tell them that they noticed that we came out and spoke out for democracy. I think it was the right call.

VD: Alright, so to transition into the chapter called "The Relationship Blossoms," it seems that by the time you get there, you were happier with the relationship and things were going in a more productive

direction. Those were very difficult early years it should be remembered. At one point IMF economists wondered publicly why the Ukrainians hadn't all starved to death.

SP: The years 1995-1998 were probably the high point of U.S.-Ukraine relations. The nuclear issue was solved. Bill Clinton goes to Kyiv in May 1995 for the post-nuclear summit. And in his briefing book, which is an inch thick, he has one talking point on nuclear weapons — it just says, express gratitude. But we and the Ukrainians began talking about other things: Ukraine's place in Europe, economic relations, U.S. assistance programs. In 1996 you have the declaration of the strategic partnership and the establishment of the Gore-Kuchma commission. So once a year the vice president's going to meet with Kuchma, and those issues that could not be resolved at the working level got kicked up to the political level for resolution. And so you've got a lot of high-level contacts. Kuchma came to the United States four times in 1997 alone. You have assistance in the second half of the 1990's so that Ukraine ranks number four in terms of assistance globally from the United States. It's things like democracy promotion, economic reform. I'm not going to argue that we used the reform dollars wisely in every case, but there was that effort. There was also money coming to Ukraine to help Ukraine eliminate the nuclear bombers and missiles and infrastructure so that Ukraine didn't have to pay for any of that. And then the United States is working with the G7 to help stabilize the sarcophagus over the destroyed reactor number 4 at Chernobyl and to help build a new one.

VD: America did help pay for the new sarcophagus?

SP: Yeah, the G7 bore the brunt of the expenses to build it. And the idea was, if Ukraine wants to build new power plants, they should do that on commercial terms, but in terms of dealing with the legacy of Chernobyl that there should be a major international assistance project. So you have a blossoming of relations bilaterally. Then there was the question of Ukraine's place in Europe, which came up when Borys Tarasiuk came to Washington in the fall of 1994. He saw Deputy Secretary Talbott, and he says, "Look, we see NATO getting ready to enlarge". Tarasiuk expected that in four years we are going to have NATO on our western border. We expect the Russians not to be happy. Where do you Americans see Ukraine in all this? And at that point in time, within the U.S. government we're thinking in terms of a NATO enlargement track, and also NATO-Russia track...hopefully, we could persuade the Russians that NATO would not be a threat and could be a security partner.

VD: There was a moment when it looked like the Russian Federation was not as concerned about it as they are now.

SF: Exactly. Talbott told Tarasuk, he said look, Borys, I don't have a good answer for you right now, but we need to have one. And the answer that was framed in the next couple of years was one that thickened U.S.-Ukraine ties and included asking Europeans to develop ties with Ukraine, but also institutionally we began thinking about a third track for NATO which was a NATO-Ukraine track. And so in the summer of 1997, in Madrid Kuchma and the secretary general of NATO, Javier Solana, they signed the Charter on a Distinctive Partnership which builds those links between NATO and Ukraine. And the idea there is to make Ukraine feel it's got an anchor to the West, that it's not being cast into a no man's land between NATO and the European Union and Russia. So, a lot of success in those 3 years. When I got to Kyiv we had some success but we had some bumps begin to appear. The problematic election and another problem that we had was a small issue, but what could've been big was the business disputes. A small number of American investors who got to Ukraine had disputes. I can't speak of every case because I'm not sure we ever had the full facts, but in most cases it appeared they were taken advantage of by Ukrainian partners or Ukrainian state institutions. And this became a big deal for Congress, because the Congress mandated for two years that the secretary of state had to certify that progress was being made to solve those cases or the Congress was going to cut assistance to Ukraine in half.

VD: And those cases were pushed through and you were successful in helping American investors?

SF: The first time we got a minimum number of cases pushed through, where we could go to the secretary of state and say go ahead and certify it. But we also said to the Ukrainians, you have to be better. In 1999, as I wrote in the book, a day before the State Department made the recommendation, I told State: do not ask the embassy for a recommendation, because our recommendation would've been that we hadn't seen enough progress. And I said, we should certify Ukraine — it was the right thing to do — but the embassy's recommendation would not have been helpful.

VD: So what happens after that in, let us say, 1999? The parliamentary elections happened on your watch?

SP: That was in '98, so early '98. The parliamentary elections happen, the presidential election was in the fall of '99. On the parliamentary elections, we sent in a report terming them "free, fair and ugly". We came to the conclusion that the elections were actually pretty well run. And what to us was the main evidence was there were two parties, one was, I forget the name but it was linked to [Ukrainian prime minister] Pavlo Lazarenko. They just barely crossed the 4% threshold. There was a second party, I think it was called the Agrarian Party that was very much pro-Kuchma, and it came in just below the 4%. It would not have taken a lot of work to put the Agrarian Party above 4%, and knock Lazarenko's party below 4% and so beneath the threshold and so out of the Rada. And the fact that Lazarenko's party won and got seats was to my mind pretty good evidence that it was a free and fair election.

VD: They did not fudge the vote count in that case.

SP: They would not have had to fudge the numbers a lot. To get the pro-Kuchma Agrarian Party in and get the Homrada party out.

VD: I have been an international election monitor in Ukraine and to say that Ukrainian electoral law is flawed would be a great understatement. The system is designed for gerrymandering votes. It is really quite bad.

SP: Whenever the foreign observers would show up, we figured you know, they're not going to violate the rules while we're there. But they would always have 10 or 12 domestic observers. The first thing I would do was to go talk to the domestic observers and say how long have you been here, have you seen any problems? In most cases, the local poll commissions were trying to do the right thing. I remember one case where they had mobile voting and the requirement was that the mobile voting people had to register a week or 3 days in advance. We got there and we asked to see the mobile voting list. We got the typed list and we saw 3 names handwritten at the bottom. So we asked, what's this? And the commissioner said just a minute, and they had this handwritten protocol, they said you know, after we got the list, this guy's wife, this guy's son came in and said my relative is sick, they want to vote, it was after the deadline but in each case we sat down, and the commission debated this for several hours. And then we wrote out this 6-7 page handwritten protocol explaining what we did and we all signed it. So I'm thinking ok, you broke the rules, but they did it with the right intent in mind. I was actually pretty heartened by what I saw.

VD: Ok so things are really great you say between 1995-98, which you see as a high-point of America-Ukraine diplomatic relations, what happens next? Why do things get bad, why do you have a chapter called "And Then Problems Appear".

SR: The beginning of 2000 was actually pretty optimistic, because Victor Yushchenko had been appointed prime minister, and there's an expectation for some radical economic reform. But unfortunately, within a couple of months, Yushchenko and the presidential administration are at odds with each other. So Yushchenko is not getting political support for what he wants to do; there's fighting back and forth, and the reform track goes off the rails...

VD: ... and that process never quite got back on the rails until 2014-2015.

SP: It didn't really take after the Orange Revolution. That was the disappointing thing. September of 2000 was my last full month in Kyiv before I returned home in October. Dan Friedt, who was the senior official at the State Department for Ukraine, came, and he spent 2 days in Ukraine, taking 6 or 7 meetings and all he was doing was saying that the Presidential Administration needs to work to support Yushchenko, and Yushchenko needs to be working with the president. They didn't listen. The problems begin at the end of 2000 with problem number one being the disappearance and eventual murder of journalist Georgiy Gongadze.

VD: The killing of Gongadze was on your watch or right after you left?

SP: I interviewed with him about ten days before he disappeared. And he disappeared about two weeks before I left. One of the last things I did and one of the happiest things that I did before I left was to sign a $25,000 grant from the embassy democracy commission to his media outlet, Ukrainska Pravda.

VD: That was a very good investment.

SP: It was a good investment. It's paid off well in terms of bolstering independent media. In any case, [the next US ambassador Carlos Pascual] tried to find ways to help the Ukrainians with Gongadze, because it was a difficult issue for the United States. One was to ask the FBI for assistance. Also advised the Ukrainians to give a press conference where they should really explain what was going on. And of course Gongadze's body was discovered in the woods and then you have the recordings come out which implicated people very close to Kuchma in his murder and disappearance. That's a problem. In early 2001, [presidential bodyguard] Mykola Melnychenko, who was the source of these recordings, was granted political asylum in the United States. The State Department only got one day's notice. Because asylum requests are handled in a very closed way. They don't talk about people because they don't want to be susceptible to political influence. In 2001, George W. Bush is president. My impression was that the Kuchma government was hoping for a win by Al Gore, because they knew Gore. Gore worked on the Gore-Kuchma commission. They then desperately tried to find ways to have face time with President Bush.

VD: That story sounds familiar [with the outcome of the Clinton-Trump election].

SP: The first big visit from a Bush official to Kyiv was when Condoleezza Rice, the national security advisor, went to Kyiv and I was with her. At the top of her list is the concern that NATO is about ready to deploy a peacekeeping force in Macedonia, at the request of Macedonia, and Ukraine is selling tanks and armored personnel carriers to Macedonia. NATO doesn't want a lot of heavy weapons around if they're going to Macedonia. So the number one request she has is that they please stop this. Kuchma tells her that they will. A month later, his chief of staff in writing confirms to her, "We'll stop this". But the arms continue to flow for another 6-7 months. So in Washington, our reaction was: "wait a minute… they said 'yes,' but it's not stopped". That killed a chance for a Bush-Kuchma meeting in the fall of 2001. This was a frustrating Ukrainian tendency. I spent some time in my first months in Kyiv in 1998 explaining to the Ukrainians, "don't tell me "yes," unless you can deliver".

VD: So they were not willing or able to cease providing weapons to the Macedonians?

SP: It finally stopped in about February 2002. Early 2002 there was another parliamentary election, and the senior official Volodymyr Horbulin comes to Washington and meets with Deputy Secretary of State Armitage. He was told by Armitage "that if this election can be a good election process-wise, we can turn the page and there will be an invitation for President Kuchma to come to the White House this spring". That did not happen. The election was problematic as before. And that was probably an overreach on our part, trying to use an invite to leverage a better election process.

VD: You boxed yourself in.

SP: Yes, we got boxed in. But other times we would set the standard much lower, or at least, the ask would be much lower. And we would get no sense that there was any work in Kyiv to make things happen. The real problem in 2002 was Mr. Melnychenko. Right before the election, his lawyer came to us and said we have a recording in which Kuchma is approving the transfer of 4 Kolchuga air defense systems to Iraq. But this is a time where, under U.N. sanction, American and British fighters are flying over Iraq. And so, the first thing we said, as a command decision was that we are not going to touch this until after the election. Because there was some suspicion, are we going to get pulled into the election? But after the election we agreed. We had Mr. Melnychenko come in, hand over the recording and the recording device. Those get sent over to the FBI forensics lab. I think it was August. They come back in. The FBI people tell us there is nothing on the recording to suggest it was tampered with, and we've had 3 people listen to it and they all conclude this is Kuchma's voice. So, the first thing, we consult with Congress, and there's a lot of nervousness within State that, when Congress hears about this, they're going to cut the assistance money off in a heartbeat. We went out to Ukraine. The Ukrainians denied it and they invited the Americans and British to send a team to Kyiv and said they would prove that this did not happen. Which is an important point for clarification. We never said the transfer happened. Because we didn't know at that point. It was that the transfer had been authorized by Kuchma.

VD: Right, that is indeed the point.

SP: A week or two before the team went I was having lunch with Ambassador Gryshchenko and Deputy Foreign Minister Chaliy. I said it's really hard sometimes to prove a negative, so what's going to be important to me is does the team come back and say they got full cooperation and full transparency. And when the team came back, they said we got fantastic cooperation from the ministry of defense and the ministry of foreign affairs, but not so from the presidential administration and not so from the security service. I believe it was the security service that said they investigated this, it never happened, they prepared an 8 chapter report detailing their work. And our team said fine, give us a copy of the report. They got 3 chapters – 5 chapters were held back. Somebody else said we had a report, so our team asked, "Can we see the report?" No. Somebody else said they had a report but only offered a 2 page excerpt. I talked to one team member, who said, "I didn't think this happened, but when I came back, I thought, maybe it had". And that had consequences. The following month, at the NATO summit in Prague, NATO decides to express displeasure by reducing the NATO-Ukraine event down from a summit to a foreign ministers meeting. Right, and that was aimed at Kuchma. Now what I think happened, I think Kuchma said yes as on the recording, and then thought better of it, you know, within a couple of hours or a couple of days. The U.S military never found the Kolchuga system in Iraq. And had Ukrainians told us in September of 2002, "Look, you know the president sometimes gets a guy out of the office by saying yes when he doesn't mean it". We wish he wouldn't have said yes in the first place, but we understood Kuchma enough to say that this wasn't unusual. But no one said that to us.

VD: But no weapons were actually transferred, this was just nonsense. If no technology was transferred that would have changed the way we reacted to it?

SP: It wouldn't have been a big problem. I had a conversation with Viktor Pinchuk when I was in Kyiv about 2 weeks after the team was there. And he said, "You know how Kuchma is, he says yes a lot of the time, but then he reverses himself". And I said, "Viktor, I think that could've happened. Nobody on the Ukrainian side though told us that happened".

VD: And the American side would have been more understanding of that?

SP: I think so, yeah. We would've wished they said no in the first place, but we would have said Kuchma sometimes does that. So that was a problem – no meeting in 2002. And in 2003-2004 the focus of US policy is can we begin to do things to help shape conditions so that the election in 2004 for Kuchma's successor is free and fair. But the relationship was in pretty difficult straits. The thing that saved the relationship, quite frankly, it was in 2003 when Kuchma agreed to send a couple of battalions of Ukrainian troops to Iraq as part of a stabilization force. In 2004, there was another NATO summit in Istanbul, and the recommendation that went to the secretary of state from the interagency group was that election preparations were going so badly in terms of process, we recommended it not be a NATO-Ukraine summit but another NATO-Ukraine ministerial meeting. Secretary Powell said no, we need Ukraine's help in Iraq, so they kept it at the summit level. You sometimes have competing objectives, and the secretary gets paid the big bucks to make those decisions.

VD: So we're up to the Orange Revolution.

SP: The thing that was interesting to me about the Orange Revolution was, first of all, how quickly there was information out that indicated there were problems in the run-off ballot. And you had very quick reactions both in Washington and in Europe. So when the Central Electoral Commission was considering declaring Yanukovych the winner, Ambassador [John] Herbst in Kyiv is telling the Ukrainians, do not formally declare Yanukovych the winner. That will cause problems. And when they went ahead and did it anyway, the U.S. press guidance was strong but was going to be used by the spokesman. But the secretary said no, I'm going to use it. So the secretary went out and sent a pretty sharp message.

VD: The Secretary of State himself?

SP: Yeah. And an interesting development was the Europeans stepped in the leading mediation role. Javier Solana, who had been the Secretary General of NATO and who was now the high representative for European Union Foreign and Security Policy, and President Kwaśniewski of Poland, they came in with several other Europeans to mediate. The U.S government said, "We're going step back and let the Europeans take the lead". There were several reasons, one was Kwaśniewski and Solana had relationships with Kuchma that nobody in the U.S. government had at the time. Remember, at this time Bush had only met Kuchma once and that was a private off the record meeting.

VD: So the Poles, Kwaśniewski personally, had to intervene and be the point man?

SP: Yeah. He had a pretty well-established relationship with Kuchma as did Solana. I think another reason we let the Europeans take the lead was that, if the United States gets involved, then there was concern that the Russians were going to be nervous. The Russians were probably more comfortable with European mediators than Americans. And the third reason was that this was sort of an issue that Europe ought to be able to deal with. So it was encouraging the Europeans to step up to the plate. But there was still close coordination: daily phone calls between Beth Jones, the assistant secretary, and my successor John Tefft and their European counterparts. They're talking to Brussels, they're talking to Warsaw all the time. Ambassador John Herbst in Kyiv is very active, and there's a huge stream of reporting coming back out of him. When it looked like the Ministry of Interior was going to send force into Kyiv, Herbst was the one who was calling people. He got the secretary to try to call Kuchma. Kuchma wouldn't take the call.

VD: Why?

SP: He wasn't available. John gets on the phone to his son in law Victor Pinchuk and says, "We know he wouldn't want to take the call, but if force is used, that's going to be a really bad turn in things". Then he was called back and assured that force would not be used. At that point, the end of the Orange Revolution, I kind of stop the narrative because I step out of somebody with insider information to someone who's watching from the outside.

VD: Your successors will write the successor volumes?

SP: Yeah, I did have a chapter on 2005 up to the present, because I thought you had to talk about it, buts it's fairly brief. So you have the failure of the Orange Revolution in delivering real reform in Ukraine. Which is really the story of Yushchenko's inability to work with Tymoshenko. One thing I think: Ukraine could have gotten a NATO membership action plan (MAP) in 2006. The Russians hadn't come up on the net against it yet. What happened though was Yanukovych, who was then prime minister, as a result of the deal that was worked out in the summer of 2006. And Yanukovych goes to Brussels to meet with the European Union, stops at NATO and says, by the way, I and my government don't want a membership action plan. And NATO's not going to do a membership action plan when the executive branch in Kyiv is divided. In 2008, when Yushchenko wanted to try again for a MAP and got Tymoshenko to sign off on it as well as Yatsenyuk, the speaker of the parliament. At that point, the Russians were much harder up on the net against it. And the Germans and the French and others were not comfortable going forward with a MAP for Ukraine.

VD: It was too late by that point?

SP: And you know the return of Yanukovych, it was interesting to me, the Yanukovych election in 2010 was seen as a free and fair process, and the U.S government said we're going to give this guy a chance.

VD: President Yushchenko lost that election fair and square.

SP: Yushchenko lost it, and Tymoshenko. I think it's quite remarkable she only lost by a couple of points given that she had been prime minister when the economy crashed and contracted by 18%. But very quickly you begin to see problems with Yanukovych, growing authoritarianism at home, the investigation against Tymoshenko, bad local elections, so the relationship became pretty difficult. The only time that Yanukovych saw Obama was on the margins of the nuclear security summits or the NATO-Ukraine summit, and even when they came to Washington for the 2010 nuclear security summit, people were still a little leery of him. Yanukovych got to see Obama, but he didn't get to the White House.

VD: To zoom out from the micro details, what are the lessons and the overarching themes of your ambassadorship?

SP: Two big lessons that I took away from this after I finished the narrative and looked back at U.S.-Ukraine relations. One was that I think the U.S. government put together the right combination of carrots and sometimes sticks to achieve big foreign policy aims. So, it got the nuclear weapons out of Ukraine in the 1990's. It got Ukraine to align its policy on nuclear and missile proliferation in 1998. It pressed Ukraine to provide troops for Iraq. But it was much less successful in getting Ukraine to pursue the domestic reforms, economic reform, anti-corruption, things like that, that would have made Ukraine move more quickly to realize what I call the American vision for Ukraine. We wrote it back in 1995, one sentence. "We want to see an independent stable democratic Ukrainian state with a robust market economy and growing links to the West. That was written for the Clinton administration, but the Bush and Obama administrations would agree with that. And then the book talks about why we were less successful pushing for reform. And part of it was we had a Ukrainian government where the bureaucratic structure often hindered things; it was hard to get things done. You had a president and a prime minister, and reform was hard to achieve if they were not on the same page. But the big issue was a failure of leadership. For reform to work, you had to have the leadership and a large portion of the elite committed to reform. Because it is going to be painful. A lot of times presidents didn't do things even though they knew that the economic reform made sense economically, but it was going to cause political pain and they were looking at the next election. So the fact that they didn't raise the tariffs to cover heat until 2016 meant every year there was a huge hole in the Ukrainian government budget.

VD: Up to 10% of GDP I've heard at some points.

SP: Yeah I've heard it's anywhere from 6-10%. So I can understand why they didn't do it, because you're hitting every household from the richest to the poorest with a price increase. But it was necessary. But the big problem was corruption, the failure of rule of law, the failure of good governance. Yanukovych was the epitome. He stole what, billions of dollars? The others, I mean Yushchenko, Kuchma and Kravchuk, they weren't nearly as corrupt personally as Yanukovych.

VD: You wouldn't be the first one to say that, but you know this is a structural problem with Ukrainian politics.

SP: Yeah. I would've argued there was an opportunity in 2014 for President [Petro] Poroshenko, who was the first president since Kravchuk in 1991 to win an election in the first round, to have a mandate, to say: Look, the next years are going to be pure hell, we're going to do a lot of reform, it's going to hurt, but we need to build on and to realize the promise of the Revolution of Dignity on the Maidan. I give him credit. They did some major reforms, but they didn't do what they needed to do. Right now Ukraine continues to muddle through. They didn't put the country on a path to success.

And my recommendations are two-fold. One is to be supportive of Ukraine in the conflict with Russia, and that means things like maintaining sanctions and keeping up the pressure on Russia. Because you need to get the Russian government to change its current policy, which seems to be a continuous simmering conflict in Donbas to put pressure on the government in Kyiv and undermine it. Don't forget about Crimea. Donbas has killed 10,000, Crimea hasn't had nearly as many deaths, but Crimea was more destructive to the European security order, because it was taking territory by force. Support NATO allies because allies that are confident will be more supportive of Ukraine. And then caution Ukraine to be realistic about what they can do with NATO and the European Union now. Do practical things, implement agreements, but you're not going to get a NATO membership action plan in the near term.

And then the second part is talking to Ukraine in a tougher way on reform. Basically recognizing that we're asking the Ukrainian political elite to do things they don't want to do. So everything becomes transactional: we'll do this assistance, but you have to do this this and this first. My worry is, if Ukraine doesn't succeed now, if you look at Ukraine historically in 1994 when Kuchma became president, there was a burst of economic reform, and after about a year it dissipated. In 2000, Victor Yushchenko is prime minister, everyone excited there's going to be a burst of reform and then Yushchenko and Kuchma part ways, Kuchma gets nervous about Yushchenko's popularity, so nothing happens. Orange Revolution, here we have Yushchenko as president, Tymoshenko as the prime minister. She was the most effective minister that he had in the cabinet in 2000. One Ukrainian told me, she's the only one in this cabinet who has any balls. But they fail to push hard reform.

VD: For the good and the bad, she may be the Golda Meir of Ukraine.
SP: But now a fourth time there's the Maidan and a burst of expectation and hopes, and if Ukraine then just keeps muddling through, the risk I see

for Ukraine is, you're going to have people in the West, especially in Europe, say, "This country can't be fixed. I've seen the movie before and I know the outcome, so why should we put time and energy into Ukraine when we know it's not going to succeed, and we know it's just going to cause problems with Russia?" And you've got people saying, "Let's get back to business as usual with Moscow." I'm not sure that's a risk that the Ukrainian government understands that it faces.

VD: Extrapolating from that, it sounds like what you think the American diplomatic corps should have done more of over the last 20 years is put more pressure on the Ukrainians. Less ambassador more viceroy?

SP: Not viceroy, but we should have been more transactional early on. We should have pushed harder in the '90's and early 2000's for reform. Had we succeeded, Ukraine might well have been a more resilient state when it came to the crisis of 2014.

A Conversation with Ukrainian Writer Yurii Andrukhovych On Literary Translation And Beat Poetry

Yurii Andrukhovych is perhaps the most renowned prose writer, poet, essayist, and translator in contemporary Ukrainian literature. He was born in the city of Ivano-Frankivsk and first came to prominence after he co-founded the Bu-Ba-Bu poetic group in 1985. He is a fierce defender of Ukraine's democratic path. An early adaptor of post-Modern literary techniques to Ukrainian literature, he has published five novels, four poetry collections, short stories, various volumes of essays, as well as literary translations from English, German, Polish, and Russian. We met in Odessa, in the 2K Dva Karla Bessarabian Bodega — a legendary restaurant now sadly closed — for a long lunch and many glasses of white Bessarabian wine.

Vladislav Davidzon: You are well known as a literary translator. Let's speak about your translations from the German language. I especially adore the work of Robert Walser and I know that you are also a fan.
Yurii Andrukhovych: Well, to say I am a fan may be an exaggeration, but Robert Walser is someone who truly changed European prose in the 20th century. He is in the same class as Kafka or Musil. In terms of the German-speaking world, Walser has not received the recognition that he deserves, and there are many reasons for this, his fate being among them. But I know all of this thanks to the fact that in his homeland of Bern there is a certain "Walser Center," which displayed not only some of the manuscripts but also publications of his work, translations into many languages. Whenever something related to Walser appears, the Center obtains it, and this center initiated a project — because they found few of his works translated into Slavic languages — which is connected with a key work, his short novel (or long story), "The Walk." There are several versions of it, a few editions from different years, but there is one that is considered fundamental, canonical, and the center conceived of a project wherein the texts would be translated into Slavic languages across Eastern Europe, not by translators as such, but rather by well-known writers from from these countries who would be able to become translators and agree

to take part in the project. For instance, the Russian translation was undertaken by Mikhail Shishkin, the famous writer, who now lives in Switzerland. He was at the first festival here in Odessa. In any case, I worked within the coordinates of a certain commission, taken up from Switzerland and elsewhere, and I was very happy to be invited to be involved in the translation, because I discovered an outstanding writer as I began to work on the translation.

VD: And how was the Walser translation received in Ukrainian literary circles? More precisely — do we need Walser in Ukrainian prose today, and did he have some kind of visible impact on Ukrainian prose in the past?

YA: Effect? Well, there was no sensation or bombshell. I can speak about an unanticipated effect upon myself, related to another of my translations and another author — Bruno Schulz, the Polish author. The Walser translation was my next work after Schulz, and, well, there wasn't the kind of impact that there had been with Schulz. Schulz was at the time a widely-read author, and his book sold fairly well, and continues to sell. But Walser, he worked in such narrow literary circles, you might say that he is a delicacy for "gourmets," connoisseurs. So I was very happy to somehow participate in this. He can already be said to have been part of this community in our country as well.

VD: It is interesting that we in Ukraine are entering a kind of, one might say, renaissance of early modernism, and that Ukraine, as a literary culture is absorbing all of those forgotten or obscure authors.

YA: Yes, there was such a phase, but it was either incomplete or resulted in catastrophe, in the 1920's, when all of this happened synchronously...

VD: Along with the West. With Vienna, with Prague.

YA: Precisely. And maybe also Paris, and in this way somehow symbolically in Odessa, through the Odessa film studio, which was called "Hollywood on the Black Sea." The young and creative flocked here, even from the capital, which was then Kharkiv, and from Kyiv, in order to be closer to our own "Hollywood." At the time, filmmaking seemed more interesting than anything in the world; to be engaged in cinematography, to write screenplays was considered more interesting than writing novels.

VD: And more profitable as well.

YA: Yes, yes. And at that time, this was true as well. And this was happening alongside similar processes in Western Europe, but it all ended, as we know, with the Stalinist repressions. That which you are asking about, it now has a hint of anachronism to it — that is to say, we must succeed in mastering what we did not achieve at that moment, what failed to become part of the cultural discourse at the time, but we also need to break new ground.

VD: Of course.

YA: Not simply to switch over to translating Bruno Schulz, Joseph Roth, Walser et cetera, et cetera and nothing more — now we need to advance forward, as well.

VD: Well, this problem is not unique to Ukraine. In the West too, there is a process of remembering the forgotten modernists.

YA: I think that many of these authors came back into fashion, but at first during the Belle Epoch, I mean between the First and Second World Wars. At that time, many interesting things occurred, not just Hitler and Mussolini, but many other things in the Western world, and it seems to me that even...

VD: Writers such as Vita Sackville-West or Wilfred Owen who were mostly forgotten 30 years ago. People in the West are beginning to read them again also.

YA: Yes, I found this to be true when, fairly recently, I taught for one semester in Berlin, at Humboldt University. My task was to deliver a kind of original seminar, a kind of special course, and I focused on a theme that could be described as "contrived poets." That is to say, my students had to invent a poet, complete with the era in which he or she wrote, his or her language, culture, and in the end, ideally, they were to write poetry on behalf of their fictional poet. In my view, the most successful of these projects was created by a German poet, who invented a certain Christian Lodal, who supposedly created German surrealism in the 1920's, being half German and half French. And as for where the student got this idea, it is because in German poetry, surrealism is a niche that has yet to be filled. They had expressionism, yet it was widely believed that surrealism was not possible in the German language, i.e. that it is a purely French phenomenon, maybe Spanish, but that the German language simply does not allow for it. My student set out to invent a poet who established German surrealism because he himself had translated Breton, and was his friend. So he thought of a fictional biography and I must say that he wrote about forty poems on behalf of "Lodal." And if you were to read them, comparing them with the work of their supposed "era," I have a feeling that if such a poet had actually existed, these poems would be in any anthology of 20th century German poetry.

VD: A very talented student, then.

YA: Yes, very talented. He wrote not only on behalf of fictional poets. But my point is this, that at the beginning of the 21st century, there appeared a tendency to return to that which had been confusing or unintelligible to us formerly.

VD: At what stage would you say is the craft of the translator of Western literature in Ukraine, and what kind of specific problems do you see?

YA: Fundamentally, the problem remains that there are many classics and works of modernism which have yet to be translated, because if we were to translate a relatively large number of works, the translations would appear thanks to the fact that cultural institutions financed in these countries — the Goethe Institute, the Austrian Cultural Forum, the Polish Institute, British Council — they accentuate, and I think that this is true, accentuate topical literature, contemporary authors. Yet we should ask why is this so? It is because these authors will come back. You can invite them to appear, they can deliver a presentation in a way that can sell books; it is publicity, it is media appearances on television, et cetera. Ezra Pound won't be making any appearances or doing any more readings.

VD: He is in Venice now, where he's been for a long time. He isn't interested in leaving.

YA: One must be a fan, an expert, everything in the world. Well, I don't know if you know about my project, it is somewhat of a different time, a different kind of poetry, but thanks to the fact that I received a Fulbright grant in 2000, I was able to work on my own anthology of American Poetry, of Beat poetry. But it covered not only the Beat poets, but also others in the '50's and '60's, encompassing nine different authors.

VD: Which poets, exactly?

YA: Gregory Corso, Allen Ginsberg, Gary Snyder, as well as several from the New York School, including Frank O'Hara and some poets from the Black Mountain School. The anthology was released in 2006. It was named after a line in a Frank O'Hara poem — he has a poem about the death of Billie Holliday, "The Day Lady Died," for which I have the interpretation "The Day of Mrs. Day's Death" And this anthology garnered a cult readership, but again, if I did not conduct this research through the Fulbright Program— to study the writing of American poets of those decades— I would not have accomplished this. I needed a year in America in order to get access to all of those publications.

VD: And where did you live?

YA: I was in Pennsylvania, at Penn State. Of course, it would have been preferable to be in New York City or San Francisco. By the way, Lawrence Ferlinghetti is also in my anthology.

VD: And he's still alive, you know; he must be nearly one hundred years old! (Ed: the poet died while this volume was being prepared for publication)

YA: Yes, he and I were in contact. I had wanted to meet him for a long time, and went to San Francisco just to meet him while I was in California.

VD: At the City Lights Book Shop.

YA: Yes, and I started speaking with one of the employees, probably a bookseller, and I said that I am translating the works of Mr. Ferlinghetti, I am working on an anthology and I'd like to speak with him. I sent him emails for several months.

VD: And he didn't answer, naturally.

YA: Not once. And this guy told me, "Well, yes. I understand you perfectly, but you know that he is (at that time) 84 or 85 and he doesn't have the time to answer every email." But that was almost 20 years ago, and he is nevertheless still around. And then I left, but I did actually catch sight of him there. We were simply crossing the street at the same time, passing each other at a red light.

VD: Like a scene from a movie.

YA: Yes, exactly. That is how I encountered Ferlinghetti, though I didn't detain him there on Broadway, when we only had a few moments.

VD: And you didn't introduce yourself?

YA: I decided that it had already happened in the most interesting possible way, exactly as it needed to have happened.

VD: Then you are a true poet. If you were a literary critic, you would have run after him.

YA: I am not a professional translator. At one point I will be translating American poets from the second half of the 20th century, and then Schulz or Walser. In this sense, I am a selective translator. I was in the U.S. in what turned out to be the last few months of Gregory Corso's life. I loved him very much. When I was still in the States with my grant, I read in the news that he had died the night before. I became friends with an American, a friend of mine there, whom I would often consult about American slang…

VD: And who was this?

YA: A local poet from Penn State. I think his name was Jim Brassfield. So, I visit Jim and I tell him, "Look, once again I was unlucky — Corso is no longer alive." He told me, "But you wouldn't have been able to learn anything from him anyway, as he had been in a vegetative state for many years."

VD: He was a heavy drug-user.

YA: Yes. Ah well, such stories. The point being that it was an ambitious project for me in the sense that — this might be interesting to you — I wanted it to be a sort of sabotage in Ukrainian poetry. I wanted to show Ukrainians how dark things can be.

VD: It is fairly conservative, Ukrainian poetry.

YA: Yes, yes. I wanted to present a kind of non-conformist poetic volume in which there is pornography, drugs, hooliganism. And this is the poetry that changed America, meaning it has the power to change a country.

VD: Your anthology is also your subversive statement, your protest.

YA: I don't presume to judge, but it seems to me that many poets of the next generations have started to write in a very relaxed fashion. It's the sense that, "Hey, we can do that too. We are the beatniks of our time." That's something.

I would not explain this by saying that my anthology was released and suddenly everyone's eyes were opened. Simply that it was released at the right moment, when the time was ripe for such a thing.

VD: You were telling me about the 175th anniversary of the great poet Ivan Kotliarevsky before we turned on the tape recorder.

YA: Yes, he was a landowner from Poltava. He became an author, which even he had not expected, the first author in the world, in history, to write a literary work which was released in the contemporary Ukrainian language rather than Church Slavonic. We can even consider him to be a modern author. Although he was writing at the end of the 18th, beginning of the 19th century, you can practically read his work without a dictionary, it is all intelligible. He wrote a great parody, a parody of the Latin epic of Virgil. He rewrote the story of the six parts of the Aeneid. The first three parts were published in St. Petersburg — by plagiarists — without his knowledge, but it was released in 1798, the same year that Pushkin was born.

VD: He was of the older generation.

YA: Yes, yes. So in the middle of the 18th century the "Onegin Verse" was written, this verse can actually be said to be "Kotliarevsky Verse," but I'll speak about it at some point. In general, it is this very funny work, comical, parodying the world of ancient heroes, and transferring them to the soil of late 18th-century Ukraine. The Trojan War becomes the battle of the Zaporizhian Cossacks with the Turks, featuring many realities and artifacts of that time – it becomes, one could say, an encyclopedia of life in that era. It is filled with the names of different dishes, there are dozens of kinds of alcohol: vodka, mead. In general, it is a very bright thing, which would later become baroque, but was already in classical verse. In his life, the author was never a loser in the sense that he didn't succeed in publishing own work. Plagiarists published his work in St. Petersburg, the first three parts of his work, and he died while writing the last three. Only four years after his death was the first edition published, and this year, 175 years later, the complete edition will be published for the first time.

A Conversation With The Odessa Philharmonic Orchestra Conductor Hobart Earle

Hobart Earle has been the Music Director and Principal Conductor of the Odessa Philharmonic Orchestra for as long as independent Ukraine has existed. A cosmopolitan figure from the cradle onward, he was born to an American family and grew up in Venezuela. He was educated in a boarding school in Scotland, before attending Princeton University and concluding his studies in Vienna, Austria. He has led the Orchestra for thirty years, during which he has kept it together as an institution during extraordinary and difficult times. We met for this conversation on the stage of the Odessa Philharmonic, a great monument of Venetian Baroque Revival movement.

Vladislav Davidzon: Thank you for taking the time out of your busy concert schedule to speak with me today, Maestro.

Hobart Earle: Thank you. Absolutely, with pleasure.

VD: You are very much a historically minded conductor, you care about the history of the city, you care about the history of music. You are very much aware of the history of what has been played in the city and in the country and in the Soviet Union before that. What has the Odessa Philharmonic played recently that has never been performed in the city before?

HE: Right now, this week, Arnold Schoenberg's "Five Pieces for Orchestra" and his 1937 version for orchestra of Brahms Op. 25. It's safe to say that over the past year, Sibelius's 4th, 5th and 7th symphonies were most likely Odessa premieres. In general, Sibelius's music was not played very much in the former Soviet Union. If it had been played it would have been played from handwritten parts (because his music was copyrighted and the USSR did not sign any international copyright treaties) and if these parts existed, they'd be here somewhere. Aside from St. Petersburg (Leningrad) and Moscow, Sibelius symphonies really did not get played much, and certainly not in Odessa.

VD: Yes, relations between the Soviet Union and Finland being what they were, he was a symbol of nationalism, and he did live to a ripe old age. His works are still copyrighted, so it seems unlikely.

HE: Yes, he died in 1957. Over the years we've played a lot of pieces that haven't been played here before. But how to determine what has and what has not been played here is an art of its own, sometimes a little bit of guesswork is needed. Edward Elgar is another example of a composer, who for whatever reason, was just not played in the Soviet Union. Maybe the violin or cello concerti from time to time, but not much more. Way back in 1993, when I conducted what was most definitely the Odessa premiere of the "Enigma Variations," to my amazement it wasn't just a premiere, but at the time, the musicians didn't know the piece existed.

VD: Elgar, is not a particularly Soviet taste! But what do you think that you have added to the history of the city, what do you think you have brought here that did not exist here before? It is, after all, a deeply musical city, it has a deeply rich musical history, and has produced world-class musicians for a century.

HE: No question of that, yes. I think we've broadened the repertoire during my tenure. Just last week, we played some Tajik music – all of which would have been Odessa premieres – Tolibkhon Shakhidi and his father Ziyadullo Shakhidi (who founded the Professional Tajik Academic Music) who is considered to be the father figure of Tajik music. We've also done a lot of contemporary music never played here, as well as a great deal of American music.

VD: A remarkable Porgy and Bess which we heard you play a week ago.

HE: Indeed, the symphonic picture from "Porgy and Bess" hasn't been played for at least 30 years by this orchestra, that's for sure, but the older members of the orchestra certainly remember playing it. We did Gershwin's "Concerto in F" way back in 1992. We played a lot of Aaron Copland and also the Ukrainian premiere of Leonard Bernstein's 'Jeremiah Symphony,' but also pieces like Gustav Holst's 'Planets' and various Mahler symphonies. I can't claim to have conducted the Odessa premiere of Mahler's 1st and 5th symphonies, but certainly his 2nd, 3rd, 6th and 9th, yes, those were Odessa premieres. I don't think Mahler's music was played a great deal in the former of Soviet Union outside of Moscow and St. Petersburg. With both Bruckner's 7th and 8th it's highly unlikely they had been played here before.

VD: He had a bad reputation in the Soviet Union for the obvious historical reason of his appropriation by Hitler.

HE: Yes. To come back to your question of what I might have added to the history of the city, there is certainly the geographical component: the list of the world's halls in which the orchestra has played. Carnegie Hall and the Kennedy Center in the United States. Five times in the Musikverein in Vienna. I studied in Vienna and I think everyone who studies in Vienna remains very attached to the city. To perform in the Musikverein is very special for any musician, and the fact that this orchestra has played there five times in the past twenty five years is wonderful. I think we've also managed to create various traditions locally. When I speak of Vienna, and think of Johann Strauss and our new year's concerts (ed: these include usage of toys, mini explosive devices and confetti), these are actually much more sophisticated than they seem. As any Viennese music student knows, it's very easy to play Strauss badly and really hard to play him well! I often try to explain it as follows: it's as if Strauss, in particular the waltzes, are like a kind of "nineteenth century Jazz" – in other words, music that's not played the way it's written. The waltzes are written evenly, but like Jazz, they have a rhythmic lilt to them which is very free. The Viennese have the very unique rhythmic "flow" of this music in their blood, in a way that even the Germans do not. For the Germans – and for everyone else outside the borders of Austria – it's a foreign art form. We have built this tradition over the years and the orchestra has become really quite good at playing these waltzes. The polkas and the marches are much easier because they are in two and four, while the Waltzes are in three. Three is always an uneven element in music.

VD: Your Strauss concerts which I attended were all very popular with Odessans. People really enjoyed them and they really like Strauss as well as the little theatrical twists that you brought in with the firing of the little popguns.

HE: You know, I caught a lot of "flak" for these concerts in my first years here. Strauss's music, being a very specific repertoire, was a vehicle to develop the orchestra's flexibility and sense of ensemble. In the early nineties I was criticized most heavily for these Strauss concerts, and for using these "tricks" you mention. Although these "tricks" have always been part of the New Year's concerts in Vienna, in Odessa when we implemented them in the early 90s, they were considered to be horrendous!

VD: Savagery!

HE: Well, we decided to bite the bullet, and unbeknownst to those criticizing us, with those Strauss concerts we were actually improving the orchestra's sense of ensemble!

VD: That is a very good note, a liminal note to bring us to the question of connoisseurship. After the collapse of the Soviet Union, a great deal of the social capital ebbed away, a lot of people from here moved away. They moved to the West, to Russia, Canada, Israel and Germany. It seems to me that a great deal of the cultural traditions that were passed down from generation to generation dissipated. Much of that spirit of connoisseurship goes all the way back to the nineteenth century.

VD: Yes, there is no question that times change and generations change. I'm not sure one can trace the tradition back from recent Soviet times all the way to the nineteenth century. That is of course a very interesting topic. In Soviet times, Odessa was very much closed off from the outside world. So in effect our sense of history is diluted – even now, the archives for this orchestra go back only to 1936. We don't really know what happened in terms of orchestral music in Odessa before that. Typical situation not only for the Odessa Philharmonic but for many performing arts organizations in the former Soviet Union. The 1930's were the time when many of these institutions were created, or officially "re-organized". For example, the State Orchestra of the USSR, now renamed after [conductor Yevgeny] Svetlanov was created the same year, so was the orchestra in Kyiv, as well as a myriad of other institutions. Of course orchestral traditions existed here in Odessa before 1936, but it's a tough nut to crack – and there's no question each generation breathes its own air and drinks its own water. No question, too, that the emigration from Odessa, beginning in the 1970's, meant there was less of a bridge to older times – and what those older times were before the 1970's becomes guesswork. We don't really have that many recordings – we have recordings of some of the great soloists performing, but almost no recordings of the orchestra here in Odessa. For example, with the Berlin or Vienna Philharmonic you can listen to them in the 30's or 40's, and there is so much more historical material. Here, it's missing. I often make historical connections purely by musical instinct which seem to be controversial at first but then turn out to be true.

VD: Give us an example of that sort of dynamic.

HE: Classic example, I conducted Shostakovich's 5th symphony on this very stage, way back in 1994. At a particular moment during a rehearsal I suddenly stopped, and said to the orchestra: "I'm convinced there's no way he could have written this passage, had he not heard Alban Berg's opera "Wozzeck"! I could just feel the musicians thinking "here he goes again" and "what's he going on about this time? Our foreign friend telling us about Shostakovich and "Wozzeck" ?!?"... The next day the principal cellist came to the rehearsal telling me that he consulted, opened a book and found out that indeed "Wozzeck" had been performed in Leningrad in 1927 and that the young Shostakovich went to all the performances, met Berg, and was very taken by him and his music. My observation was just a gut feeling of musical instinct – neither I nor the musicians knew this fact at the time.

VD: I always ask you about the much heralded Odessa School and the imprint it has left here.

HE: Yes, but you see, what is the Odessa School? If you can find me a definition, or someone who can persuasively explain in words what it was, please let me know.

VD: So maybe it's a spirit?

HE: The thing is if you look at the great musicians from Odessa...

VD: ...they were all born here and left.

HE: Right. But look at David Oistrakh and Nathan Milstein, they are very different violinists. Look at Gilels and Richter: they are completely different pianists. Take Shura Cherkassky, he is different yet again. They are all representatives of Odessa, but they were all very different. That's normal in any city, soloists are very individual. What unites them could well be this sense of "spirit," that word you mention. Odessa, being a port city, this unites them – at least in their character "offstage" – with a certain kind of typical Odessan "joie de vivre".

VD: So there is no technique that unites them all? Nothing that Gilels gave to Richter? No Odessa Stolyarsky musical school magic?

HE: They were all very original. That unites them. A lot of them had their childhood in Moscow and then came to New York City, for example, after studying in Moscow. Cherkassky left very young. Yet the city produced many great musicians, so there is indeed something about the city that was very special. During the time when Stolyarsky was teaching it was very fashionable to play the violin and in every courtyard there were young kids playing the violin.

VD: So what is the difference for you between a city like Vienna and Odessa? You came here as a young man at twenty – nine, given an opportunity to conduct your own orchestra right after the collapse of the Soviet Union. What is the most rewarding part about being the conductor of an orchestra in Odessa rather than say a city like Vienna?

HE: In a city like Vienna there are so many established traditions. If you are a music director, it's harder to create new traditions, or, let's put it this way – it would take more time. Here, over the years, I think we've managed to change a lot.

VD: What were some of the negative, pernicious traditions or issues that came along with the positive legacies of Soviet musical training? Personnel issues? Cohesion issues?

HE: Ironically, the Soviet Union tended to create people who were not always interested in the general good. More often than not, there were the sorts of people who were attuned more to their own personal interests than to the collective good. A classic example here on stage was the war over getting the curtains (which were horrible for acoustics) down in 1996. After the curtains finally came down, it was hard to make the musicians understand that they needed to fight to make sure the curtains stayed down when I was away. It was hard to get them to insist to the bureaucrats who ran the hall that the curtains needed to remain removed when the orchestra was on stage. And the bureaucrats did not want to have to expose the ill-repaired walls hidden behind the curtains on stage. My attitude to that issue was : "don't hide this under the rug – open it up and show the public that the walls need to be repaired".

VD: This is a good moment to transition into your personal crusade over the much needed repair work needed for the hall.

HE: The previous governor, Ihor Palytsia, of his own initiative upon hearing the story from me, said: "Let's get this fixed". Way back in 1996, we had the legendary American acoustician, Russell Johnson, come here to compile a major report on the hall. In that report, Russell wrote that "this concert hall could rival the great European halls" if the proper acoustical repair work and structural changes were made. Some elements of Russell's report have been implemented. The stage was rebuilt, using a single layer of wood, for example (before that, they kept adding layers of wood one on top of another from the 1930's onward, and that was horrible for the acoustics). New seats were installed throughout the hall – this is important because the seat backs need to reflect the sound. In every good hall the back of the seats are made of a hard material, such as wood, that reflects the sound. Johnson's vision has yet to be fulfilled. The main issue is, the windows have yet to be properly repaired: one can still hear some of the traffic sounds coming through. We can't record here unless we stop traffic in the surrounding streets, which we did on two occasions over the years, including rerouting the trolley buses.

VD: What are you most proud to have accomplished during your tenure as the musical director?

HE: To be honest with you, I would go straight to the way the orchestra sounds. I like to use the phrase 'dark sound' and we also search for a kind of transparency. It is a special sound and it is a sound which is very different from that of any other orchestra in Ukraine. It is also different from the great Russian orchestras in Moscow and St. Petersburg, in that there is a 'southern', warm element to the sound. Perhaps not many people are aware of this, but every conductor is different, and every conductor has a very powerful effect on the sound of the orchestra he/she is conducting. Whether that effect is tangible or intangible, minor or major, if you look at the great conductors, they all had their own sound. Just compare Leonard Bernstein and Herbert von Karajan, for instance – they both conducted the Vienna Philharmonic, and each of them elicited their own different sound from the same orchestra! Every music director brings his imprint to the sound and that is what I can be proud of – this very particular sound which the orchestra has today. Another positive note should be that we have maintained the size of the orchestra, despite all the concerted efforts to reduce it over the years. Our orchestra is full-time and plays at least sixty concerts a year. In the nineties in particular there was a push to cut the size of the orchestra by as much as thirty percent and hire ringers. I resisted that effort with every bone in my body. When you do that it, it is the beginning of the end. You have to have a full sized orchestra! Today, no other orchestra in Ukraine has eight double basses full-time, and even some of the great orchestras in Moscow have only seven.

VD: What are your regrets if any?

HE: Well, the first regret must certainly have to be the hall, which of course has a somewhat tragic history. People in Odessa do not really understand to a full extent that the hall is architecturally as unique and significant as their rightly beloved Opera house. The Odessans are funny people in that to all of them the opera house is a symbol, which is of course wonderful. It is a wonderful building, but even Russell Johnson made the point that he would not rank this building that far below the Opera house in terms of its architectural importance. He said to me: what sets this city apart is that it has both a great Opera house and a great hall. Most cities only have one or the other. For years, we have been fighting this terrible legend, spread by Leonid Utesov's joke on this very stage, that the acoustics are bad, because the hall was built as a stock exchange and built so that nobody standing over there could overhear our conversation here. A wonderful story, but the trading room was elsewhere in the building, and today's concert hall was used as a hall for banquets and ceremonies. According to Russell Johnson, there is nothing about this hall's soul which is anti-acoustical, only a few specific elements – such as the windows – that do need to be changed. We need to install wooden shutters over the windows to reflect the sound, and the windows need to be isolated, so the ambient street sounds stay outside. I can't say that I have been able to get the local government to focus on the windows. I can't say that we have achieved what we wanted to. If this hall was to be redone correctly it would become a real destination for classical music. Secondly, the international market is very difficult, and – despite the clearly established success that the orchestra has had, both in Europe and North America for a number of years now – we have been unable to establish ourselves on a regular basis with Western tours.

Unfortunately, and also kind of unfairly, this is in part because the orchestras from St. Petersburg and Moscow have a huge lion's share of that market and those cities have the kind of name recognition that Odessa just doesn't have. I think the orchestra has deserved its fair place in the international market, but alas, we don't seem to have it. This I do genuinely regret.

VD: Yet you have had some remarkable world class musicians perform here despite all the difficulties.

HE: Getting big names to Odessa is a whole problem. A lot of the names of stature internationally, with whom I perform abroad, such as Ivo Pogorelić or Steven Isserlis, Daniel Mueller Schott, the orchestra simply cannot afford to pay them to come here. There is a very limited budget for guest artists. I have had conversations with people like Yo-Yo Ma, Gil Shaham and Joshua Bell about coming to Odessa. They are all interested. We have had some major artists come to perform here, like Yefim Bronfman and Piotr Anderszewski, who are great pianists and very well known worldwide, they have certainly never come to play with the orchestras in Kyiv or elsewhere in Ukraine. They enjoyed being here, but they came as a gesture of friendship, basically for pocket change. We have a serious financial problem.

VD: The local government does not help very much?

HE: We pay taxes into the local budget without receiving one Hrivna of subsidy – all of our subsidies come from Kyiv and all our taxes go back out to the Oblast (regional authorities). So bearing that in mind, the local government should at the very least be giving moral support to the orchestra which costs them nothing and which is a major tourist and cultural attraction. They have not really understood the value of the orchestra's ambassadorial role for the city. In terms of support, we have had private charitable funds both here and in the United States, and these funds did all sorts of things. We even did dental work for wind players so that they could continue to play fifteen years ago. It turned out to be a very important issue, I had one horn player who had a number of teeth pulled by an idiot dentist and so he could not put his dentures in and was completely unable to play.

VD: That is not the kind of problem we have in the west.

HE: We were very fortunate and found a French-Swiss dentist who told us he could fix this. Our man is still playing the horn and his son is our principal horn player. While we were at it, we decided to do the same for all the other wind players as they all had serious dental issues. We also did things in the 90's like bring vitamins for the musicians. That was all funded by a charitable fund, a 501 C3 that we had in the U.S. – the American Friends of the Odessa Philharmonic Orchestra. We no longer have it because the IRS closed out many of those foreign funds which were not functioning for long periods because of money laundering and terrorism concerns. You need an entire team of people to operate that sort of structure properly, and we were not able to maintain such a team from a long distance, that is unfortunate. The new class of nouveau riche here in town also don't seem to be interested in traditional philanthropic endeavors, and it is true that there is no legal framework or tax deduction structure for it here either. The general apathy here has been disappointing. Even though we've had support from time to time, there has been a general indifference over the years from the local government, and also from local business.

VD: And what about the effects of recent events? Have they been detrimental?

HE: We are just now beginning to see proposed budget cuts – for the first time since the start of the war – of almost 10%, and this is very unfortunate. The national government is the only institution in this day and age here in this country who can properly support the arts. Ukraine is a country of a very high culture, and I'd like to think of it as a country where this is one of the best things it has going for it. If the federal government starts to cut funding for culture and to go down the road that a lot of European governments have gone down... well that is a very bad road to go down. Very sad news. Which is not going to solve the budget problem of the country either. The amount of money that the government spends is significant – if you add up the total of all the national level arts organizations – but it's not significant at all in terms of the percentage of the national budget. People who are leaders in society need to lobby against these proposed budget cuts, only that way can we resist them.

VD: So let's conclude on a happy note. You and the orchestra defy all the expectations of fussiness and conservatism often associated with classical music. You put on popular music, in the good sense of popular, and in fact you were the first to bring film scores to the classical scene here, which is of course common in the West.

HE: Correct. And yes, film scores are also easy to play badly. They are very demanding on the orchestra, and we need to be good to play them well. For the annual "city day" concert, we have played a diverse repertoire of Western European, Hungarian, Latin and North American, Romanian, Greek and Turkish music, as well as pieces representing Asia and almost all fifteen former soviet republics. Multi-national music for the multi- national city of Odessa. A lot of it is easy to listen to but hard to perform.

VD: Odessa and the many musicians who worked here had a great tradition of creating some of the best of Soviet popular music. There was the aforementioned Utesov, Isaac Schwarz as well as my own composer ancestor – Isaac Dunaevsky.

HE: Sure, the two Issacs! When I speak of the two Isaacs however, this being Odessa, I think of a third. We had a very special concert with the third Isaac, who was of course Babel. We had a wonderful evening with Babel's grandson Andrei Malaev-Babel, he read some of the Babel stories interspersed with music by Isaac Schwarz. But Dunaevsky – he was a wonderful musician and we've played much of his music, including his "Concert Waltz" – which, by the way, is purely a concert piece, not from film or operetta. It is sad to note that Dunaevsky is almost completely unknown outside of our neck of the woods, despite his great talent as a musician. But that's the way life goes. There is so much – on all sides – that we don't know about each other. Would you believe that the orchestra did not know who Stephen Sondheim was? I discovered that last week, while explaining the lyrics of "Porgy and Bess" to them. I also explained to them something that most people, even in America, don't know: Sondheim was Milton Babbitt's last private student. For that matter, many people don't know that Leonard Bernstein's parents were from Berdichev and Shepetovka …

VD: How remarkable it is to have a Venezuelan born, Scottish and Viennese-educated American, a student of Babbitt and Leonard Bernstein (whose own family was from this part of Ukraine) explaining Sondheim to the Odessa orchestra! That really brings the circle all the way back around.

CPSIA information can be obtained
at www.ICGtesting.com
Printed in the USA
JSHW010008060722
27815JS00005B/91

9 781680 539677